Francophone Sub-Saharan Africa 1880–1995

This new edition of Patrick Manning's established text includes two new chapters that discuss developments in the region since 1985, emphasising the democratisation movements of the 1980s and 1990s, the Francophone movement, and the crises in Rwanda and Burundi. Focusing on the French-speaking countries in west and central Africa, the book brings out the way in which the precolonial African heritage shaped new societies, in interaction with French and Belgian colonial rules, and with global economic and cultural forces. Three eras of change are described: the transition to colonial rule from 1880 to 1940, the transition to independent states from 1940 to 1985, and the reconfiguration of post-colonial society after 1985. It presents a strong line of interpretation and clear summaries, as well as considerable detail. The first edition of this book has been widely used in courses in African studies and African history.

PATRICK MANNING is professor of History and African-American Studies at Northeastern University, Boston, Massachusetts. He is the author of *Slavery, Colonialism and Economic Growth in Dahomey, 1640–1960* (1982) and *Slavery and African Life* (1990), and the editor of *Slave Trades 1500–1800: Globalization of Forced Labour* (1996).

Francophone Sub-Saharan Africa 1880–1995

PATRICK MANNING

CAMBRIDGE
UNIVERSITY PRESS

To Pamela and Gina

PUBLISHED BY THE PRESS SYNDICATE OF THE UNIVERSITY OF CAMBRIDGE
The Pitt Building, Trumpington Street, Cambridge CB2 1RP, United Kingdom

CAMBRIDGE UNIVERSITY PRESS
The Edinburgh Building, Cambridge, CB2 2RU, United Kingdom
40 West 20th Street, New York, NY 10011–4211, USA
10 Stamford Road, Oakleigh, Melbourne 3166, Australia

First edition first published 1988 as *Francophone Sub-Saharan Africa 1880–1985*
Reprinted 1989, 1994
Second edition 1998

First published 1998

Printed in the United Kingdom at the University Press, Cambridge

Typeset in Times 9.5/11.5pt [vn]

A catalogue record for this book is available from the British Library

Library of Congress Cataloguing in Publication data

Manning, Patrick, 1941–
Francophone Sub-Saharan Africa, 1880–1985 / Patrick Manning.
p. cm
Bibliography.
Includes index.
ISBN 0 521 64255 8.   ISBN 0 521 64519 0 (pbk.)
1. Africa, French-speaking Equatorial – History – 1884–1960.
2. Africa, French-speaking Equatorial – History – 1960–
3. Africa, French-speaking West – History – 1884–1960
4. Africa, French-speaking West – History – 1960–   I. Title
DT532.5.M36 1988
966'.0097541 – dc19   87-26550

ISBN 0 521 64255 8 hardback
ISBN 0 521 64519 0 paperback

Contents

Illustrations

Figures

Maps

Acknowledgments

Elizabeth Wetton suggested that a book such as this would be of interest, and then guided it expertly to completion. The Northeastern University Instructional Development Fund provided support for travel, research, and duplication of a draft for use in class. I am grateful to students at Northeastern University for comments on the initial draft of the book, and particularly to Gina Baskerville, Danielle Delince, Janine Alpizar, Sasha Fiato, Joycelyn Christopher, Marit Ratner, and Maureen Grady. Several colleagues gave me valuable suggestions for improvement of a more advanced version: Bogumil Jewsiewicki, Jan Vansina, Richard Roberts, Tom Reefe, Myron Echenberg, Catherine Coquery-Vidrovitch, and an anonymous reader for Cambridge University Press. Ballard Campbell urged me on in a spirit of friendly competition. Marjorie Murphy provided inspiration through her example, numberless practical suggestions, and comfort at all times. Jean Suret-Canale provided valuable information through his writings, an example of remarkable personal resilience, and some delightful African stories.

To all of these I am grateful. With such support from others, I am happy to assume responsibility for the inaccuracies and ambiguities that remain.

Patrick Manning
March 1988

NOTE ON THE SECOND EDITION

This volume extends the first edition by ten years. A new chapter 8 emphasises the democratization movements of the 1980s and 1990s, the Francophone movement, and the crises in Rwanda and Burundi. A new epilogue, chapter 9, addresses urban issues of the 1990s and prospects for the future. I am grateful to Jean-Marie Makang for guidance on these chapters.

In May of 1997 forces loyal to Laurent Kabila drove Mobutu Sese Seko from Zaire and occupied Kinshasa. Kabila declared himself president and announced that the country would again be known as the Democratic Republic of Congo. In this text, meanwhile, I retain the term "Zaire" for the period from 1971 to 1997.

Patrick Manning
August 1998

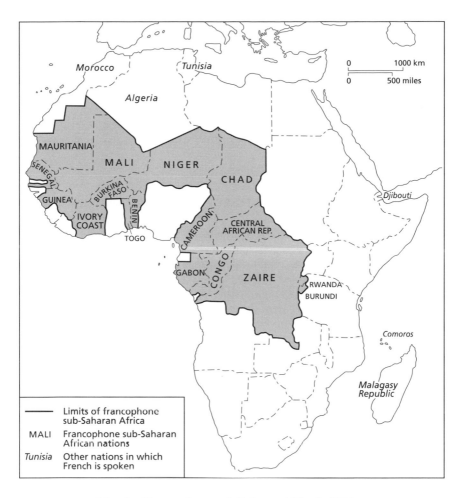

Map 1   Francophone sub-Saharan Africa in 1995

1

Prologue

Francophone sub-Saharan Africa consists today of 17 countries of West and Central Africa in which French is the language of government. These 17 nations range in a contiguous semicircle from Mauritania in the west to Chad in the east and to Zaire in the south. They were colonies of France and Belgium from the late nineteenth to the mid twentieth century. (Other former French territories outside of West and Central Africa are not included in this book.) Francophone sub-Saharan Africa, defined in these terms, has existed for just over a century; it was brought into existence with the European conquest of Africa which reached its height in the 1880s.

Francophone sub-Saharan Africa covers an area of ten million square kilometers, which is 40% of the area of sub-Saharan Africa, or 35% of the area of the entire African continent. The 1995 population of the 17 countries was estimated at over 100 million, or one-fifth of the entire African population. The area of francophone sub-Saharan Africa is 17 times that of France and Belgium combined, and its population is today almost twice that of France and Belgium combined. Zaire is the largest of the francophone African countries – it is the second largest African nation in area, and third largest in population. Rwanda is the smallest and most densely populated country in francophone sub-Saharan Africa. It is equal in area to Belgium, and had a 1995 population two thirds that of Belgium. France is slightly larger in area than Cameroon, while the 1995 population of Zaire, Cameroon and Ivory Coast taken together were nearly equal to that of France.

French, English, and Arabic are the main languages of government in Africa today. Map 2, which shows African countries according to their main language of government, provides a simplified portrait of the colonial history of the continent. The English-speaking (or *anglophone*) countries include the former British colonies plus Liberia, and accounted for 40% of Africa's population in 1995. Anglophone Africa includes Africa's largest country (Sudan), its most populous nation (Nigeria), and its wealthiest nation (South Africa), as well as most of East Africa. Arabic-speaking Africa includes the nations of North Africa plus the sub-Saharan countries of Sudan and Mauritania; these countries had 20% of the African population in 1995. The Portuguese-speaking (or *lusophone*) nations, all of which are former colonies of Portugal, accounted in 1995 for another 4% of the African population.

2   *Francophone Sub-Saharan Africa 1880–1995*

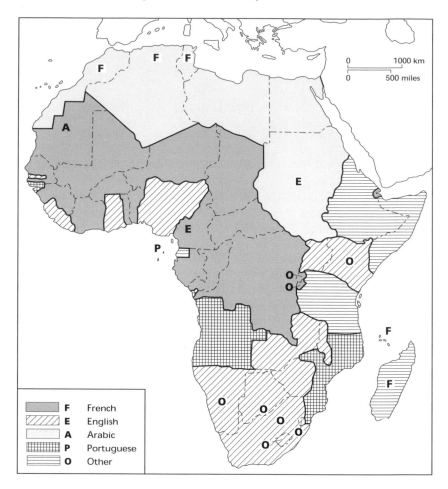

Map 2   Official languages in Africa, 1995

Two types of exceptions are governed in yet other languages: Ethiopia is
governed in Amharic, Tanzania is governed in Swahili, Somalia is governed in
Somali, and Equatorial Guinea is governed in Spanish. These nations accounted for 13% of the African population in 1995. Secondly, in a number of cases,
nations have more than one official language: Arabic and English in Sudan,
Arabic and French in Mauritania, Kirundi and French in Burundi, French
and English in Cameroon, English and Afrikaans and others in South Africa.

This book concentrates on one area of the continent for a century in time. It
includes all of the former Belgian colonies and most of the former French
colonies in Africa. Excluded from the book are eight former French colonies
(Djibouti on the Red Sea, the North African nations of Algeria, Morocco, and
Tunisia, and, in the Indian Ocean, the nations of the Comoros and the

Malagasay Republic, and the island of Reunion, now a department within the French Republic). This is because their histories, while important, are quite different from those of the 17 nations on which we shall focus.

What is unique and characteristic about francophone sub-Saharan Africa? Partly it is the common ancestral heritage of West and Central Africa – the centuries of development and interaction in the valleys of the Senegal, the Niger, the Shari, the Ogowe and the Zaire. Partly it is the French and Belgian imprint on this immense region – the French language and the accompanying traditions of law, administration, and education. It is true that these territories were French-speaking only at the elite and administrative levels during much of the past century, because the colonial regimes kept education and political participation at a minimum. But in the era of decolonization, since World War II, the French language has come to be spoken very widely.

The third set of links among these 17 nations is that, in the years since independence, they have chosen to draw on and to develop a broad cultural unity which is worthy of the term "francophone African culture." Francophone African culture emerged from a fusion of French culture with African culture. At the elite level, African poets, political figures, and philosophers carried out this fusion. Their achievement is mirrored, for instance, in the pages of the literary and scholarly journal *Présence africaine*. At the popular level, an equally important cultural fusion was carried out by village school teachers, musicians, merchants, and preachers. The songs of the Zairian musicians Franco and Rochereau (or Luambo Makiadi and Tabu Ley, as they are now known) provide examples of the strength of this popular culture.

In contrast with anglophone Africa, the francophone countries use the metric system and drive on the right; they also have more centralized administrations. In contrast with Arab Africa, francophone sub-Saharan African countries emphasize their recent history rather than the glories of their medieval histories. In contrast with lusophone Africa, the francophone countries gained independence without having to go to war for it, and are left with a tradition giving relative emphasis to moderation and compromise. In contrast with the nations of eastern Africa, where Amharic, Somali, and Swahili define specifically African linguistic communities, the francophone nations emphasize their participation in a world linguistic community.

The experience of francophone sub-Saharan Africa in the century from 1880 to 1985, while unique in these and other respects, also has important parallels with the experience of English-, Portuguese-, and Arabic-speaking Africa. As a result, while the story to be told in these pages is primarily about the specific experience of francophone sub-Saharan Africa, it illustrates many of the issues and the trends which have been important throughout Africa. In some cases, as with the Great Depression of the 1930s or the influenza pandemic in 1918, the history of francophone Africa can scarcely be separated from that of the rest of Africa. In other cases, as with language policy or political rights, the history of francophone Africa is unique and distinct.

The colonial experience and decolonization brought changing identities for Africans at both individual and collective levels. This is reflected particularly in changing names of countries and colonies in francophone Africa. Thus, the nation known today as Mali was known as French Sudan from 1922 to 1959, as Upper-Senegal-Niger from 1900 to 1922, and by other names in earlier periods. The nation known today as Zaire was given its boundaries as the Congo Independent State in 1885. It became the Belgian Congo in 1908, then became the Republic of Congo in 1960, the Democratic Republic of Congo in 1965, and became Zaire in 1971. Across the Zaire River (also known as the Congo) lies the People's Republic of Congo (or Congo-Brazzaville, after its capital), as it has been known since 1963. This territory was known as French Congo beginning in 1885 and as Middle Congo from 1910 to 1958, when it became the Republic of Congo. In the text we shall refer to these countries by their modern names as frequently as possible, but it will often be necessary to use their earlier names. Four maps in this chapter should help to clarify the changing names of African political units: map 1 (1995), map 3 (1880), map 4 (1900), and map 5 (1940).

The book traces three types of influences over the course of a century. First, it presents African society, its history and its changes. Secondly, it describes colonial rule in Africa, and the French and Belgian nations which were behind the colonial administrations. Thirdly, it discusses African consequences of the industrial transformation of the modern world. This industrial revolution goes beyond the influence of any European or African nation, and has led to the internationalization of the economy, of politics and of culture.

The objective of this history is, first, to present the main facts of the historical development of francophone sub-Saharan Africa. A second objective, perhaps equally important, is to convey the outlook and the identity of the peoples of francophone Africa. In the pages below, the reader (with the assistance of a little imagination) may re-enact the historical experience of the peoples of francophone Africa. Through participating indirectly in that experience, one may seek to understand and articulate the viewpoints, hopes, and fears of those who actually lived it and who live it today.

THE AFRICAN LANDSCAPE

The landscape of francophone sub-Saharan Africa stretches in three broad belts from west to east. The *northern savanna* or the *sudan* is the largest and most populous of these belts. The *equatorial forest* lies astride the equator in the Zaire River basin, and smaller patches of forest stretch along the West African coast to Bénin, Togo, Ivory Coast, and Guinea. The *southern savanna* covers the southern half of Congo and Zaire and extends into neighboring Angola and Zambia. In addition, the *highlands* of Rwanda, Burundi, and the Kivu region of Zaire are a small but densely populated region of open grassland and regular rains. In 1880 the lands of francophone Africa supported roughly 30 million people, almost all of them in rural settlements. About 15 million lived in the northern savanna, some 6 million lived in forest zones, about 4 million lived in the southern savanna, and about 3 million lived in the highlands. These great landscapes, and the many variations within them, reflected and in turn conditioned the rainfall, the temperature, the vegetation, the animal life, and above all the forms of human habitation of each. Since much of the story to follow will be told in terms of these land-scapes, we shall begin with a more detailed description of each, as they appeared a century ago.

The northern savanna, a great expanse of grassland with trees dotting the river valleys and the wetter lands, is bounded to the north by the Sahara Desert and to the south by dense forest hugging the coast. This broad savanna, known as "the bright country" by the Mandingo people of Mali, is covered with fertile soil, but most crops must be grown during the short summer rainy season. The savanna stretches 3,000 kilometers from the coast of Senegal to Lake Chad in the center of the continent and another 3,000 kilometers to the Red Sea. The desert edge of the savanna, known as the *sahel* (Arabic for "coast," since the Sahara can be seen as a sea of sand), has short grass and fluctuating rains. Some years it could be farmed, other years it was grazed, and some years it had to be abandoned.

The northern savanna is often called the *sudan*, from the Arabic term for "the land of the blacks." The sudan is divided into three sections: the Western Sudan (the Senegal and upper Niger valleys), the Central Sudan (the lower Niger valley and the basin of Lake Chad), and the Eastern Sudan (the Nile valley). We shall be concerned with the Western and Central Sudan. Only a small portion of this vast area is drained by the westward-flowing Senegal and Gambia rivers. Most of it is drained by the mighty Niger, which rises in the mountains of Futa Jallon in Guinea, flows northeast to the desert edge at Timbuktu, and then curves in a great bend to flow southeast. From its bend the Niger flows across the savanna toward the coast where, after passing under the forest, it finally discharges its waters through a maze of creeks into the Bights of Benin and Biafra. Further east, in the very center of the continent, the Shari River rises just beyond the northern fringe of the forest and flows gently northward into the landlocked basin of Lake Chad. The lake, salty and shallow after millions of years of receiving the Shari, still supports a large fish population.

Each year, summer rains brought the savanna to life. Intense labors of the farmers, working with hoes, resulted in preparation of fields and planting of millet and sorghum, the main grain crops. Within two months of sprouting, millet stalks reached heights of two meters. These and other crops covered the landscape with a carpet of green. But after the millet harvest in September and the end of the rains in October, the savanna turned back to the brown, grey, and gold which dominated its colors for most of the year. In one sense the farmers of Senegal and the savanna stretching to the east were repeating an annual cycle that had been carried on for the thousands of years since millet had been domesticated. But the rains were not always regular, and in too many years they did not come at all. Farmers planned accordingly, and built the granaries whose conical forms became a dominant feature of savanna architec-ture. In another sense, the basic patterns of savanna agriculture and life generally had changed from generation to generation in response to the many movements, innovations, and reverses of Africa's long history.

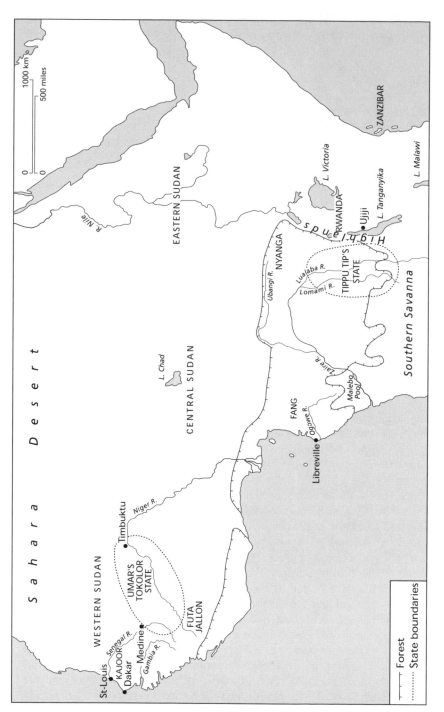

Map 3 Africa in 1880

The forest, which skips along the West African coast from Guinea to Cameroon, with a breadth of 100 kilometers at most, expands to nearly 1,000 kilometers in breadth in Central Africa, and extends eastward over 2,000 kilometers from the Atlantic to the highlands of Kivu and Uganda. The western portion of the equatorial forest is drained by the Ogowe River. The great majority of the equatorial forest is drained by the Zaire River and its tributaries: the Ubangi in the north and the Lualaba and the Lomami in the east. The Zaire flows in a great semicircle through the forest and emerges into the southern savanna before flowing to the sea. Its level rises and falls in a complicated pattern in response to rains north and south of the equator. Forested areas have two rainy seasons each year, with the heavy rains in late spring and lighter rains in late summer. For the forest south of the equator, the spring rains begin in October, and the summer rains begin in February. Despite the luxurious and dense foliage of the rain forests, the underlying soils were poor and weak in nutrients. Winning a livelihood from this land required farmers to plan and to work energetically.

Crops varied significantly among regions of the forest. In the most westerly regions, from Guinea to Ivory Coast, the main crop was rice. This was not the paddy rice of Asian origin (which is today a favorite staple in most African cities), but the dry rice native to Western Africa. Further east, along the coast from Ivory Coast to Cameroon, the main crops were yams and maize. Finally, the peoples of the Zaire and Ogowe basin forest lived primarily on plantain and bananas. Aside from these basic crops, the farmers of the forest region grew a variety of other crops (farmers in the Zaire basin grew as many as 30 different crops at once), and they also raised poultry and small domestic animals such as goats and sheep.

The mouth of the Zaire River lies in the southern savanna, an expanse of grassland extending from the southern fringes of the equatorial forest, at some five degrees latitude south, to the Namib Desert in modern Namibia, and ranging eastward to the great lakes. In the west, the lower Zaire is fed by the Kasai and Kwango rivers. To the east, the Luapula River flows north across the savanna and feeds ultimately into the upper Zaire.

The millet-growing peoples of this savanna had formed themselves into states much larger than those of the forest region to the north. But they had also been involved deeply in slave trade during the eighteenth and nineteenth centuries. As a result, many people had begun to grow manioc as well as millet, since they found this tuber easy to grow and productive. In addition, it could be left in the ground for over a year before harvesting.

The highland areas of Rwanda, Burundi, and Kivu, in the midst of Africa's Great Lakes region, form quite a different ecology. This area averages 1,500 meters in elevation and towers above the Zaire basin, 1,000 meters below and to the west. The region's ample rains drain into Lake Kivu and Lake Tanganyika, and then flow down to the savanna and the Lualaba River. The main crops in the highland savanna were several varieties of beans, and they permitted the growth of francophone Africa's densest populations.

The labels on map 3 indicate the main geographical regions within francophone sub-Saharan Africa. First, it is divided into its West African and Central African halves. West Africa includes all the countries from Senegal to Niger. Central Africa includes all the countries from Chad and Cameroon to Zaire. Secondly, each of these great regions is divided into three (or four) large ecological zones reflected in the crops, the peoples, and in socio-economic patterns. In the more populous West Africa, the zones are the sahel, the savanna, and the coast (where the coast includes the forest and the adjoining wet savanna). In Central Africa, the four zones are the northern savanna, the forest, and the southern savanna, and, to the east, the densely populated highlands.

THE ANCESTRY OF FRANCOPHONE AFRICA

Francophone sub-Saharan Africa was born of an African mother and a European father; from the union of two old civilizations emerged a new civilization. This new civilization matured under the influence of both parents, and it is marked by the characteristics of each parent (although, as with all offspring, it developed its own unique characteristics). To understand fully the nascent francophone African civilization, one must know something of the background of the parents. In this section (and in other sections later in the book) the reader will find summaries of some key aspects of earlier African and European history. For more background on earlier African life, and also on European history, the reader should consult the guide to further reading at the end of this book, which lists a number of excellent introductions to precolonial African society, as well as surveys of French and Belgian history.

The distant histories of peoples serve to establish their ethnic identity and their national character. The French honor the emperor Charlemagne (who died in 814) as an early hero, and they still chant the *Song of Roland*, an epic history of France focused partly on the influence of its Catholic church. Even more important was the rise and expansion of the French monarchy, which conquered and assimilated a large area of Western Europe. With time, the rise in France of a strong intellectual and literary tradition served to reinforce the strength of the monarchy. Under François I, French (rather than Latin) became the official language of government in 1515. Louis XIV (1643–1715) was France's most powerful and brilliant king; he and his ministers did much to make the French monarchy the dominant power in Europe during the seventeenth and eighteenth centuries. During these centuries, France established colonies in the Americas, Asia, and Africa, which set precedents for later African colonization.

The Belgian tradition looks back not only to monarchs such as Charlemagne (his capital was at the edge of Belgium), but also to *Everyman*, the anonymous hero of the great medieval Flemish morality play. The Belgian inheritance from the ages is not one of such unity and central power as the French, but is rather one of continuing economic leadership and regional identity despite social conflict. Since early medieval times, the lands of Belgium have been shared by people speaking French and Dutch languages, peoples now known as Walloons and Flemings. Late in the Middle Ages, the communes or towns of Belgium were centers of commerce and industry, whose leaders prized their independence from the feudal lords who remained on country estates. For a brief time in the fifteenth century, all of the French- and Dutch-speaking areas of the Netherlands were united under the leadership of the dukes of Burgundy. Philip the Good, Duke of Burgundy from 1419 to 1467, maintained his court in Brussels and made his realm one of the powers of Europe. The Low Countries, as they are also known, boasted Europe's most prosperous economy and a brilliant cultural life. But the perils of royal marriage soon awarded the Netherlands to Spain, and the great conflicts of the Reformation split the area in half. The northern half became the independent Republic of the Netherlands, a Protestant area. The southern half remained staunchly Catholic and remained under Spanish (and later Austrian) rule; thus did Belgium gain its identity.

African traditions are equally deep and far more numerous. In the Western Sudan, for example, the thirteenth-century epic of *Sundiata* (who died in about 1250), the conquering founder of the empire of Mali in the Western Sudan, is still recounted today. The Guinean scholar D. T. Niane recorded it and translated it into French, so that this epic has now become part of the heritage of all Africa. It tells of Sundiata's youth in exile, his devotion to his mother, the wars in which he matched battlefield skills and supernatural powers against the tyrant Soumaoro, and his establishment of a greatly expanded Mali empire. Quite a different epic is from the forest: that of *Mwindo*, the hero of the Nyanga people of northeastern Zaire. Mwindo, a small man with great powers, was born miraculously (through his mother's side) to a chief. The chief rejected his son, and Mwindo escaped to the safety provided by a paternal aunt. Through adventures under water, underground, and in the skies (where lightning became his protector) Mwindo made his way back to his birthplace. There he settled accounts with his father, and accepted half the state as his compensation.

Another measure of African tradition is the list of kings of Rwanda in the highlands at the eastern fringe of Central Africa; a list remembered in precise detail for a period of over three centuries, and including all major personages of the court. In the southern savanna the Lunda kings imposed their influence over a wide region beginning in the sixteenth century, with bracelets made of human nerves as a key symbol of royalty. The rise of the Lunda empire, in the southern savanna, is recounted through the story of Chibinda Ilunga, who immigrated to the Lunda homeland, married queen Rwccj, became king, and began a tradition of sending emissaries to found subject kingdoms in nearby areas.

These stories of ancient origin establish the ethnic identity of African and European peoples. More important in determining their outlooks and actions as they came into close contact with each other, however, were the experiences of the late eighteenth and early nineteenth centuries. France and Belgium each experienced revolutions and a strengthening of national identity. Germany emerged as a European power and established African colonies which later became part of francophone Africa. The African territories experienced change as revolutionary as that in Europe. Strong states emerged, new directions of commerce developed, religions gained new converts, economic life was reorganized, and new family structures and social classes formed. In sum the French, the Belgians, and the African peoples collided with each other in the 1880s, but they all were undergoing great internal changes even as they encountered each other.

In France, the Revolution of 1789–99 overthrew the monarchy, wrote a charter for the universal rights of man, and gave birth to the first French republic, to modern nationalism, and to a new sort of empire under Napoleon Bonaparte. With this, France began the oscillation between revolution and autocracy which has characterized its politics ever since. French domination of Europe ended with the defeat of Napoleon in 1815. In political and economic affairs, France lived thereafter in the shadow of Britain and later of Germany.

By the time of the revolution, France had lost most of its old colonies to Britain. France also lost its valuable sugar colony in Haiti. There the ex-slaves who had gained their freedom in 1794 threw out Napoleon's troops and proclaimed the independent nation of Haiti on New Year's Day, 1804. But a quarter-century later, France began a new venture in African colonization with the 1830 invasion of Algiers. After taking over this port town, the French military soon found itself involved in a long struggle with the brilliant Arab general Abd al-Qadir. After 15 years the French emerged supreme and began sending settlers to take over the best land.

France's second revolution and Second Republic came in 1848. French slaves were freed a second time, and this time for good. But in 1852 the republic gave way to the Second Empire, under Emperor Napoleon III. The emperor, Louis Bonaparte (a nephew of the earlier Napoleon), had served as president of the republic until he seized complete power. Napoleon III built a strong and reforming administration within France. His colonial ventures included some expansion in Africa, and support for the conquest of Mexico by the Austrian prince Maximilian.

Meanwhile the Prussian statesman Otto von Bismarck led in consolidating dozens of small German states. To complete this process, Bismarch provoked war with France in 1870, and the combined German armies won easily. At a victory celebration in Paris, Bismarck proclaimed the united German Empire, and annexed to it the industrial French provinces of Alsace and Lorraine. In an instant, Germany had become the predominant economic and military power in Europe. Meanwhile, the Second French Empire collapsed and was followed by the revolutionary upheaval of the Paris Commune. The Commune was suppressed by French and German soldiers, and in 1871 the Third French Republic was formed. The French, humiliated in war and riven by social conflict, thirsted for revenge and for glory. Some sought to quench this thirst through African conquest; Jules Ferry and Leon Gambetta became the leading parliamentary spokesmen for French imperialism.

The Third Republic lasted until the next German conquest of France in 1940. The republic was dominated by a coalition of republican parties, though the monarchists remained a political presence, and the socialist party (based on a growing working-class movement) grew steadily in influence. With World War I and the Russian Revolution, the socialist party split in half, and the more revolutionary half of it became the communist party. For a brief time in the 1930s the socialists, with the support of the communists and some republicans, formed a Popular Front government. All of these parties and tendencies influenced the policies and realities of the French colonies in Africa.

Belgium, which had remained a province of Spain and then of Austria until its conquest by Napoleon, owed its national independence to the aftermath of the Napoleonic wars. The Congress of Vienna made Belgium part of the Kingdom of the Netherlands, under the Dutch king, in 1815. In 1830, just as the French were overthrowing another king, the Walloons and to a lesser degree the Flemings rose up to declare their independence from the Netherlands on grounds of their regional autonomy and their identity as Catholics. The victorious Belgians then achieved recognition from their powerful neighbors – England, France, and Germany – by promising to remain a neutral nation. They won appointment of Leopold of Saxe-Coburg as their king. Leopold was of German birth and had lived his adult life in England; he soon married the daughter of the new French king. Their son Leopold II became king in 1865.

Belgian industry, now strengthened by national independence, continued its European leadership; for a brief time Belgium had the second largest industrial output in Europe. The expansion of Belgian industry meant the growth of both a powerful proprietary class and a large wage-labor class. The power of the proprietary class was reflected in the *Société Générale*, a gigantic holding company (formed in 1822, even before Belgium's independence) which came to control the nation's major industries and banks. The working class expressed its growing organization in trade unions and in the socialist party. The dominant political party in Belgium, however, was the Catholic party, and its main challenger was the liberal party. Meanwhile, Belgium had no previous history of colonization and, as a neutral nation, could not join in alliances or undertake conquests. Yet in 1885 Belgians found themselves associated with one of the largest colonies in Africa, the Congo Independent State.

For Africa, the great events of the early nineteenth century included the decline and eventual end of the Atlantic slave trade, the concomitant expansion of slave trade and slavery within Africa, and the rise of militant Islam. The countries of West and Central Africa had been economically tied to the Atlantic and to the Muslim world for centuries through slave exports. Now a new sort of connection arose. Slaves remained in Africa, and they supplemented the work of free Africans in producing commodities – grains, ivory, peanuts, palm oil, and textiles – some of which were exported to Europe. In exchange, Africa imported larger quantities of money, textiles, salt, and manufactures than ever before. Along with these great changes in African social and economic life came the reorganization of government in many African areas.

These transformations, however, affected the various African regions in different ways. West Africa had been in relatively intensive economic contact with North Africa and the Europeans for centuries, and benefitted from a nineteenth-century decline in the severity of slave trade. Life in the West African savanna and sahel was dominated by movements of Islamic renovation which led to the creation of such great states as Masina and the Sokoto Caliphate. Domestic and external commerce expanded at the same time. Slave exports declined to a trickle along most of the West African coast, and this region underwent sustained economic growth, as reflected in the growth in exports of peanuts and palm oil, but also as reflected in the growing number of domestic slaves. West Africa faced the Europeans with many divisions, but with a relatively resilient social and economic order.

Central Africa was less integrated into the world economy than West Africa. (The exceptions were its northern and southwestern fringes, which had been in long contact with North Africans and Europeans, respectively.) In addition, the Central African slave trade grew rapidly in the nineteenth century, and continued in some areas into the twentieth century. In the northern savanna, Muslim states such as Bagirmi and wandering raiders such as Rabeh ibn Abdullah captured slaves to be settled in the region or to be exported to Egypt. In the southern savanna and parts of the equatorial forest, slave raiders sought captives for the markets of Cuba and Brazil and for local use as well. At the same time, adventurers from the east and south – such as Msiri and the Chokwe – took over large areas of the southern savanna. These factors, combined with the sparse Central African population, made the region malleable and yet fragile in comparison to West Africa. On the one hand, Central African societies could be moulded by the touch of colonial masters who sought to remake them; on the other hand, they were in danger of shattering irreparably under the new colonial pressures. Only the Central African highlands remained isolated from the impact of slave trade and political transformation, until the Europeans arrived.

CONTENDING VISIONS OF AFRICAN DESTINY

The bearers of African and European traditions met, clashed, and at times cooperated; the emergence of francophone sub-Saharan Africa during the past century was one result of this interaction. This section, in a prologue to that story as told in the chapters below, focuses on the dreams and actions of a few key individuals in the years leading up to 1880. These were individuals who had great influence on the creation and evolution of francophone sub-Saharan Africa. The narrative in this prelude focuses on their visions of African destiny. We shall return at the end of the book, revisit their terrain, reconsider their vision, and see to what degree their hopes for Africa were realized.

Louis Faidherbe, a captain in the naval infantry, assumed leadership of the tiny French colony of Senegal in 1854. The area under his rule was limited to the island of St. Louis, in the estuary of the Senegal River, and to a few outposts along the banks of the river inland. His vision was of the *assimilation* of West Africa into a growing and reforming French empire. His energy and drive launched the French conquest of much of West Africa.

Faidherbe was a young man, full of energy and drive, whose actions reflected his devotion to three traditions of French life. First, he was devoted to the liberal and universal tradition of revolutionary France, He was thus a supporter of the assimilationist vision which caused the French National Assembly, in the course of the 1848 revolution, to grant French citizenship to the inhabitants of French colonics, including St. Louis. Secondly, he was a military man, an officer in the naval infantry – for it was the navy which ruled the French colonies – but he had developed his outlook during service in Algeria, where the French has been involved in a massive effort at conquest since 1830. Out of his Algerian service he developed an anti-Muslim missionary zeal which colored most of his policies in Senegal. Thirdly, he was a devoted servant of the Second French Empire and of Emperor Napoleon III's campaign for efficient administration, French nationalism, and imperial expansion in Indochina, in Mexico, and in Africa. Faidherbe laid out a strategy of French expansion up the Senegal valley, and was inspired by Paul Soleillet's dreams of a railroad across the Sahara to Algeria. He hoped to expand French influence to the interior, perhaps as far as the fabled Timbuktu, the center of trade and religious scholarship at the desert edge. He hoped to extend the liberal vision of the French revolution, but also the autocratic and reforming power of the Second Empire; and he sought finally to add to the glory of the French military.

But across Faidherbe's intended route to the interior lay the growing sphere of influence of al-hajj Umar, a man who had launched a campaign as universal in its vision as that of Faidherbe. His was a vision of *dar al-Islam* – that West Africa should be fully converted into a land of the believers in Islam. Umar was not a young man, but he was as full of energy and reforming zeal as any person in West Africa. He had grown up in Futa Toro, an ancient center of Muslim influence in the middle Senegal valley, and had spent his youth and middle age as a pilgrim, a cleric, and a scholar, traveling and studying in Mecca and in the capitals of the great states of Muslim Africa. Now in his old age he sought to establish a pious kingdom, worthy of almighty God. Having retired to a retreat at Dinguiray on the headwaters of the Niger River, he called upon the faithful to join him. He built his theocratic community and then, after the manner of the prophet Muhammad, in 1853 he declared a *jihad*, a holy war, against the unbelievers and slackers around him until they submitted to him and to the will of God. Though Umar's Tokolor state was to be centered primarily in the Niger Valley, most of his early supporters came from the Senegal valley, and even from St. Louis itself.

Faidherbe and Umar fought to a draw in 1854, as Umar was unable to take the French fort at Medine on the upper Senegal. The intolerance of each met its match in the other. The battles between the successors of Umar and of Faidherbe continued until 1898, when the French conquest of the Western Sudan was completed.

Millet dominated the fields of the Western Sudan and provided the basis for the region's nutrition, but another crop grew steadily in importance throughout the nineteenth century: peanuts. Alongside the fields of millet, often alternating with millet to improve soil fertility, fields of peanuts had expanded since the 1830s, as farmers used the increasingly available slave and servile labor to produce a crop which could be sold to Europeans, now willing to pay a high price for this oil-bearing seed. European demand for peanuts led to the development of Dakar as a port and the metropolis for the region. In 1868 French troops landed at this village facing the island of Gorée, and by the mid 1870s they had built the beginnings of a modern port there. In 1885 the French had completed a railroad – the first in West Africa – from Dakar north to St. Louis, across the fertile but still independent lands of Kajoor, and peanuts flowed in steadily increasing quantities from rapidly expanding farms to Rufisque, a port just east of Dakar, and to Dakar. Shortly thereafter, the French took control of Kajoor and many other areas of Senegal. Faidherbe's dream of combining military expansion and economic growth seemed to be turning to reality.

Eastward along the Atlantic coast, in what is today the Republic of Bénin, lay the kingdom of Dahomey, with its capital at Abomey and its port of Ouidah. There too a range of visions contended for influence. The Marseille merchant Victor Régis had set up a trading post in Ouidah in 1840 to purchase palm oil in exchange for a range of imports. As his trade became successful, he opened posts to the east and west of Dahomey. His vision of the African future was one based on *free trade*. He thought of himself as an efficient merchant who would dominate the trade of the coast, if only French influence could eliminate the restrictions placed on trade by the rulers of Dahomey. (Other French merchants, earning smaller profits but harboring similar visions, traded along the coasts of what are today Guinea and Ivory Coast.)

King Glele of Dahomey (1858–89) had no intention of placing himself under French influence. He was ready to grant small concessions of land to Régis and to missionaries, but he envisioned the future of Africa as one based on *African sovereignty*. He did not seek to conquer a wide area, as did Umar, but he insisted firmly on the integrity of his kingdom, and he sought relations of diplomatic equality with France and Britain, as with his African neighbors. The most difficult aspect of diplomacy was the European (especially British) insistence on his abandonment of slave trade. Glele was willing to do so, but insisted that it be done in a manner that gave full recognition to his sovereignty. No such arrangement was ever made.

In 1860 Catholic missionaries added another vision of the future to Bénin. The SMA Fathers of Lyon, a newly founded mission organization, sent Father Borghero and two other Italian priests to open a mission in Ouidah. Their vision was of the religious *tutelage* of Africa. They expected to teach Christianity and to save the souls of people along the African coast.

Borghero and the SMA Fathers found, to their surprise, that a significant Catholic community already existed in Ouidah and along the coast. These were known as Brazilians: Africans who had lived in Brazil, often as slaves, some 4,000 of whom had emigrated to the Bight of Bénin in the mid nineteenth century. They spoke Portuguese, professed the Catholic religion, and used Brazilian names. This community dominated the fledgling mission, and it insisted that the mission school be run in Portuguese rather than in French.

The Brazilians, along with other leading figures of Ouidah, were merchants and landowners, and their vision of the African future was based on *African enterprise*. They sent their children to the mission school and they traded with Régis, in the hope of profiting from the expanding commercial economy. They fully intended, however, to remain masters of their own enterprises, and did not see themselves as subordinate to the Europeans.

Nearly two decades after Faidherbe's arrival in Senegal, another adventurer began the work of carving out France's empire in Central Africa. Pierre Savorgnan de Brazza was born in Rome to an aristocratic family from the Italian kingdom of Piedmont-Savoy, but at age 18 he adopted France as his homeland and the French navy as his career, and he devoted his life to extending the frontiers of France. After service in the Franco-Prussian war of 1870, he came to Libreville in Gabon in that same year, at the age of 21. In 1875 he began his explorations of the Ogowe River, whose waters rise in the far interior of what is now Gabon, and which he saw as a potential trade route of importance. There he developed his vision of *association* – peaceful French penetration of Africa and development of a commonwealth of interest between Africans and Europeans.

Brazza managed to work his way up-river in 1875 to Lambaréné, and there he met with leaders of the Fang people and gained permission to conduct trade. Based on these peaceable and cordial contacts, Brazza readily concluded that European penetration and domination of Africa could be achieved without conflict and perhaps even with oppression. Brazza's expectations of peaceable relations contrasted with the view of the American Protestant missionaries who had become influential in Libreville: they saw the Fang as a fierce people.

The families who populated the forest and plied the Ogowe river, and who have come to be known collectively as the Fang, envisioned a future based on *autonomy*. Each group would be left to pursue its own destiny without imposition by others. The distinction between this vision and Brazza's notion of *association* became clear only gradually. These people lived in small villages and their economic life combined farming, hunting, gathering and fishing. They were in the process of migrating from north to south, and were reputed to be fierce. Their economic life, based on cultivation of bananas and tubers, was busy, because they had two growing seasons, one for each of the two rainy seasons in the equatorial forest, and because of their additional hunting and fishing activities.

Brazza, meanwhile, pushed inland from the Ogowe in search of the Zaire River. He reached Zaire from the west in 1877, only a few weeks after Henry Morton Stanley had sailed down it from the east. Brazza then sought to establish French influence over the lower Zaire basin. He focused particularly on Malebo Pool (known in colonial days as Stanley Pool). This ten-kilometer wide pool in the Zaire River, which lies 300 kilometers from the mouth of the river and just above a long stretch of rapids, had served as a central place on Central African trade routes for centuries. There Brazza bested Henry Morton Stanley in a treaty-signing race for the interior, and signed in 1880 a treaty with Iloo I, king of the Tio.

Iloo was an elderly king whose power was limited by the power and energy of several great lords who owed him allegiance and yet acted with great independence. Iloo, against the advice of some of the lords, signed a treaty with Brazza in which he agreed to cede land for a commercial station to France. Iloo's vision of the African future was based on a *balance of forces*, in which outside influences (in this case Brazza) could be added to the equation of local forces. He considered the treaty to be an alliance with France, not a subordination to French authority (as the French later claimed it to be). As long as Iloo reigned (until 1890), his vision of the treaty remained valid, except for the area of Brazzaville which came under French domination. In addition, the treaty (which the French called the "Makoko" treaty, after a term for the Tio king) was not even in force until 1882, since the French National Assembly initially rejected it out of reluctance to acquire new colonies. Then came a public Paris meeting at which both Brazza and Stanley spoke: Brazza appeared as the peaceful colonizer and Stanley appeared as the ruthless conqueror. With such favorable publicity, Jules Ferry was able to get the Makoko Treaty ratified by the French National Assembly.

If Brazza rose to the occasion in this new imperial competition, it was Stanley who had set the terms of the game and whose activities brought King Leopold II of Belgium into African colonization. Stanley, the English-born, American-naturalized journalist, had become famous as leader of the *New York Herald's* expedition to find the missionary-explorer David Livingstone. In 1871, Stanley and his well-equipped caravan met Livingstone at Ujiji, on the eastern shore of Lake Tanganyika. Stanley brought back news of his travels to a reading public increasingly interested in African affairs. He returned to African exploration in 1874, leading an expedition of 200 inland from the east coast of Africa. He followed, as had he and Livingstone before, the roads dominated by Swhaili traders based on the island of Zanzibar. These merchants – who dealt in slaves, ivory, imported American cloth and many other goods – had expanded their influence across a vast area of East Africa only a few decades before Stanley's journey. Stanley passed over the highlands and into the headwaters of the Lualaba River.

There he met Tippu Tip, the greatest of the Swahili merchants, who had set up a large state in the Lualaba Valley, where he gathered great quantities of ivory to be sent to Zanzibar in caravans every two or three years: this was the influence which eventually caused Swahili to become the *lingua franca* for eastern Zaire. Tippu Tip's vision of African destiny was that of the *merchant principality*.

Stanley resolved to push on down river, into the forest, and Tippu Tip agreed (in return for a fee) to accompany him at least part way down the Lualaba, which Stanley eventually found to be one of the major sources of the Zaire. Explorer and merchant prince parted ways at the bend in the river where the Zaire turns west. Stanley and his caravan continued slowly down river, sometimes trading their goods for food and at other times fighting off attacks or initiating attacks in order to seize supplies. After 999 days of travel, Stanley and his expedition reached the port of Boma on the Zaire River estuary in 1877.

Stanley's vision was that of the explorer and tamer of wild Africa. His was a vision of *incorporation* of Africa into the broader world economy. His view and his destiny was soon to be linked to those of Leopold II, king of Belgium. Leopold, the energetic and ambitious sovereign of a small country whose constitution limited him to a ceremonial role, had been seeking an opportunity to become a builder of empire for a decade, making various attempts in Indonesia, the Pacific, and East Africa, all to no avail. His vision was centered on the search for *imperial glory*. But in 1879 he formed the International African Association with a particular interest in the Zaire basin, and by the end of that year he and Stanley had formed a tight, contractual relationship. Stanley was sent to the mouth of the Zaire at the head of a typically large expedition to sign treaties in the name of the association. Leopold, who never saw his African possession but followed it developments on a daily basis, expressed anguish when Brazza passed through Stanley's camp in 1880 and then went on to sign the Makoko treaty.

Stanley, meanwhile, focused on construction of a long road around the rapids of the lower Zaire. This work, carried out by Zanzibari and local laborers, took two years to complete. Once completed, it enabled him to bring steam boats from the coast to Stanley Pool. From there, once the first steamer was launched, his agents could reach the immense extent of the navigable Zaire and its tributaries. In the course of building the road, Stanley acquired the nickname of *Bula Matari* ("Rock Breaker") from the workers. Stanley gloried in the term, and it was later adopted to refer to the colonial state – both the Congo Independent State and the Belgian Congo. *Bula Matari* was a most apt and colorful term, for it crystallized at once the European and African appreciations of the vision of *incorporation*.

A CENTURY OF CHANGE

A century ago European and African cultures faced each other in conflict and contradiction. White was distinct from black, and the powerful were distinct from the weak. Europeans and Africans differed in language, religion, economic system, and in their visions of the future. In the conflicts and conquests of that time it was forgotten that Europeans and Africans had traded, worked, warred and played together for hundreds of years along the African coast. European conquerors, and many Africans as well, could see only two alternatives before them. Either Africans would retain their old ways but remain permanently weak and under the thumb of Europe, or Africans would give up their old ways and assimilate to the ways of Europe.

In fact, neither alternative took place. Out of the conflict there emerged new cultural syntheses. Both European and African traditions have bent and accommodated to the pressures of the other. This book tells the story of the emergence of a new cultural synthesis in the areas ruled for a time by France and Belgium. The details of the story are broken into two time periods: from 1880 to 1940, and from 1940 to 1985. Each of the two periods is discussed in three chapters. They address economic and social affairs (chapters 2 and 5);

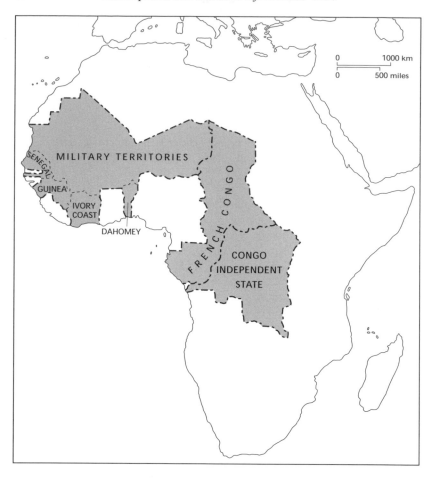

Map 4   Francophone sub-Saharan Africa in 1900

government and politics (chapters 3 and 6); and cultural and religious issues (chapters 4 and 7). The new chapter 8 traces politics from 1985 to 1995, and chapter 9 concludes in 1995.

In each of the chapters, the primary emphasis is on change and transformation rather than on continuity. This is not to deny the importance of continuities in modern Africa, nor to argue that ancestral African society has disappeared without a trace. It is, instead, to argue that African societies have renewed and reformed themselves in response to new challenges and that the strengths in the old African civilization can be seen in the strengths of the new.

Let us summarize the transformations to be detailed in the pages below. As we have said, the history of francophone sub-Saharan Africa begins with the European conquest. The conquest had two main stages. The 1880s were the

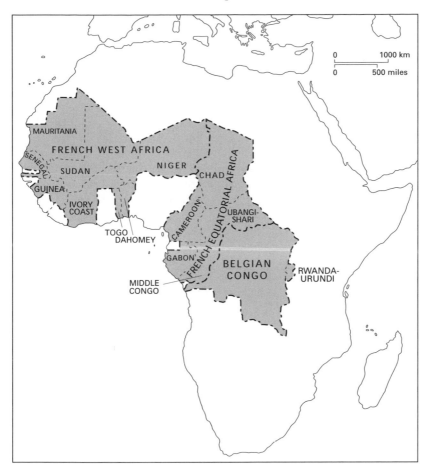

Map 5   Francophone sub-Saharan Africa in 1940

high point of the *diplomatic partition* of Africa, in which the European governments, after races to collect treaties, military confrontations, and long negotiations, agreed on how the African continent was to be divided among themselves. The actual *conquest* of Africa – the physical subjugation of its
inhabitants – was not completed until the turn of the twentieth century, and in
fact large areas of Central Africa and of the West African sahel escaped regular
European administration until after 1930.

In the early days of francophone Africa, the colonies were administered in
an informal and haphazard way, as conquest was still the main agenda of the
new rulers. It was only in the first decade of the twentieth century that a
rationalized administration was set up. This reorganization placed most of
francophone Africa into three great colonial units, each ruled by a governor-

general. French West Africa (Afrique Occidentale Française, or AOF) consisted of the colonies from Niger to the west and had its capital at Dakar. French Equatorial Africa (Afrique Equatoriale Française, or AEF) consisted of the colonies from French Congo to Chad and had its capital at Brazzaville. The Belgian Congo, a single gigantic colony, had its capital initially at Boma and then after 1920 at Leopoldville.

One final step in the territorial constitution of francophone sub-Saharan Africa took place with the French, Belgian, and British conquest of the German colonies in Africa during World War I. The French conquered most of Togo in 1914 and most of Cameroon in 1916, dividing these captured territories with the British. Similarly, in 1917 the Belgians conquered Rwanda and Burundi in the highland portion of German East Africa, and ruled them jointly as Ruanda-Urundi. With the establishment of the League of Nations, these new francophone colonies became French and Belgian Mandates from the League beginning in 1923. With some exceptions, the French and Belgians governed the mandates as appendages to their larger colonial units.

The francophone African territories were administered from this point to the 1950s with considerable continuity. Then in 1956 came a French administrative reform, the *loi-cadre*, which soon dismantled the governments-general in Dakar and Brazzaville and gave growing power to the governments of the individual colonies. This balkanization of the federations was followed by the independence of 14 sovereign nations from 1958 to 1960. In the Belgian Congo, independence came very suddenly in 1960, and the country nearly broke up into conflicting regions in the civil war which followed. Finally Ruanda-Urundi, on gaining independence in 1962, broke into two nations conforming to the boundaries of the precolonial states which had made it up.

The political systems, first, have changed in dramatic fashion. A century ago African governments ranged from tiny independent villages and families, as in southern Cameroon, to great empires with elaborate administrations, as under al-hajj Umar. The more than half-century of European rule brought a uniform system of administration, but it was utterly autocratic, giving the Africans almost no formal say in their government. African influence over their local governments was mainly through informal systems of representation and pressure. The return of African self-government by 1960 brought great hopes for freedom and democracy, but these hopes encountered many frustrations. Neocolonialism – the continuation of European power over Africans even after African political independence – was recognized as a problem shortly after independence. Corruption in African governments rapidly emerged as another problem. And autocracy – often through military government, but also by civilian leaders – returned to haunt many African countries. Africans paid a high price for the loss of their political rights in the colonial period.

The political changes in modern Africa, however impressive, are exceeded by the physical change which Africa has undergone in the last century. Africans now travel not only on foot but in cars and airplanes; they ship goods by truck rather than by head porterage. Radio reaches everywhere, and most tools are now machine-produced. The ecology of Africa has changed dramatically, though often for the worse. Great dams and hydroelectric projects provide electric power for millions, but the growth of population and short-sighted use of resources have caused the loss of much of Africa's forest, and the loss of much valuable grassland to desert. Water and firewood, crucial resources for urban and rural populations, are often in short supply.

The social life of Africans has changed almost as much as have physical conditions. The most positive change has been the dramatic lengthening of human lifespans. Infant mortality – the proportion of infants who fail to survive their first year – has declined from over 300 per thousand births a century age to about 100 per thousand in 1995. African mortality remains high by world standards, but the declining impact of death has enabled family size to grow even though birth rates have remained stable. In the same period, the expectation of life at birth rose from under 30 years to nearly 50.

African families remain strong, though they are structured differently now, partly because of the rise of cities (francophone Africa was roughly 30% urban in 1995) and also because of the development of economic structures and new social classes. The peasantry remains Africa's largest social class. (Alongside the millions of small farmers may be found smaller numbers of rural artisans, herders, fishers, and hunters.) The peasantry, however, has been gradually giving way: to the rise of a wage-labor class, the increase in numbers of small proprietors, the formation of a large bureaucracy, and the development of a small but powerful capitalist elite.

As the domestic economy has changed, so also has the nature of Africa's ties to the world economy. The African economy is much more dominated by world-wide forces than it was a century ago. The relation of Africa to the world economy has changed from a mercantile relation (in which Africans sold slaves to Europeans as workers, and then sold peanuts and other goods to Europeans), to an industrial capitalist relation (in which Africans sell their own labor to capitalist employers, European and African). Multinational corporations – Nestlé, Mobil, Toyota – are today as familiar to citizens of Togo and Zaire as they are to the French and Belgians.

The greatest changes in Africa during the past century, however, were in the area of culture. Most Africans are now Christians or Muslims, where a century ago most were neither. The philosophy of Africa, self-assured if isolated in the nineteenth century, then inundated and defeated by colonialism, has recently emerged to assert the value of African civilization in new and persuasive terms. African music, art, and literature have expanded to completely new forms: electric guitars as well as koras and xylophones, painting as well as sculpture, novels in French as well as epics in Mandingo and Kinyanga. The success of this transformation was revealed clearly in the first World Festival of African Arts and Culture in Dakar in 1966.

Francophone sub-Saharan Africa emerged as more than a convenient geographic bloc of territories, and more than a set of administrative units. It is a cultural community defined today by language, but also by traditions of education, religion, law, politics, social and economic structure.

Yet, lest the notion of francophone Africa come to seem as too logical, it should be emphasized that the term was not widely used until the 1960s. The colonial terms for Africa referred not to language but to empire: French Africa ("l'Afrique française") and Belgian Africa. French writers also spoke of "Black Africa" ("l'Afrique noire") when in practice they meant the French-speaking areas of sub-Saharan Africa. The terms "French-speaking Black Africa" (l'Afrique noire d'expression française") and finally "francophone Africa" ("l'Afrique francophone") did not become commonplace until the years after independence. African writers played an important role in spreading these new terms, as they sought to assert their independence without denying their historic ties to France. Further, it was only with the passage of time that the term was applied easily to the former Belgian colonies as well as to the former French colonies. In short, the notion of francophone sub-Saharan Africa is one which we read from the present back into the past.

Nonetheless, as we shall see, the events of the past century fit into patterns which justify the notion of francophone sub-Saharan Africa as a valid historical category. The creation of francophone sub-Saharan Africa was initiated with the conquests of the nineteenth century. It was taken a step further with the consolidation of the French and Belgian colonies in the early twentieth century, baptized with the independence of Africa and it continues to develop.

Not all of Africa's great changes have been equally successful. Cultural accommodation, while difficult, has been achieved more successfully than economic transformation. Africa's social and family structure, while imperfectly adjusted to the needs of today's world, functions far more effectively than Africa's political structure. New technology has been adopted, but the environmental impact is devastating in many areas.

In this study of a century of life in francophone sub-Saharan Africa, we will learn of the transformation of these 17 nations, and of the pressures for further change. In some senses the histories of francophone African nations are unique, and we will emphasize their uniqueness by contrasting their evolution with the experiences of anglophone, Arab, and other African nations. In other senses the history of francophone nations is representative; it gives an idea of the nature of change throughout Africa and in the modern world generally. The African countries are small in population and poor in material wealth by world standards, but they are not necessarily any less revealing of the essential problems of modern growth and change. The potential for destruction is clear there; the ecology of Africa is as badly threatened by economic change as that of Europe or North America. The hope for reconciliation is also to be found there. African countries include large numbers of Christians and Muslims who coexist within national boundaries, and they may be able to lead in resolving the world-wide conflicts between Christians and Muslims. Finally, the experience of African countries poses the question of economic equality which divides North from South: will Africans be able to overcome their conditions of poverty and dependence?

It is not necessarily true, however, that francophone sub-Saharan Africa will continue to expand and deepen its identity. The French language will doubtless remain important in these countries for the foreseeable future, especially for communication at an international level. More and more people will become literate in French. In some Central African countries French is on its way to becoming the universal language. On the other hand, more and more people will become literate in African languages – for instance, Wolof in Senegal and Lingala in Zaire – and thus limit the expansion of the influence of French. Further, the collective identity of 17 nations as specifically *franco-phone* African nations will be limited in the future on two sides. They will be drawn, on one side, to emphasize the narrower identity of their own individual national traditions. At the same time, there are still powerful forces drawing them to adopt a broader identity which goes beyond the limits of language and colonial heritage to emphasize continental, pan-African unity. Our story, then, is of the rise of francophone sub-Saharan Africa during the past century. Its future is yet to be created.

2

Economy and society, 1880–1940

The European conquerors of Africa believed that Africa changed only by fits and starts, and only as a result of external stimulus. These colonizers believed themselves to be developing a backward continent. They thought their new colonial regime was imposing great changes from outside, suddenly and powerfully, on a continent which was previously static, stagnant, and isolated. These Europeans chose to see themselves as the cause of positive change, and saw Africans as the cause of backwardness.

Some colonizers saw themselves as saviors of their fellow humans in Africa. They offered spiritual salvation through Christianity, or social salvation through Western eduction and capitalist enterprise. Other Europeans saw themselves as superior beings. They passed judgment on African civilization and found it to be morally inferior, economically backward, and incapable of achieving equality with Western civilization. Most Europeans in the late nineteenth century spoke of Africans as children – and therefore as people without maturity and without history. Not all Europeans considered that Africans were capable of growing up.

While Africans rarely spoke of themselves as children, many Africans did accept an apocalyptic view of colonialism. Certain of them accepted colonialism enthusiastically in hopes that it would create a new Africa more to their liking. Such a person was Joseph Tovalou Quénum, the wealthy Dahomean merchant and political figure who sought to expand his family fortune by allying with the French against his king, Behanzin. Others agreed that colonialism was an ultimate challenge to African traditions, but fought against it fiercely to preserve their own heritage. Samori Touré, ruler of a great state in the Western Sudan, has become a modern African hero because he fought with such determination against French conquest.

The European myths of European dynamism and African changelessness were self-serving and misleading. The beginning of colonial rule in Africa, as dramatic as it appears from the sudden changes on the map, was not the explosive collision of the irresistible force and the immovable object. The African "immovable object" had been in great change during the eighteenth and nineteenth centuries, particularly through the developing influence of slavery. Africans has been in regular contact with Europeans, especially through commerce. The European "irresistible force" was not one force but a variety of conflicting and evolving forces. The conflicts among European nations are reflected on the map with the formation of modern Germany and Italy in the era of colonial conquests, and with the recognition of more than a dozen new European nations after World War I. Within each European nation, society was dividing into conflicting social classes, especially the bourgeoisie and the proletariat – that is, the proprietary and wage-owning classes created out of the rapid expansion of the new industrial order.

Africa did, in fact, have its instances of sudden change, particularly in its government and politics. The European conquest of previously independent Africa was sudden indeed, as most of it took place in the two decades from 1880 to 1900. The independence and recognition of new African nations took place even more rapidly; all of francophone sub-Saharan Africa gained independence between 1958 and 1962.

Change in African history, however, involves far more than the rapid reorganization of political life. It includes the slower but more fundamental changes in economic organization, in social structure, and in the ecology of the continent. Thus Africa's involvement in world trade is marked not by sudden shifts, but by a slow decline in the volume of slave exports over a period of a century, and a slow expansion in exports of peanuts, palm oil, and coffee, paralleled by a slow expansion in African imports of cotton textiles and hardware. Neither the changes in the structure of African families nor the progressive deforestation of African lands obey the chronology set by the political events of colonization and decolonization. These small and slow changes in African economic and social life, taken together, provide the most basic explanation of the modern transformation in African life.

Colonialism is important in the modern history of Africa not because it created change, but because it exaggerated changes which were taking place already and because it revised the terms on which the changes took place. For these reasons we shall not begin the details of our story with governments, diplomacy, and war. Instead, we investigate first the changing conditions of daily life in francophone sub-Saharan Africa, to obtain a grasp of the material economic and social conditions which have been most basic to the lives of Africans, and which provide the context for the politics and culture to which we shall turn in later chapters.

This investigation begins with a review of the tumultuous social conditions of nineteenth-century Africa, as seen through the rise and fall of slavery. We turn next to the technology and ecology of francophone sub-Saharan Africa from 1880 to 1940. With this background, we review aspects of life in town and country: population, health conditions, social structure, and economic activity. We give particular attention to the nature of ethnicity and social class and turn subsequently to patterns of commerce and to the impact of colonial government on the economy. The conclusion to the chapter notes some important economic differences among francophone, anglophone, and Arab Africa, but also points out their common absorption into a capitalist world economy.

THE HERITAGE OF SLAVERY

Slavery and slave trade conditioned life in Africa as nowhere else in the world in the nineteenth century, and the heritage of slavery marks African life even today. The Atlantic slave trade reached the peak of its volume at the end of the eighteenth century and then declined. Some regions, especially the areas now included in the nations of Bénin, Congo, and Zaire, continued to be greatly influenced by the export of slaves until after 1850. The slave trade across the Sahara and the Red Sea reached its peak somewhat later, in about 1850, and it influenced seriously the areas of modern Chad and Central African Republic until after 1880. The total number of slaves *exported* from Africa declined steadily after 1830. But the number of men, women, and children enslaved remained high, because of the continuation of African wars, raids, and famines. Because of this excess supply of slaves, the prices of slaves in Africa fell, and African purchasers of slaves were able to buy many more slaves than before. As a result, the institution of slavery *in Africa* expanded during the nineteenth century as never before. Male and female slaves were captured and purchased for use as agricultural laborers, as servants, as artisans and, in smaller numbers, as soldiers and officials.

Surveys by French officials just after 1900 showed, for vast areas of the Western Sudan, that two-thirds of the population was enslaved, and that the great majority of adult slaves were women. Among such Central African trading peoples as the Chokwe and Bobangi, most of the population was servile. For the territories of francophone sub-Saharan Africa as a whole, one may speculate that as many as ten million people lived in servile status in the late nineteenth century, and that most of them were female.

This expansion of slavery was accompanied by significant economic change. In Senegal, especially beginning in the 1830s, landowners settled down thousands of slaves to grow peanuts for the expanding export trade. In Dahomey and in Cameroon, slaves were put to work in the harvesting and export of palm oil and palm kernels. Along the upper Zaire River, Tippu Tip's great trading expeditions included large numbers of slaves carrying tusks of ivory. In the savanna states of Bagirmi and the Sokoto Caliphate, landowners, officials, and merchants put captured slaves to work in the production of grains, textiles, and as porters on caravans. The Bobangi of the middle Zaire River and the Chokwe of the Kwilu valley expanded greatly their territory of influence through the wealth and power they gained in slave trading.

The social changes brought by this expansion of slavery included the creation of a slave class, and the further enrichment of a class of slave owners. Slave owners now found that their prosperity depended on strong state support for the institution of slavery, and they began to organize themselves into a conscious class. The increase in numbers of slaves made it difficult for masters to claim, as they had done before, that slaves became members of masters' families simply because they lived in the same compounds. As slaves took on more and more of the agricultural labor, they came to live apart from their masters and to have distinct families of their own. These slave families began to coalesce, as the depth of their common interests grew, into slave classes. The masters responded with a new form of the ideal that slaves were "part of the family," in order to restrict the growth of slave consciousness. Masters argued that slave families, now living separately, were lineages affiliated with the lineage of the master.

The expansion of slavery, and the defense of the expanded slave system, also brought political changes to Africa. In the Western Sudan, Samori Touré turned a commercial state into a great warlord's realm, and used slaves as the currency for financing it against the attacks of the French. In the Central Sudan, the roving adventurer and slave-raider Rabeh arrived to seize control of the kingdom of Borno in 1893. Further east and south in the savanna, Dar al-Kuti rose as one of the last major slaving states, and preserved its independence from the French until 1913.

For centuries, since the rise of sugar plantations in Brazil and the West Indies in the seventeenth century, European purchases of slaves for New World plantations had been the main reason for the expansion of African slavery and slave trade. But a new movement of opposition to slavery emerged late in the eighteenth century. The opponents of slavery included the New World slaves themselves, certain Christian thinkers who found that slavery could not be reconciled with their religion, and economic leaders who believed that wage labor was destined to replace slavery. Africans too, both slave and free, added their weight to the anti-slavery movement from the first. But the opponents of slavery in Africa had to be content with small and infrequent victories until late in the nineteenth century.

The Quakers in America and England were among the main early opponents of slavery, and the English abolition of Atlantic slave trade in 1808 was one of the main achievements on the road to ending slavery. The most spectacular anti-slavery actions occurred in France and the French colonies. France, at the high point of its great Revolution, abolished slavery in all its colonies in 1794, and maintained for some years an alliance with the former slaves of its richest colony, St.-Domingue (now Haiti), who had risen in revolt beginning in 1791. But in 1802 Napoleon decided that slavery was to be reinstituted, and sent armies to subjugate St.-Domingue. The former slaves suffered initial defeat, but then rose to expel the French, and declared independence for Haiti in 1804. The black people of the other French colonies, however, found themselves back under the yoke.

In the 1830s, Victor Schoelcher emerged as the leader of a revived French humanitarian movement dedicated to the abolition of slavery. This movement finally achieved its goal in the early days of the Revolution of 1848, as all slaves in French colonies were liberated. From this time on, religious missionaries took the lead in the French anti-slavery movement. Cardinal Lavigerie, head of the White Fathers, devoted himself to anti-slavery campaigns in Algeria and East Africa.

By the 1870s, the European anti-slavery movement had become linked fatefully to the movement for European conquest and colonization in Africa. That is, Europeans who wished to conquer Africa for other reasons seized on the work of anti-slavery activists and used opposition to slavery as a justification for conquest. The Belgians, for instance, had no history of colonization nor of slavery, so it was logical enough for them to oppose slavery in principle. But for King Leopold II, who was seeking a way to obtain a colony for himself, the anti-slavery campaign was a means toward the end of colonization. For Leopold's Congo Independent State (CIS) and for the French in West and Central Africa, the conquests and treaties were all conducted under the banner of anti-slavery. Two great conferences of European nations, the Berlin Conference of 1884–5 and the Brussels Conference of 1889, were nominally devoted to the humanitarian aim of ending slavery in Africa. In fact, however, they did more to ensure European conquest of Africa than to abolish slavery in the conquered territories. The new European governments of Africa did make serious attempts to prevent the capture and sale of slaves. But slavery itself remained a common fact of life for over a generation after colonial rule began, and in some cases it lasted much longer.

The colonial governments tended to protect the institution of slavery, opposing the liberation of slaves on grounds that it would bring about unwelcome social disorder. Further, the new governments used slaves in their own service. Thus the French military, in establishing its base at Bamako on the upper Niger in 1883, refused to release slaves from service. The French demand for grain to feed the troops, further, encouraged landowners at such nearby towns as Banamba to buy slaves in order to grow more grain. Some slaves, however, fell directly into French hands. Military authorities in the West African savanna settled them down in over 150 "liberty villages." (Missionaries set up another 30 liberty villages.) In these liberty villages, however, the ex-slaves were called upon to work under restrictions so severe that the condition was a small improvement over slavery. In 1904 the French civilian administration condemned the liberty villages, and they disappeared by 1911.

The slaves themselves sought to use the colonial conquest as a means of freeing themselves. Many slaves ran away from their masters the moment French or Congo Independent State troops arrived. Others appealed to the new administration for their freedom. Many others simply took their freedom after some reflection: the slaves of Banamba announced in 1905 that they would no longer be slaves, and thousands of slaves, individuals and families walked back toward their homelands east of the upper Niger. As they passed the French post at Bamako, the commandant recorded them as explaining "that they had no animosity to their masters, they simply wanted to return home." The escape from slavery was generally easier for male slaves than for females, as women were often tied by children and by marriage to their adoptive homes. And for many slaves, there was no home to return to. These slaves had a greater tendency to escape to French and Belgian administrative posts and towns.

The slave owners too were faced with an adjustment once the colonial era began. As slavery gradually lost the force of law, they sought to transform their control over their slaves in order to maintain it. To the degree that they could become landowners, they could exchange ownership of the slaves for payments of rent from tenants. In this way, many informal renegotiations of the relations between masters and slaves were worked out. If the owners were able to maintain their wealth, they could become entrepreneurs – capitalist leaders of the growing colonial economy, rather than slave-owning relics of the past.

Slavery itself died out over the first half of the colonial era. Shortly after 1900, both French and Belgian administrations decreed that, thereafter, all children would be born free. For those already enslaved, they could petition the courts for their liberty, or they could purchase their liberty, but otherwise they would remain in slave status until their death. In this way, the nature of slavery changed from the vicious and expanding system of servitude it had been in the late nineteenth century to a more benign system which was now declining. Slave families now became lineages attached to the lineages of their masters.

After World War I, the great powers declared slavery illegal. The victorious Allies agreed, in the 1919 Convention of St.-Germain-en-Laye, to update the 1889 Brussels Act by pledging to abolish "slavery in all its forms." The League of Nations, formed in 1921, supported a 1926 convention in which 40 nations adopted the same language. But the harnessing and abolition of slavery in the twentieth century could not remove the knowledge of what it had been. The stratification of society into master and slave remained in the minds of Africans for succeeding generations, as did the privileges achieved by the masters and the disabilities thrust on the slaves.

TECHNOLOGY AND ECOLOGY

African technology changed dramatically in the years between 1880 and 1940. Most of the changes were the result of new industrial technology introduced from Europe, but the new technology became integral to the African way of life in this short time. Changes in the technology of transportation and communication were among the most visible and the most significant.

Steamships came early to the African coast. In the mid nineteenth century, when sailing ships still dominated the trade of the North Atlantic, steamships had all but driven the sailing ships out of business along the African coast because of the advantage of their speed and their regular schedules in an area where contrary winds made sailing difficult. Steamships came to the navigable reaches of Africa's rivers early – the Niger expedition of 1854 is one such example. The most important breakthrough in river transport was in December 1881 when Stanley launched the first steamer at Malebo Pool and began charting the thousands of kilometers of the Zaire and its tributaries. Telegraphs and postal systems were set up, linking colonial capitals to Europe, and linking military and administrative posts in the hinterland to the capitals. From the first, African workers operated the telegraph and postal systems, and African customers were an important part of the clientele. Senegalese telegraph operators, for instance, served all over the French African colonies, and they were sometimes able to use the information they collected on prices of goods or political decisions to advance their own business or political careers.

The colonial regimes built roads and railways. The railways were almost always to serve economic purposes, carrying African products to the coast for export, but they were also used for military and administrative purposes, as with ferrying troops to trouble spots. Railroad construction was capital intensive and thus required raising large amounts of money either in Europe or by taxation of the African colonies; once constructed, they could be operated for smaller maintenance expenses. Road construction, on the other hand, was more often political than economic in its objectives. Roads were built with labor alone, and usually with unpaid labor. The annual requirement of clearing roads was therefore more of a statement of submission to the colonial government than it was an investment for economic advantage.

The first railroad in francophone sub-Saharan Africa was built in the years from 1883 to 1885, and linked the ports of Dakar and St.-Louis in Senegal. The next major railroad in francophone Africa covered the nearly 300 kilometers from Matadi to Kinshasa in the Congo Independent State. This railroad paralleled the road carved out by Stanley in 1880–1; it bypassed the rapids of the lower Zaire and provided the essential link from the coast to the navigable portions of the Zaire River. Financed by investments from Belgian, British, and German investors and from the government of Belgium, it was built by workers drawn from Senegal, Dahomey, Gold Coast, Barbados, and China. It was completed in 1898 after a considerable loss in life to the work force. Joseph Conrad described a scene in construction of the railroad, in which some workers had left the work site to rest, while the noise of blasting continued in the background.

> Black shapes crouched, lay, sat between the trees leaning against the trunks . . .
> They were dying slowly – it was very clear. They were not enemies, they were not criminals, they were nothing earthly now, nothing but black shadows of disease and starvation, lying confusedly in the greenish gloom. Brought from all the recesses of the coast in all the legality of time contracts, lost in uncongenial surroundings, fed on unfamiliar food, they sickened, became inefficient, and were then allowed to crawl away and rest.

Other major railroads, all constructed before World War I, included the extension of the Senegal railroad from Kayes on the upper Senegal to Bamako on the Niger in the 1890s, and later a link from Kayes to Dakar. The French state built railroads in the Ivory Coast, in Guinea, and in Dahomey; private firms built further railroads in the Congo Independent State to supplement the river transport network. Finally, the German administrations of Togo and Cameroon built rail networks in the prosperous coastal regions of their colonies. All of these railroads were designed to link a seaport to a hinterland. They were not designed to link major African centers to each other, but to link African sources of raw materials to European purchasers, and to link European manufacturers to African purchasers. Once the railroads were there, however, they began to play a role in the local economy. In Dahomey, for instance, salt merchants began shipping their wares on the railroad, and cattle merchants used the rail line as a convenient path to march their herds through a marshy area.

Railroad construction slowed after World War I, except in the southern savanna. The Belgian Congo added 2,450 kilometers of new lines to its rail network, through private investment with state participation, and thus extended an efficient system for shipping mineral resources out of the colony. The French state in Equatorial Africa concluded that they must have a separate link to the coast, rather than use the Belgian railroad. It therefore constructed, from 1921 to 1934, a long and difficult rail link between Brazzaville and Pointe Noire on the Atlantic. As with other railroad construction, this work required large numbers of workers – many of them forcibly recruited – and built up a wage labor force for its later operation. The high death rates for the construction workers on the Congo–Ocean railroad, as it was known, became a major colonial scandal.

Africans paid most of the costs of railroad construction; they subsidized the construction of their railroads through payment of taxes and by performing underpaid and unpaid labor. In the French territories, purchase of the capital equipment was funded by tax revenue and by bonds sold in Europe. These French railroads were all government-owned; they thus prefigured the nationalization of rail lines in Europe. The few efforts of French colonial governments to give concessions permitting privately owned railways failed. In the more heavily capitalized Belgian Congo, however, most railways were constructed and operated by private firms, with the state owning a portion of the stock. These railroads thus prefigured the later expansion of joint private-government enterprise in Africa and Europe.

Internal combustion engines followed steam power promptly in Africa as elsewhere. Trucks were imported for transport in small numbers beginning about 1910, first by government and then by private merchants, European and African. The limits on imports of trucks were not the lack of interest in them, but the lack of roads (trucks had to make their own), the high cost of purchase and the cost of maintenance and repair. During times of war and depression, gasoline became scarce or prohibitively expensive, and the trucks stopped rolling: African goods could then move only in the slow, painful, and expensive old way, by head transport, or by donkeys, oxen, and camels.

Internal combustion motors powered cotton gins, which enabled the export cotton industry to get under way in Sudan, Dahomey, Ubangi-Shari, and the Belgian Congo. During the 1930s, small motors came to be used to power mills for grain: West African families purchased grain in the market, and had it milled upon purchase.

Through these and other developments, Africans were drawn firmly into the world of industrial technology. The Africans did not produce the industrial goods, but they operated them (in the case of railroads and copper, gold, or diamond mines) and they used them in daily life in ways which profoundly changed their technical tasks. This reliance on imported tools and technology had roots in the distant past. The Tio of French Congo, for instance, had given

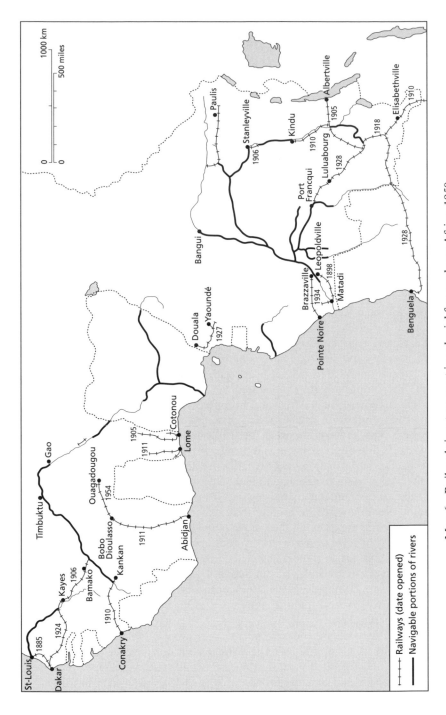

Map 6 Rail and river transport in colonial francophone Africa, 1950

up mining iron as long ago as the eighteenth century, since they found it possible to purchase iron from European merchants at lower cost; the same was true for other peoples as well. Similarly, long-established salt-manufacturing industries along the Atlantic were outcompeted in the nineteenth century when European merchants began importing salt at low cost in order to sell it for palm oil. As time wore on, industrial innovations were marketed with success to African purchasers. Matches reduced the necessity to keep a fire going at all times. Kerosene was a much more efficient lighting oil than palm oil or shea butter. Imported casks of jute sacks were used for packaging the exports of peanuts, palm oil, and palm kernels. Hand knives and long matchets were marketed throughout Africa. The arrival of sewing machines enabled a new line of tailoring work to begin, and the arrival of bicycles made transportation easier.

The changes in African technology during the colonial period, however, were not limited to the adoption of industrial technology, and they were not necessarily improvements. In Central Africa, agricultural technology underwent massive changes which left the population with an inferior diet. The main reason was the recruitment of men to labor for the state and concessionary companies (a continuation, in effect, of the turmoil and displacement brought by the nineteenth-century slave trade). With the men absent for much of the year, women had to take on more responsibility in clearing and fencing, and they had to give up cultivation of many crops. As a result, they restricted their fields to a few starchy staples, maintaining calories but losing nutritional balance. At the construction sites and in the mine compounds, the colonizers fed their recruits a diet based almost entirely on starchy staples, thus reinforcing the trend. As a result, manioc (cassava), a root crop which produces starchy tubers in almost any tropical soil, spread widely throughout forested and wet savanna areas. It is productive and easily preserved, though not especially nutritious.

Despite such difficulties, the increased contacts among African farmers and with Europeans meant that many new crops and techniques were tried, with occasional success. Techniques in fishing and herding also changed. One remarkable development was the expansion of fish shelters in the lagoons of Dahomey. These shelters, made of branches thrust in the bottom of the lagoon in areas from five to 100 meters across, attracted fish which were periodically harvested with the aid of nets.

Aside from technical change, the growing importance of the world market had its impact on African ecology. Market prices and the pressure of colonial taxes encouraged many farmers to focus on producing goods for export, and to cut back their production of foodstuffs. In some cases even foodstuffs were exported. In the years between 1906 and 1913, farmers in Dahomey and Togo exported large amounts of maize to German producers who used it in production of liquor and were willing to pay a good price. The colonial administration in Dahomey complained that farmers were cutting down forests – even sacred forests which were thought to be the residences of important spirits – in order to plant new maize. While the farmers ignored the pleas of the government to save the forest, the government had already sought to undermine the power of the priests who had earlier been able to preserve the forest.

The growth of non-food exports influenced the African landscape as well, if only because they caused farming people to put their efforts into different tasks. Exports of rubber were important in heavily forested areas. Exports of ivory from the savannas of North Central Africa remained significant as long as the elephants survived in numbers. The forested areas of West Africa produced palm oil, palm kernels, cocoa, and coffee for export; and the northern savanna produced peanuts and cotton for export.

The natural limits on resources sometimes put pressure on the ecological system. In savanna areas, water was in short supply for much of the year, and people had to choose among living close to waterways, carrying water for long distance, or trying to gain access to more water through cisterns and wells. As towns grew in size, the shortage of water became even more serious, and it was steadily compounded by shortages of firewood. Ouagadougou in Upper Volta, for instance, a town of over 10,000 but with few nearby forest resources, could supply its needs for firewood only through the efforts of hundreds of women who scoured the countryside for wood and carried it into town.

Human strains on the limits of tropical ecology were often more serious. One serious new pressure brought on African ecology came from the enforced concentration of settlement by colonial governments. Particularly for forested areas such as southern Ivory Coast and the Belgian Congo, European governments were unhappy with the dispersed settlements of the inhabitants, who preferred to live in small hamlets rather than large villages. In the early twentieth century, many forest dwellers were forced to move to large villages near to roads, where they could more easily be called upon to make tax payments and do road work. The Gouro of Ivory Coast, for instance, were required to consolidate their hamlets into large villages after the 1910 rebellion in which some of them participated. These larger and more permanent settlements interfered with their pattern of shifting cultivation. Shifting cultivation had been a successful adjustment to the poverty of African soils; a newly cleared field typically provided good harvests for two or three years, after which it required many years of fallow. But when farmers were required to stay in one place, they had to develop new adaptations to offset the rapid decline in the fertility of the fields near their residences.

TRANSFORMATIONS IN TOWN AND COUNTRY

The towns of precolonial Africa had grown up at centers of commerce and centers of political power. There were few towns in heavily forested areas, because both political and economic life were decentralized there. In the savannas, however, towns were common and at times large. Jenne and Timbuktu, for instance, were two great commercial towns of the Niger valley; the port town of Ouidah on the Atlantic coast of Dahomey had a population of about 10,000 in the mid nineteenth century, and nearby Porto-Novo had twice as many. Political capitals were sometimes more impressive than the commercial towns; the court of the Mangbetu kings in the upper Ubangi was decorated with burnished copper which dazzled the beholder and glorified the king. But political capitals were less lasting because patterns of politics changed more rapidly than patterns of commerce. In the Kuba kingdom of the Kasai valley in the southern savanna, each king engaged an architect to lay out an entirely new capital town. The capital of Bagirmi, in the heart of what is today Chad, moved periodically with the king.

Although towns stood out as centers of power and exchange in precolonial Africa, the population remained overwhelmingly rural. So while the story of transformation in social and economic life must include an emphasis on the rise of new cities and new conditions in cities, most of the transformation of African life has taken place in the countryside. For instance, cities have grown rapidly in population during the past century, but most of Africa's population growth has taken place in the countryside.

African populations have fluctuated widely in size and composition during the past century. West African populations were growing as the French took over, and continued to grow at modest rates. For much of Central Africa, population declined during the nineteenth century as a result of the captures and mortality associated with the slave trade. For these same areas – the French colonies of equatorial Africa and much of the Belgian Congo – population continued to decline to the 1920s. The medical causes of population decline were reinforced by social changes. Venereal disease, endemic to the area, brought sterility to many inhabitants. These and other diseases were spread further as a result of the greater mobility that occurred under European rule. Forced labor and forced cultivation interfered with the normal African work patterns, and cut nutritional levels to the point where health was impaired.

The disease conditions of Africa raised the level of mortality to an unusually high level, even given good personal hygiene. The greatest killer was malaria, a disease carried by a microscopic fluke transmitted to humans by the *anopheles* mosquito. The fluke causes fever, nausea, and death of as many as 30% of children in their first year, and recurrent sickness thereafter. The mosquito reproduces in puddles of water so tiny that no efforts have been successful in eradicating it. Yellow fever, also transmitted by mosquitoes, came in periodic epidemics. Smallpox epidemics killed many and scarred many more.

Sleeping sickness, transmitted by the *glossina* or tsetse fly, struck the populations of Central Africa especially. There and in forested regions of Ivory Coast, sleeping sickness spread from the beginning of the twentieth century, as labor recruitment and tax collection brought people into closer contact with the flies. Colonial experiments with methods of control, involving quarantine and clearing of brush, were not successful until about 1940. Other diseases with which Africans had to contend included yaws, bilharzia, measles, and influenza. The 1918 influenza epidemic, for instance, carried away an estimated 5% of the population of francophone sub-Saharan Africa. Parasites laid people low with dysentery or with guinea worm. The generally high level of disease in this tropical environment reduced the certainty of life, and forced people to remain prepared for sudden and drastic changes in their lives, or for the end of life.

Just as diseases affected the human population, they also affected the plant and animal populations. Tsetse fly and sleeping sickness prevented horses and cattle from living in large areas of the continent. A great epidemic of rinderpest or cattle plague swept across Africa from east to west in the 1890s, and drastically reduced the cattle population of the savanna. Smaller epidemics wiped out populations of chickens and pigs in some regions.

Populations grew as well as declined. Towns and missions tended to attract population because of new types of employment, and the populations of towns tended to grow not only through immigration, but because health conditions were somewhat better there than in the countryside. The health conditions were better because of public health measures rather than because of actual medical care; towns had better water supplies, latrines, and fewer mosquitoes. In the countryside, colonial governments contributed to population growth once they took an interest in halting local famines by arranging shipments of food; at the same time, colonial governments also caused famines. Thus, the relatively efficient administration of Governor Brevié brought population growth and prosperity to Niger during the 1920s. Then the heavy collection of taxes compounded the effects of drought to bring about a major famine in western Niger in 1931.

The family was and is the basic unit of African social life. Most families in francophone Africa defined themselves as lineages: patrilineages or matrilineages. Patrilineages consist of all male and female persons descended from a single male ancestor through the male line; matrilineages consist of all male and female persons descended from a female ancestor through the female line. They are known as *corporate* descent groups because each person is theoretically a member of only a single lineage group. Lineage leaders, usually drawn from the oldest men, handled decisions on allocation of land, presided over marriages and funerals, and resolved disputes.

In practice, lineages did not operate as neatly as in theory. For instance, the rules of inheritance in matrilineages required that a man pass his goods and titles to his sister's son rather than to his own son. (A man's own son is in his wife's lineage, not his own, while a man's sister's son is the nearest male in the next generation who remains in his lineage.) Many men in the southern savanna, an area where descent is mostly matrilineal, were able to violate this rule through the use of slaves. Since a slave woman had no lineage of her own, a man's children by a slave woman could be considered as being in his own lineage, and he could pass goods and titles on to his own sons without reducing his family's possessions. In fact, slavery and this sort of marriage became so prominent in the nineteenth-century southern savanna that it was matrilineal in theory only.

In this sense marriage, rather than the lineage, was the most important aspect of African families. While the rules and institutions of marriage varied widely in francophone Africa, almost all societies allowed for polygyny or multiple wives. Women married early and began having children while still in their teens; men did not usually marry until well into their twenties, and rarely took a second wife until their thirties. In this way men could hope to have multiple wives, but only by postponing marriage. The women, in turn, often had multiple husbands, since they were still young when their husbands died, and they could remarry (or were required to remarry). Multiple wives were common in southern Ivory Coast, but in Rwanda few men had more than one wife.

While lineages and polygyny remained the basic pillars of African families, they underwent great changes in the twentieth century. The colonial system of taxation, for instance, tended to break up lineages. Lineage chiefs paid the same taxes as any other adult, yet the lineage chiefs often held the treasury for all the families under their leadership. Younger men became aggrieved that the chiefs would not pay taxes on their behalf, and broke away to form their own, smaller lineages. In other cases colonial governments created lineages where none had existed; both Belgian and French governments required appointment of family chiefs who would be responsible for collecting taxes and recruits.

The spread of Christianity brought a challenge to polygyny, since Christian missionaries argued that no Christian man could have more than one wife. In some cases, as in southern Cameroon, the conversion of most families to Christianity meant the near total abandonment of polygyny. In other cases, as in Ivory Coast, independent Christian churches sprung up which followed the European interpretation of the religion on most lines, but permitted polygyny.

Islam, too, spread during the colonial period. Islam did not challenge polygyny – indeed, it served to legitimize multiple marriage, though with a limit of four wives per man. But the spread of Islam did change the relations of men and women within the household. African women did not put on the veil, as did many women in the Middle East, but in some cases they were removed from public view and secluded in compounds, as among the wealthy Maraka merchants of the Middle Niger.

Family units produced most of the food and household goods on which the people of francophone Africa relied. Each area relied on starchy staples to provide most calories, and on a range of vegetables, fruits, and condiments for variety and nutritional balance. Millet, a tall and rapidly growing grain crop, was the main source of food all across the northern savanna and in the southern savanna as well; sorghum, another grain, was second in importance among the northern savanna peoples. Rice was the main crop in the western forest and nearby savanna: in parts of Ivory Coast, Guinea, and Senegal. For the remainder of the West African forest, for portions of the equatorial forest, and for nearby savanna areas, yams were the main crop. These yams were grown in mounds and produced large cylindrical tubers which could be boiled and eaten in chunks or pounded into a paste. For most of the equatorial forest, bananas and plantains were the main crop, while beans dominated in the highlands of Rwanda and Burundi. Two American crops, maize and manioc, had come to be widely grown even before the colonial period, especially in wet savanna areas, and have spread further since then.

The timing of the rains governed production of these major crops. The agricultural calendar of savanna peoples involved intensive preparation of fields as the first rains came, planting (and replanting in cases when the rains failed), weeding, and then harvest, all within a period of less than half a year. Production of the many other crops and care of domestic animals had to be worked into the same calendar. All other activities, such as house construction, textile work, basketry, and repairs, tended to be concentrated in the dry season. Peoples of the forest and of the highlands, on the other hand, had two rainy seasons and two harvests per year, so that their activities were spread a little more evenly through the year.

There were a number of types of specialization of work. Most basic was the sexual division of labor. In southern Cameroon, men cleared fields, while women did most of the farming. Women's farming was centered on peanut fields, while men's farming centered on melons, from which the seeds were eaten. When the men were called away to do road work or perform military service, food output declined and nutrition suffered. In Senegal and Niger, men and women divided up the farm labor, while along the West African coast women tended to specialize in marketing work.

Ethnic specialization in production was another way of dividing up the work. The Fulbe people specialized in cattle raising all across the northern savanna from Senegal as far east as Lake Chad. Other ethnic groups specialized in fishing: the Buduma of Lake Chad, the Bozo on the Niger River, the Alladian on the lagoons of Ivory Coast.

The transformations of rural Africa under French and Belgian colonial rule were subtle yet fundamental. An inexperienced visitor to the countryside in 1940 might have taken away an image of a simple and unchanging country life, rather than of a life recently transformed through the influence of taxation and labor recruitment. Our visitor might not have noticed how numerous were the small changes in technology, farming patterns, residence patterns, and family organization. In the cities, however, the changes brought by colonial rule were impossible to ignore.

The Europeans founded new towns such as Dakar and Brazzaville, laid out with straight, twentieth-century streets, central plazas, and imposing Victorian buildings. Their populations included roughly half of the tiny European population of each colony, which was employed in government and mercantile offices; Europeans, in turn, comprised roughly 10% of the total population of these new towns. In 1900 these colonial capitals did not exceed 5,000 in population. In time they grew, but without great rapidity. By 1940 Dakar was the largest city in francophone sub-Saharan Africa, with a population of 60,000 Africans and 10,000 Europeans, and in the same year Leopoldville (now Kinshasa) had reached no more than 40,000. Both the European and African populations of these towns were heavily male; Leopoldville was only 30% female in 1940. Residential segregation was never a matter of law in French and Belgian colonies, but it was always a practice. The new towns were divided into the "European city" (or the Plateau in Dakar) and the "African quarters" (Poto-Poto in Brazzaville, Treichville in Abidjan, the Medina in Dakar). The Europeans lived in spacious houses with surrounding gardens in the vicinity of the government buildings; they had electricity and often running water, and bought provisions at European-owned stores. The African quarters were laid out in adjoining areas to receive the steady stream of immigrants seeking work in the city. The immigrants built small homes, closely packed, on land whose title was often in dispute; they carried water from public fountains, often located at the great market places.

Wage labor was the usual form of employment for Africans in these towns. The elite were interpreters, clerks, teachers, railway and port workers; a much larger number held such positions as servants, runners, day laborers, and janitors. But the towns, as centers of European enterprise, were also centers of African enterprise. Tailors, bicycle repairmen, hairdressers, and many other entrepreneurs opened up shops alongside the many small retail outlets in the cities' market places.

In three cases, the French placed their colonial capitals in old African towns, with populations of from 10 to 20,000. In Porto-Novo and Ouagadougou, the French built their European city at the outskirts of the African town. In St.-Louis (which remained the capital of Senegal until 1958), Governor Faidherbe rebuilt the town entirely, much as Baron Haussman was then rebuilding the city of Paris. The end result in the old African towns was similar to that in the new towns, except that the sex ratio remained more equitable in the old towns.

The colonial governments, while they were centered in the towns, were not content until they had extended their influence throughout the new colonies. And in fact they had great influence, over a period of decades, especially in the creation of a wage labor force. Important as this creation of a wage labor force was, however, it is often misrepresented. Colonial officials often spoke of "drawing Africans into the money economy" as if the people of the colonies were ignorant of the use and the meaning of money. Officials also spoke of "teaching the natives the value of work."

In fact, Africans worked quite as hard as farming peoples the world over, and almost all the peoples of francophone Africa used money before the Europeans took over. In some cases the money was even European (Maria Theresa silver dollars, British sterling, French francs), while in other cases it consisted of gold dust, cowrie shells, copper rings and crosses, or standardized strips of cloth.

What the Europeans meant by trying to draw Africans into the "money economy" and the "cash economy" was that Africans should be discouraged from using their own money, and they should work for wages from European firms, or sell their goods to European merchants, and that they should spend their money on imported European goods. What the colonizers meant by teaching Africans "the value of work" was that they should be willing to place greater value on working for a European employer at a low wage than on working their own land. Bringing about this willingness required a great deal of coercion. The result was forced labor on highways, railroads, and public works, taxes requiring people to earn European cash, and a steady program of indoctrination.

Production in the mines of the Belgian Congo was a special case of labor recruitment. Gold exports began in 1905, copper exports in 1909, and diamond exports in 1914. Because of high demand for these minerals, large sums of European capital were attracted to the Belgian Congo as nowhere else in francophone Africa, for purchase of mining and processing equipment, and for railway construction. In 1906 the Congo Independent State approved the formation of three great companies, whose rights were confirmed with the Belgian takeover. These were Union Minière du Haut-Katanga (UMHK), formed to mine copper; the Lower Congo–Katanga Railway Company (BCK), formed to build a railroad to Katanga, and with mineral rights in Kasai; and FORMINIERE, formed to exploit the forests and mines of the diamond-bearing areas of Kasai. All were dominated by the Société Générale, the Belgian trust. UMHK also included a substantial investment by a British group headed by Robert Williams, a former associate of Cecil Rhodes in South Africa, and UMHK gave a substantial block of stock to the Katanga Special Committee (CSK) which had earlier obtained the concession of the land from the Congo Independent State. Finally, the colonial state obtained some UMHK stock, and once the mines became profitable this stock provided the Belgian Congo with additional revenue. This pattern of interlocking ownership persisted throughout the colonial period.

In the early stages of mining work, only surface deposits were worked, and with very elementary technology. As a result, great numbers of workers were recruited, and received very low rates of pay. This was especially true for the gold deposits of the Uele valley, where as many as 100,000 recruits labored in mines and in the refineries at Kilo and Moto. In these early days, recruits on their way to the mines were at times linked with ropes about their necks. By the 1930s, as mining became more capital intensive, working conditions improved, and smaller numbers of recruits were required.

The Katanga copper mines, for the first 20 years of their operation, were in practice part of the British-dominated southern African mining complex. Most of the African miners were Bemba from neighboring Northern Rhodesia, and the European staff was mostly English-speaking. Copper ore was shipped to the south, after the opening of the railroad in 1910, via Northern Rhodesia and South Africa. Only gradually did the Belgians gain control. They bought out the British investors by 1920, they linked Katanga to the Lower Congo with the opening of the Kasai railway in 1928, and in the 1920s they replaced the Bemba miners (especially when they carried out strikes for better working conditions) with recruits from the Congo.

The mines had a significant effect on their surroundings. They stimulated demand for food, construction material, clothing, and entertainment. Union Minière worked closely with the Benedictine missionaries to create a model community among its workers. One result was to instill in the copper miners the idea that the ideal wife was one trained by the Benedictines.

ETHNICITY AND CLASS

The peoples of francophone Africa have been drawn toward each other by a range of historical factors. But they retain among themselves social and ethnic differences as sharp as those of any other continent. The ethnic differences are reflected in the nearly 700 distinct languages spoken by the people of francophone Africa. Most of these languages are classified within the Niger–Congo group, the largest of the four great African language groups. The Niger–Congo languages include several major subgroups, including the Mande and Voltaic languages of the Western Sudan. The languages of francophone Africa may be compared to the languages of Europe, which are part of the great Indo–European group of languages. The Bantu languages, a subgroup of Niger–Congo languages, spread out to include most of Central Africa, in a pattern similar to the spread of French, Spanish, Portuguese, and other Romance languages to cover a large portion of the Indo–European language zone. In addition, a large portion of the northern savanna population speaks Afro–Asiatic languages, and a smaller but significant group in the Central and Eastern Sudan speaks Nilo–Saharan languages.

The people of francophone Africa include a large and fluctuating number of ethnic groups, which are distinguished from each other in language, in culture, in social structure, and in political organization. To recall two ethnic groups mentioned in the previous chapter, the Mandingo of the Western Sudan include today over two million persons, while the Nyanga of the Zaire forest include no more than twenty thousand persons.

In popular parlance, the peoples of Africa are divided into "tribes." Today's notion of the tribe developed in part out of the variety of African ethnicity, but also out of a nineteenth-century European determination to classify Africans. Once the European ethnographers were finished, every African could be classified neatly into one "tribe" or another, and could thus be attributed with a language, culture, and history which was unique and unambiguous. Tribal maps were drawn to show the frontiers of each. This notion of the tribe developed out of a growing sense of European national identity, for the map of Europe was then being redrawn to fit ethnic limits, and at times the people were moved to fit the lines on the map. In addition, Europeans viewed Africans as "primitives" and believed that each member of a primitive society must have a unique tribal identity.

Sometimes this artificial and simplistic notion of ethnicity could be applied to Africa with success. The Bakongo in Zaire and Congo, the Fon in Bénin, and the Wolof in Senegal were "tribes" in this sense. They were identifiable linguistic communities, they shared a common identity (which had grown up through the history of a state in each case) and they maintained religious and social customs which distinguished them from their neighbors. But at other times the notion of the "tribe" served mainly to falsify reality. Thus it is with the Bangala "tribe" and the Lingala language. As the Congo Independent State hired men beginning in 1886 from Makandza, a forested area on the middle Zaire, their language – Lingala – became a lingua franca for a growing portion of the river zone. It rapidly became the language of the army (the *Force publique*) and, later on, of government workers. It became a sort of Bantu Pidgin, a work language which absorbed new words readily and which was useful for communication among people of widely different origins. The falsification of reality came with the Belgian tendency to label all Lingala-speakers as members of a "Bangala tribe," when in fact the Bangala people were but a tiny portion of Lingala-speakers. "Bangala" was, more properly, an occupational term, referring to those working for the Belgian government. Today, Lingala has become one of the five main languages of Zaire, and it remains the language of government workers.

The notion of ethnicity as occupation (rather than ethnicity as ancestry) is reinforced by the case of the Hausa and Tuareg ethnic groups of Niger. Hausa and Tuareg languages are two very different Afro–Asiatic languages; the Hausa are farmers and merchants, while the Tuareg are nomads herding camels, cattle, and goats. But in periodic droughts at the desert edge, many Tuareg found themselves unable to live as nomads, and moved far south to take up farming. As they did so, they became ethnic Hausa and adopted Hausa language and ways. In years when the rains were good and grazing lands extended far into the desert, some Hausa became ethnic Tuareg. They turned to building flocks, which could multiply rapidly under these conditions.

Ethnicity thus provided Africans with an identity, but that identity was one of many, and it was more often flexible than rigid. The Luba and Lulua of Zaire are today known as two tribes, who fought with each other bitterly in the 1960s. Yet they are two segments of what was a single Luba people a century ago, until the wars just before the Belgian conquest caused one large group to move westward, after which they took the name Lulua. The Kuba of Zaire maintain the myth that they are all descended from one great ancestor, but an interviewer talking to many families found that most families saw themselves as exceptions, since they had different ancestors. Finally, ethnicity was sometimes simply a matter of administrative convenience; the government labelled a group or combined several groups to fit its convenience, and the label stuck. Many of the labels by which African ethnic groups are known today were given to them in the beginning of this century by the colonial officials who wrote studies of these groups in hopes of learning how better to rule them.

If ethnicity is an important but elusive term in the description of African society, so also is class. The term "class" can be used to refer to evident social groupings: slaves, commoners, and aristocrats. The hierarchy in African society, while not punctuated by the great differences in wealth and architectural display known elsewhere, is clearly marked in the social distinctions and prerogatives separating those above from those below.

Class can also refer to occupational groups in a mode of production. In late nineteenth-century Africa, a series of overlapping modes of production produced a profusion of possible classes: peasants and aristocrats for feudal Africa, slaves and masters for slave Africa, workers and employers for the embryonic capitalist Africa. In addition, merchants, princes, and clerics represented special interests, though it is difficult to describe each as a full social class. When class is thought of in this way, then the largest African class by far was the peasantry. Most African peasant families owned their own land, though some had to pay rent to landlords. They produced food and other goods for their own consumption, but they also sold their surplus on the market and bought imported and domestic goods with their earnings. Alongside this peasantry worked other occupational groups: artisans, herders, and fishers.

Class distinctions in Africa were neither absolute nor inflexible. Individuals crossed class lines, even repeatedly, during the course of a life. The overall structure of African classes, however, stands out clearly, as do the changes in the structure. The period from colonization to World War II, in particular, saw important changes in the class composition of francophone Africa. A wage working class came into existence, grew, and underwent internal differentiation. An African bourgeoisie came into existence, as proprietors of small businesses and plantations, taking its place alongside the larger but absent European bourgeoisie. A much more numerous class of petty producers and petty proprietors developed, particularly in the towns. Meanwhile the class of slaves gradually evaporated, and with it the class of slave owners. The African aristocracy too was phased out, and its more successful members took on new identity as members of the colonial bureaucracy. There was no more kings and sovereigns, but there were now many chiefs answering to the colonial administration. Aside from that, the peasantry grew as those above it and below it were pushed to the middle.

COMMERCE

African commerce was sustained by the small traders who carried out the daily exchanges needed to keep African economies going. In West Africa, these were the women and girls who sold local or imported goods in the four-day markets, and they were the *juula* traders of the Western Sudan and Hausa merchants of the Central Sudan who carried goods by head from market to market, and sometimes for hundreds of kilometers. They were the farmers who in dry season acted as porters, carrying bundles of salt for days in order to sell them and bring back a load of foodstuffs and trinkets to sell at home. In Central Africa the local marketing networks were less intensive than in West Africa, but the Zaire river and its tributaries provided paths for the flow of tons of goods in large canoes. The Bobangi, who plied the Zaire, carried fish and a wide range of goods wherever they went, and stopped to display goods at water's edge in the innumerable villages. To facilitate this commerce, buyers and sellers used a variable and often flexible system of currency. Some currencies were imported – as with cowrie shells from the Maldive Islands and Maria Theresa dollars from Europe – and others were locally manufactured – as with the copper crosses of Katanga and the cloth squares of the Kuba, Vili, and Lebou. Only the most isolated and self-sufficient of villages chose to exist without money.

Having enough money was a different matter. Money was in short supply in Africa partially because of its overseas supply, and partially because African levels of wealth were too low to warrant having more money. Slave trade, meanwhile, had provided Africans with three centuries of temptation to make a quick killing and obtain, in return for delivering a person into the hands of slave merchants, enough cash to last for a year or so.

Slave merchants were indeed some of the great old-time African merchants. In addition, the nineteenth century saw the rise of a class of merchants devoted to exporting peanuts, palm oil, ivory and other goods of interest on the world market. A parallel group of big African merchants handled trade in goods from one part of Africa to another, as with the kola trade and trade in textiles.

European merchants formed yet another layer in Africa's commercial network. The slave merchants were displaced by old trading companies in the nineteenth century. These in turn were transformed among the British into Holt, Walkden, and the giant United Africa Company of Unilever; into the Compagnie française d'Afrique occidentale (CFAO) and the Société commerciale de l'Ouest africain (SCOA) among the French; as well as the German firms of Gaiser and O'Swald. The German firms were thrown out of all of Africa during World War I. They returned after the war and built their businesses back up, but were then once more expropriated during the Second World War. A Belgian group formed the Compagnie du Congo pour le Commerce et l'Industrie (CCCI).

These commercial firms made their profits on the amounts bought and sold, in animated competition with each other. Quite different were the concessionary companies which obtained huge tracts of land in the Central African colonies. Here the firms gained power, not through investing their capital but through a grant of the state, and they made profit not by competing with each other, but by extracting wealth from the unhappy people over whom they had been granted dominion.

The idea of concessions had long existed, and the British Royal Niger company, chartered in 1880, provided a recent example of using private companies as proxies for government by imperial powers strapped for funds. Concessionary companies came to francophone Africa with railroad companies, in Senegal and in the Congo Independent State, during the 1880s. Then the British South Africa Company, chartered in 1890, took over Zimbabwe and Zambia and brought British mining and territorial interests to the very frontiers of the Congo Independent State.

Leopold responded to this British threat and to the temporary exhaustion of his personal fortune by turning to several types of concessions. First, in 1892 the Congo Independent State granted huge land concessions in its southern and eastern territories to the Katanga Company (CK), the Great Lakes Railway Company (CFL), the Kasai Company, and others. These concessionary companies were to have great importance over the long run in land speculation and mineral development. In the short run, however, their importance was overshadowed by the second type of concession, which granted land in northern and western regions, the rubber-bearing areas of the forest. In 1892 the state granted to two newly formed companies, Anversoise and ABIR (Anglo-Belgian India Rubber Company), concessions to govern and to exploit huge tracts of lands in the forested areas of the Zaire basin. These companies made considerable profits by forcing people in their territories to collect rubber.

Thirdly, and at the same time, most of the rest of the Congo Independent State was declared to be Private Domain – that is, the private domain of the state, which alone had the monopoly of its commerce. (Free trade was thus permitted only in restricted regions of the Lower Congo). The financial position of the Congo Independent State improved rapidly. The State received revenue from rubber trade in the Private Domain. Finally, Leopold's state granted one very large concession to the king himself – the Crown Domain. Rubber in the Crown Domain was collected by agents of the State, but the revenues from this area went to Leopold himself, who invested them in Belgium.

Stories began leaking out of the Congo Independent State almost immediately, documenting the oppressive measures used to collect rubber both in the concessions and in the state-controlled Private Domain. Swedish missionaries wrote home to tell of people in one village ordered to bring in more rubber than they could possibly collect, and being sent to pillage nearby villages as the only means to collect their quota. Women were captured and held as hostages until the men delivered the amount of rubber required. British consular officials began to collect systematically the stories of these abuses. An American missionary recorded the words of a State official, speaking of the work of an African corporal:

> Each time the corporal goes out to get rubber, cartridges are given to him. He must bring back all not used; and for every one used, he must bring back a right hand!

Six thousand cartridges had been used within six months of 1899 in this portion of the Crown Domain. Sometimes the soldiers lost cartridges, and brought back hands from living persons. The scandal spread wider as Joseph Conrad wrote his short novel, *Heart of Darkness*, which painted the Congo as a dark place but also made clear the exploitation of its people under the Congo Independent State. The English colonial activist E. D. Morel set up the Congo Reform Association shortly after 1900 to protest conditions in the Congo, and to try to distinguish good colonialism (as in English territories) from bad colonialism. The result of this campaign was the 1908 Belgian takeover of the Congo Independent State, and the suppression of concessionary company rule by 1912, though the companies themselves remained influential long thereafter.

The initial profits of this concessionary system encouraged the French and German rulers in Central Africa to imitate it. French Equatorial Africa (or French Congo, as it was to 1910) turned to a regime of concessions beginning in 1898. The concessionary companies were almost uniformly starved for capital, and most of the concessions were for land which the French had hardly

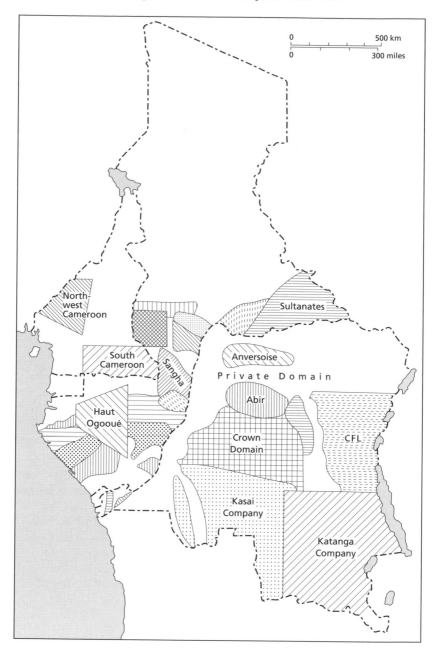

Map 7   Concessions in Central Africa, c. 1905

explored, so that many of the companies failed immediately. Among those which prospered were the Sultanates Company, the Upper Congo Company, the Upper Ogowe Company, and the Sangha–Ubangi Company. Success came either through a system of pillage, as with the Sultanates Company which achieved its profits through alliance with local rulers who forced inhabitants to collect rubber, or by investing in merchant capital (often with Belgian funds), as with the Upper Ogowe Company.

The Germans in Cameroon chose to grant land concessions as well: to the South Cameroon Company in 1898 and to the Northwest Cameroon Company in 1899. These concessions, along with smaller concessions on Mount Cameroon, were more profitable than those in the French colonies. As elsewhere, however, much of the capital invested was Belgian. The concessions in Cameroon came to an end with the defeat of the Germans in World War I.

In the French colonies, some concessionary companies survived until after 1930, though they were in decline after the collapse of the rubber trade in the 1920s. As in the Congo State, metropolitan public outcry helped to end the system; René Maran's 1923 novel *Batouala* and André Gide's 1927 *Travels in the Congo* phrased the oppression in the region eloquently. Equally important, the administration found that competitive commerce now brought higher government revenue than monopolistic concessionary companies. The competitive merchants offered better prices for imports and exports to African producers, and volume of commerce increased. One further reason for the end of concessionary companies was that the government was at last becoming strong enough to control all of French Equatorial Africa, and to set up a new system of exploitation: forced cultivation, especially in Chad and Ubangui-Chari.

Concessions in West Africa were restricted, with few exceptions, to Ivory Coast and Guinea, where European settlers built up plantations of bananas and coffee. In Dahomey, the inhabitants petitioned successfully against concessions. In the savanna, French military officials declined to hand over control of the land. And everywhere in West Africa, the domestic commercial network was sufficient to provide a flow of goods and revenue which the government found adequate.

Despite the importance of the concessionary companies for the social history of francophone Africa, the greatest volume of import and export trade was handled by merchant firms. The merchant firms were headquartered in the main port towns: Dakar, Conakry, Grand Bassam, Cotonou, Libreville, Boma, Brazzaville. These firms did not own large plots of land, but exchanged goods with African merchants who, in turn, traded with African peasants. In many parts of francophone Africa, however, an intermediate class of immigrant merchants took over an important sector of commerce. Lebanese and Syrian Christians, Greek, and Portuguese families settled in large and small towns, and gained an important role in wholesale and retail commerce. These immigrant merchants became far more numerous in colonies where the government had actively destroyed African commercial networks (such as Guinea, Zaire, and Cameroon) than in colonies where the precolonial merchants survived (as in Bénin and Mali). With passage of time, the big firms began opening up branch stores in smaller towns. In this and other ways, the commercial competition among big firms, Mediterranean immigrants and African merchants continued throughout the colonial era.

The foreign trade of francophone sub-Saharan Africa was almost entirely with Europe, though there remained small volumes of trade with North Africa, Brazil, the United States, and occasionally Asia. From the African point of view, the reason for selling goods to the Europeans was in order to purchase imports. The top of the list of African purchases was textiles; bolts of cloth manufactured in Holland, England, or France, in a wide range of patterns made to meet African tastes. Most imported textiles were cheap cottons for everyday wear, which competed with the cheapest African textiles of cotton and raffia cloth. But Africans also imported expensive velvets, which were substitutes for some of the finest African cloths.

Alcoholic beverages were the second category of imported goods: casks of distilled spirits, cheap and strong, cases of rum, gin, and absinthe in bottles. Coastal Africans had bought these beverages from Europeans for centuries, and the growing consumption was restricted only by the high taxes placed on them. The French sought to stimulate African purchases of wine, and the Belgians sought to stimulate the market for beer. Beer won out. Africans produced beer from all their starchy staples, and imported beer came to be increasingly accepted as a substitute.

Behind these leading imports came a wide range of consumer goods: tobacco, salt, sugar, wheat flour, rice, hardware, matches, and kerosene for lamps. Another category of importance was the import of packing materials: sacks for peanuts and palm kernels, casks for palm oil, and baling materials for cotton. Colonial governments imported large quantities of building materials for construction of their buildings, roads, and railroads. Finally, industrially produced goods for mining, transportation, and processing came to have a steadily increasing share of the value of imports: trucks, boats, automobiles, gasoline, coal, and machinery of all sorts.

Francophone Africa's exports were dominated by a few main agricultural and mineral commodities. The various commodities were produced under different systems of labor. An independent peasantry produced peanuts and palm oil, rural forced labor was the source of most rubber and cotton exports, and industrial labor produced copper and gold.

Senegal produced peanuts in such large and growing quantities that it appeared to be the richest colony in francophone Africa during the early colonial years. Extension of the railroad drew new areas into the market, and farmers brought new areas into production. Not all the farms, however, were peasant smallholdings. The nineteenth-century system of slave production was replaced in the twentieth century by the large landholdings of the Mouride religious order, and many of the workers received no more than subsistence. Next most valuable of the agricultural exports were palm oil and palm kernels, both of which come from the same tree. As with peanuts, the oils were used in Europe in lubrication, in soap, and as cooking oil; the pulp was used to feed

(Note: all figures are approximate)

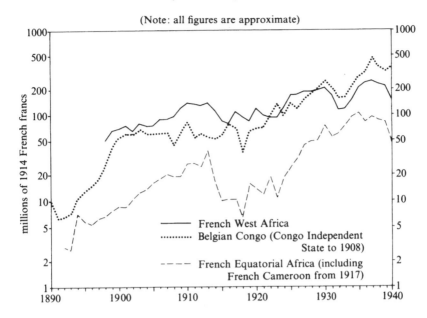

Figure 1   Exports, 1890–1940 (1914 French francs)

cattle. The largest francophone African supplier of palm oil and palm kernels was Dahomey, where the labor force was primarily free but included some slaves. Palm oil and kernels also came from Ivory Coast, Togo, Cameroon, French Congo, and the Belgian Congo. In 1911 Lever Brothers, makers of Palmolive soap, obtained five large land concessions in the Belgian Congo in order to build modern plantations of carefully bred oil palms. In fact the modern plantations were not set up until after 1950. Palm oil and palm kernel exports of the Belgian Congo passed up those of Dahomey in the 1920s, but only because Lever purchased the produce of peasant farmers, at uncompetitive prices.

The rubber boom from 1890 through World War I provides the clearest example of compulsory production. As the demand for automobile tires and other rubber goods expanded, the price for scarce wild rubber grew sharply in the 1890s. The African and Brazilian forests were the main sources of rubber, and the boom continued until the development of modern rubber plantations in Southeast Asia began to bring prices back down in 1913. In the years of the boom, European merchants and government officials did everything they could to cause Africans to collect rubber. Africans rarely benefitted from the rubber trade. The excesses to which it led in Central Africa have been described above.

Compulsory production of cotton was a less extreme form of oppression. African farmers grew cotton in most of the savanna and many places in the forest, and used it in the manufacture of cotton cloth. French and Belgian officials sought to induce Africans to produce larger quantities of cotton, and to produce it for export to Europe, in the hope that Africans would then buy more imported textiles. In Sudan, the French administration wavered between offering high prices for cotton and forcing producers to sell a quota of cotton to French merchants. In Ubangi-Shari, a much more consistent policy was implemented during the 1920s. (Félix Eboué, later governor-general of French Equatorial Africa, initiated this system.) Throughout the cotton-growing area, each local chief was given a quota of cotton to be delivered to market each year, and was also instructed to plant a certain acreage in cotton. The prices were set low enough so that the French merchant firms could pay for transportation down the Zaire River and across the railroad to the coast. While this enabled the French firms to make a small profit, the African farmers took a loss on cotton production every year, since they could more profitably have spent their time growing food crops. A similar system was set up in both the northern and southern savanna areas of the Belgian Congo during the 1920s, with the difference that the cotton was purchased not by the administration but by joint private–state firms, such as Cotonco.

The main mineral export of francophone Africa after 1910 was copper from the Belgian Congo. Here the labor system was industrial, relying first on recruited labor and eventually on a permanent wage-labor force. Gold exports from the Belgian Congo, Ivory Coast, and Guinea were next in importance. Most of the gold was mined by European firms using recruited labor, but self-employed African miners (particularly women working during the dry season) produced a portion of the gold exports. Quite a different export commodity produced with industrial labor was timber, particularly from Gabon and Ivory Coast. In Gabon the Upper Ogowe Company and the African Forestry Enterprises Company (CEFA) invested in the harvesting and sawing of *okoumé* or gaboon mahogany, whose exports grew rapidly with the expansion of the aircraft industry after World War I.

Exported in smaller quantities were coffee, cocoa, coconuts, and bananas from the coastal colonies, ostrich feathers from the desert edge (used in European hats), ivory taken from the declining elephant populations of Central Africa, as well as grain, fish, and domestic animals used as ships' provisions.

The quantity of goods traded by the French and Belgian colonies increased steadily from the mid nineteenth century through the 1930s. But the benefits from this increasing trade did not rise so steadily, because of changes in prices and in levels of taxation. Prices of such African goods as peanuts and palm oil rose to a high level in the early 1880s, only to fall very sharply by 1890. From 1890 to the outbreak of World War I in 1914, the terms of trade became steadily more favorable for Africans; the prices of African exports rose more rapidly than the prices of imports from Europe. At the same time, however, the new colonial governments were increasing taxes rapidly, so that what Africans gained through better prices they tended to lose in higher taxes.

These early fluctuations were small, however, in comparison to the changes in price levels from 1914 to 1940. Africans experienced a bust during the war, a postwar boom in 1920–21 followed by a bust, another boom, and then the great depression of the 1930s. At a time when Africans were becoming more dependent on imported goods, the cost of those goods was increasing.

African merchants and farmers, limited in their incomes by prices and taxes, were also limited in the amount of investment they could do in expanding their output. Most of the investment in African agriculture and commerce was done by the African proprietors themselves, and not by government or by private European investors. With the exception of substantial Belgian private investment in Congo mines, concessionary companies and railways, very little European capital came to francophone Africa. Thus the Banque Africaine de Bruxelles was based on Belgian capital, but the Banque de l'Afrique Occidentale of Dakar and the Banque Commerciale Africaine in Brazzaville gained most of their capital out of African commercial profits.

The Great Depression of 1929–39 struck francophone Africa as seriously as it struck Europe. Incomes collapsed, wage-earners lost their jobs, and farmers lost their markets. Governments, however, were able to collect heavy taxes even when the economy was collapsing. In the French colonies, export prices had fallen by 1934 to *one-fifth* their 1927 level, and the income of African farmers and merchants fell at the same rate. But government revenue fell by only *one-half*, which meant that effective tax rates more than *doubled* for French subjects in the worst days of the depression. Africans were able to compensate in part for their lower incomes by working longer hours; the volume of African agricultural exports rose to a peak in 1937, but declined thereafter.

GOVERNMENT AND THE ECONOMY

A good measure of the impact of colonial government on francophone Africa is the level of tax revenue and government expenditure. For the French, the main source of income was customs duties – taxes on the value of most imports, and on some exports. Although they nominally ruled huge territories by 1890, they did not begin to collect large amounts of tax revenue until after 1900. Then within a few years, the French colonial governments raised customs duties by a factor of ten, so that selling prices of imported goods increased by nearly 30%. Customs duties were paid most clearly by people near the coast, who participated most actively in foreign trade. In order to collect revenue in the interior areas, French colonial governments also set up *head taxes* shortly after 1900; every adult was expected to pay a tax in cash each year, which was to be collected by the chiefs and passed on to the government. Adults were initially defined as persons over eight years of age. In addition to the taxes there were licensing fees for merchants, registration fees for land, and fees for registering births and deaths. The revenue increases came later in French Equatorial Africa than in French West Africa, as it took longer for the government to establish effective control over the inhabitants of the equatorial colonies.

The Congo Independent State was prohibited from charging import duties by the treaty which guaranteed its existence. As a result, its revenues came

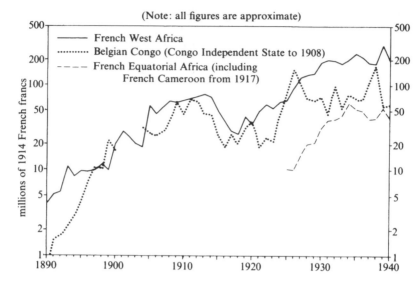

Figure 2   Tax revenue, 1890–1940 (1914 French francs)

from export duties, from taxes and dividends paid to the State by the concessionary companies, and from the sale of rubber collected directly by the state.
The first real economic impact of European rule was felt by the inhabitants of
the Congo Independent State in the 1890s, whereas the inhabitants of the
French colonies did not feel that impact until after 1900. Once Belgium took
over the Congo, the new regime established a system of customs duties and
head taxes similar to that in the French colonies, though the Belgian colonial
state retained the practice of investing heavily in private firms, and collecting
dividends as well as taxes.

Government expenditures went first to salaries for the French and Belgian
officials. (And, since the cost of living in Africa was low, officials were able to
save much of their salary and send it home to Europe.) The overwhelming
majority of government employees were Africans, but their rates of pay were
low enough that the total cost of African salaries was less than the cost of
European salaries. The categories of government activity included administration, police, courts, health, agriculture, education and public works. Expenditures on health, agriculture, and education, however, were tiny in comparison
to those on police and administration.

The colonial governments, in addition to ruling their colonies, also operated
a number of enterprises. These included the postal service, the ports, railroads,
and the provision of water supplies and electric power in the main towns.
These enterprises, particularly in the French territories, were government-
owned in Africa at a time when many of them were privately owned in Europe.
The colonial governments thus set a pattern of public ownership of enterprise
in Africa which has continued to the present. This emphasis on government

enterprise was the exact opposite to the concessions policy, and it resulted in part from the failure of the concessions in French territories. In the Belgian territories, the practice of government ownership of large blocks of private stock (in companies now known as "joint" or "mixed") set another pattern; mixed enterprises subsequently became common in Africa and in Europe as well.

One further area of government intervention in the economy was in regulating the supply of money. Official colonial calculations of the amount of money in circulation in francophone Africa show a massive increase in the supply of money between 1880 and 1940, and imply that there was an equally dramatic expansion of the money economy. This rapid growth is largely an illusion, and for two reasons: much of the increase in the circulation of French and Belgian money represented African switching from the use of their old money to French and Belgian francs; and much of the rest of the increase in money circulation is a result of the sharp increase in prices in the years after 1914. The previous moneys included British coin, Maria Theresa dollars, cowrie shells, gold, and cloth strips. This money was obtained not through government coining but by export surpluses: in Dahomey, for instance, exports of palm oil and palm kernels enabled merchants to buy cowries which were used as money in the local economy.

The French and Belgian governments insisted, once into the twentieth century, on using only their own currency. The French used metropolitan French francs, but also notes from the Banque de l'Afrique Occidentale and its equivalent in equatorial Africa. Colonial governments required all taxes to be paid in francs, they levied extra fees on the import or use of any other money, and they actually confiscated and destroyed holdings of money other than francs. Some Africans never overcame their astonishment at this apparently irrational European behavior. For instance, after the end of colonial rule, an old Maraka man from western Burkina Faso recalled a scene from his youth. The people of his town has been required by the French to hand over all their cowries, in exchange for some French francs. He and a friend decided to spy out to see what the French did with the cowrie money they had collected. They had to wait until late at night, but finally they saw the sacks of cowries loaded into canoes, taken to the middle of the river, and secretly dumped into the waters.

The new money, moreover, did not represent any significant improvement over the old. Just as with cowries, its quantity was determined by export trade rather than by minting or central bank policy. Until the end of World War II in 1945, the only way for Africans to obtain money was through an export surplus; French and Belgian coins and paper money were purchased through the export of African goods, not minted in the colonies.

Aside from this basic similarity, the monetary systems in French and Belgian Africa were significantly different. French colonies used French money, in line with the centralizing tendencies of French administration. But since the Congo Independent State was not initially under Belgian rule, its money was a separate Congolese franc, and this Congolese franc continued to be coined even after the takeover. The value of the Congolese franc could therefore deviate from that of the Belgian franc. For instance, the Congolese franc rose to a value higher than the Belgian franc during and after World War I because of growing mineral exports from the Congo, and this difference gave rise to active currency speculation in the postwar years. During the Great Depression the Congolese franc and the Belgian franc were at last fixed at equal value.

CAPITALISM

Capitalism began in Europe. It had its medieval and early modern forms, centered in the towns of northern Italy, the Netherlands, and Belgium. During the eras of merchant capitalism and early industrial capitalism, Africa was linked to the capitalist world through the slave trade, by which Africa provided labor to New World plantations and purchased goods carried by European merchants. Yet Africa in those days, though linked to the world economy, was not dependent on a capitalist economic system.

Capitalism came to Africa in the late nineteenth and twentieth centuries from three sources: European private enterprise, colonial governments, and African private enterprise. European private enterprise included the "legitimate" traders who bought peanuts and palm oil in the nineteenth century, the railroad firms, twentieth-century trading firms, and mining investors.

The contribution of colonial governments to spreading capitalism in Africa included the operation of government enterprise, such as postal systems and railroads. A more important contribution of government to developing capitalism came with the development of a wage labor force. Governments used taxation, labor recruitment, and sometimes appropriation of land to pressure their African subjects into offering their labor for wages, and low wages at that. This government enforcement of capitalist ways, while it involved a great deal of compulsion, was not unique in the development of capitalism; in seventeenth-century France, the monarchy controlled the largest enterprises, especially munitions factories.

The third source of capitalism in Africa, African private enterprise, is one that should not be forgotten. African merchants, transporters, and planters put time, energy, and all the resources they could gather into building up businesses and competing in the rough-and-tumble world market. They were not very successful, as measured by their profits. Perhaps their lack of acquaintance with the culture of capitalism was a problem, but at least as important were their shortages of funds and, especially, the fact that colonial governments and European firms used both fair means and foul to outcompete them.

A further factor drawing francophone Africa into close dependence on capitalism was the development of the world market. Revolutionary advances in technology and declining prices of industrial goods involved Africa ever more deeply in the capitalist economy. If sewing machines, cotton gins, gas-powered mills, trucks, and outboard motors first appeared as curiosities, they rapidly became necessities, and more and more African effort came to be organized around purchasing those necessities. And, in those years when the changes in prices made it disadvantageous to work for wages or buy imported goods, the colonial government was always there to compel the payment of taxes and the provision of labor.

The result was not necessarily increased welfare for the African population, but it was more capitalism. That meant more European money, and it also meant changes in social structures, as wage labor came to replace work on the family plot. But Africans did not give up their own social structure easily, and they did not all become urban wage workers.

The economy and society of francophone sub-Saharan Africa, and indeed of all African regions, underwent fundamental transformation from 1880 to 1940. The new economy was dominated by capitalism, though in a complex and contradictory fashion. African wage labor expanded dramatically in the mines and cities, though wage laborers were less than 5% of the African work force in 1940. (The much larger number of forced laborers cannot be counted as wage laborers, though they did receive some compensation). Capitalistic firms grew rapidly in number, though only a tiny proportion of African businesses were organized on a capitalist basis.

Nevertheless, African producers and entrepreneurs found themselves enmeshed by 1940 in a network of constraints and institutions which were fundamentally capitalistic. All had to pay taxes to colonial governments which were representatives of the capitalist order. Most relied on commodities produced by capitalist industry (from textiles to matches to hoes). Many relied on capitalist demand for sale of their crops. In addition, the main hopes for advance lay in wage labor or in ownership of a firm. Capitalism, in sum, had come to Africa. But the coming of capitalism to these African colonies did not necessarily mean an increase in wealth or an improvement in social welfare.

Sociologists and economists have written at length in an attempt to explain the meaning of this survival of the old alongside the new in Africa. In the colonial era, they relied on the framework of the "dual economy." In this view, the old and the new were seen as separate and isolated from each other; stagnant traditional structures sat alongside a small but expanding modern sector. The problem with this view was that it denied the contributions of the Africans to building the modern sector, and it ignored the oppressive nature of the measures by which the colonial regimes induced the Africans to make those contributions.

A more recent approach explains the African economy in terms of the "articulation of modes of production." According to this view, the European and African economics interacted, and the nature of each was determined in part by the other. This approach has the advantage of acknowledging change in African economies, and of acknowledging the long history of Africa's involvement in the world economy. Capitalism in Africa, in this view, has special forms. Rural production is in part the survival of an old system, but in part it has become a means of absorbing the cost of producing and reproducing African labor, and thus of subsidizing a system of low-wage capitalism.

The colonies of francophone sub-Saharan Africa were not among the centers of African wealth, with the possible exception of Zaire. Senegal, which began as the wealthiest of the francophone colonies, produced far less wealth than the French colonies of North Africa, or Egypt under British rule, or southern Africa under British rule, or even the British West African colonies of Nigeria and Gold Coast. Not only was the level of income in francophone Africa lower than that in most other regions, its rate of growth was also slow in the early colonial years, with the exception of the rapid growth of output after 1920 in Zaire. Partly as a result of this relative underdevelopment, the French and Belgian colonizers in sub-Saharan Africa established administrations and tax policies which were more extractive than those in anglophone and Arab Africa, and the tradition of economic regulation remains strong in those countries. If economic liberalism often gave way to coercion in francophone Africa, however, it is true on the other hand that francophone Africa never experienced the rigid, legally enforced color bar of the British territories in eastern and southern Africa. Social confrontations in francophone Africa have been more among classes than among races.

3

Government and politics, 1880–1940

The early colonial years brought political humiliation for Africans. Scores of African rulers died on the battlefield; many more were executed or exiled after defeat. Those who signed treaties and remained as protected rulers soon found themselves demoted from king to chief and required to collect taxes or recruit laborers for their French and German overlords. At a later stage most were dismissed altogether.

For the European colonizers, the early colonial years were a time of triumph and self-satisfaction. The conquest itself was high adventure for European officers. They faced great dangers, but success brought the rewards and recognition due to a hero. And even when the thrill of conquest gave way to the more mundane work of administration, the rewards remained great. A French man in his twenties, newly out of school, might find himself to be a *commandant de cercle* with complete authority over 200,000 people. He could accept, if he wished, the offers of gifts and women from subjects who sought his good will. Or, for those who refused to pay taxes, he could burn their villages and impose punitive fines in the near-certain knowledge that the governor would back him up.

Beyond this simple picture of European triumph and African humiliation, however, lies a more complicated and more important story of political change. Some Africans led distinguished and successful political careers, and some Europeans fell from power in defeat and scandal. Further, and quite aside from the ups and downs of individual political careers, the colonial era brought structural change to African politics.

In the years up to 1940, France and Belgium imposed a European administration on francophone sub-Saharan Africa. But it was not the same as the system of government in Europe. In Africa, the European colonial regimes used modern administrative technology, including telegraphs and typewriters, but they used medieval European principles of government. In Europe, France was a republic and Belgium was a constitutional monarchy. All adults were citizens with equal rights under a single code of law. Almost all men had the right to vote. The African colonies, on the other hand, were territories within an empire. Government gained its authority from Paris and Brussels, not from the consent of the governed. Adults and children alike were subjects. They lived their lives without political rights, and with legal rights given under different codes of law from that of their colonial rulers.

The European governors of colonial Africa, while imposing European structures and European ideas of sovereignty, also borrowed heavily from the structures and principles of African government. Many local territories kept their boundaries after European conquest. Kings and chiefs, while reporting now to foreign rulers, preserved many of their old methods and powers. European local administrators often found themselves ruling with the techniques of an African king rather than with those of a European bureaucrat. Thus the government of colonial Africa, while dominated profoundly by European power and desires, was both African and European in its operation.

European ideas of democracy were a different matter. These ideas spread to Africa not through the efforts of European colonizers, but through the campaigns of African critics of colonial rule. African demands for citizenship and voting rights were often treated as treasonous in the early colonial years. Only in the years after World War II did the idea of democracy come to be acceptable to colonizer and colonized alike. And only in the years after independence did a real synthesis of African and European political systems begin to be formulated.

The political system of francophone Africa in the early colonial years was authoritarian and bureaucratic, but also fragmented. Even though colonial governors held absolute power in theory, they were limited in practice by other forces. Belgian influence was limited by that of the French. Governors were limited on one side by their budget, and on another side by the distance between them and local administrators. European local administrators were limited by the power of African leaders to rebel or to refuse cooperation. African rebels, in turn, were limited by the fact that their enemies could ally with the colonizers. To get the full flavor of African politics, even in this period dominated by the growth of the colonial state, one must consider several levels at once, ranging from local to international, and from formal to informal to illegal. At the beginning of this era the strongest voices were those of European theorists and generals, but the African voices were never silenced; some spoke in resistance to the new ways, others sought to collaborate with the French and Belgian rulers, and still others sought a way out of this dilemma.

In politics and government, francophone Africa contrasted sharply with anglophone Africa. Armies were larger, and military expeditions were more important in French and Belgian than in British territories. French and Belgian colonial governments included a higher ratio of European administrators to African subjects than in British colonies. Thus their theory of direct rule (vs. British indirect rule) paralleled the numerically greater intensity of their presence. The restrictions on African political activity were much tighter in Belgian and French territories than in the British. The exceptions which granted some political rights in Senegal made that colony the early center of politics in French Africa. The real focus of politics in assimilationist French Africa, however, was Paris, just as the focus of Portuguese African politics was in Lisbon. The Belgians, in contrast, turned away from both the French vision of assimilation and the British tradition of self-government. They sought to establish a system of political tutelage, in which the African subjects would have no rights beyond the level of their own commune or village.

In this chapter we will investigate early colonial politics, beginning with the concepts of colonialism brought by French and Belgian colonizers, and also with the African interpretation of the meaning of colonialism. Then we will trace the conquest of the francophone African territories, the early stages of colonial administration, and the fate of African governments and political units once they had fallen under foreign domination. We then turn to the firm consolidation of colonial administration, the development of the colonial system, and the rise of an African political class seeking to test the limits of the colonial system. The chapter concludes with a discussion of absolutism at the political zenith of colonialism.

CONCEPTS OF COLONIZATION

France had wide experience with colonization before her sub-Saharan African colonies became significant. Neither Belgium nor Germany (which colonized four of the 17 nations of francophone Africa) had significant experience with overseas colonization. France had built and then lost a great empire. She lost territories in India and Canada to Britain, she lost St. Domingue to a revolution, and sold Louisiana to the United States. In the nineteenth century France built a new empire, with the conquest of Algeria beginning in 1830 and the conquest of Indochina beginning in the 1870s. Most Europeans, regardless of their experience with colonization, tended to share two basic beliefs about Africa in the nineteenth century. They believed that African culture was inferior to that of Europe. And they believed that Africa contained untapped wealth – wealth which could be tapped easily with European energies and knowhow.

European politics up to the eighteenth century had been based on the relations of monarchies. In the nineteenth century, however, even though many kings and queens remained on the throne, the politics of Europe came to be based on *nations*, in which the key element is the *people*. The French nation, which was galvanized during the 1790s, unified several social classes into a powerful nation. For Belgium in the 1830s, the nation was created through unification of two ethnic groups (Flemings and Walloons) who shared a common religion. For Germany in the 1860s, a multitude of separate political territories unified to form a single nation. Each of these nations was formed on the principle of the unity and the legal equality of all citizens.

As these nations sought to expand and to form colonies, a dilemma arose on the political status of the new territories and of their inhabitants. Was the overseas colony to be part of the European nation? Were the inhabitants to become citizens? In some cases the answer was yes. France, in the revolutionary enthusiasm of 1848, granted citizenship to the inhabitants of Martinique, Guadeloupe, and Guiana in the West Indies, and Réunion in the Indian Ocean. At the same time, she granted citizenship to the inhabitants of the towns of St.-Louis and Gorée in Senegal (citizenship was extended to inhabitants of Rufisque in 1880, and Dakar was separated from Gorée in 1887). But in all other cases, Europeans were reluctant to grant citizenship to the people of African colonies.

On what basis was citizenship denied to those in African colonies? The first reasoning was national; the Africans were foreign, not French or Belgian, and were members of other nations. The difficulty with this reasoning was that it assumed that European nations to be conquerors, and assumed the Africans to be subject nations. This was the reality of colonialism, but many European colinizers preferred to see themselves as liberators rather than as conquerors of Africa. The French in particular, as they grieved bitterly over their loss of Alsace and Lorraine to the German conquest of 1870, were reluctant to label themselves conquerors.

As a result, other reasons were commonly offered for the denial of citizenship to Africans. In religious terms, it was argued that Africans were heathen rather than Christian, though this implied that African Christians should be eligible for citizenship. In cultural terms, it was argued that Africans were savage and not civilized (or that they were peasants and not bourgeois). This distinction, in a century in which theories of evolution had become popular, implied the possibility that African societies or African individuals might evolve to a level at which they would merit citizenship.

The most formidable distinction, however, was racial; the Africans were black rather than white. A small but important group of Africans devoted themselves to education and acculturation so that they could achieve citizenship and full political rights. They accepted the logic and the challenge of evolution, and they were known as *évolués* by the French and Belgians. They adopted the religion, the language, the culture, the economic outlook, and the levels of achievement which were seen as ideal among the citizens of France and Belgium. What they could not change was their race, and this physical distinction served as the last defense of those who did not wish to allow the colonized to become citizens.

The Africans in the colonial era were subjects rather than citizens is made especially clear by the case of the Congo Independent State. This state was not a colony of Belgium, but an independent state under the personal rule of Leopold II. Yet there as elsewhere, the African inhabitants were subjects and without political rights. Only a few Africans who were educated or had permanent employment with Europeans were able to become *immatriculés* (registered) and live under Belgian law.

Within the framework of this general set of European concepts of colonization, we may distinguish some more specific policies. The first of these is *assimilation*, which was described in chapter 1 as the approach of Louis Faidherbe in Senegal. His approach began as that of administrative assimilation, in which the colony becomes formally a part of the mother country, rather than a separate but protected state. He went further to support political assimilation, at least in the extension of citizenship to the inhabitants of the four communes. It was consistent with this approach of assimilation that France declined to establish a separate Ministry of Colonies until the end of the nineteenth century. But Faidherbe found, early on, that his vision of assimilating Senegal into the French empire could not be accomplished without subjugating it. Subjugation by military force became an ironic but ever-present aspect of assimilation. The establishment of unified political dominion, rather than equality, was the key objective in the assimilationist view.

The alternative French approach of *association* was introduced in chapter 1 through the exploits of Savorgnan de Brazza. While he sought to expand the French empire as earnestly as did Faidherbe, he thought it could be done by recognizing the separate cultures and institutions of African peoples, and by establishing protectorates over them. In the associationist view, establishment of broad sovereignty and opening of trade relations (rather than a unified dominion) were the main objective.

The approach which Henry Morton Stanley brought to bear in the Zaire basin was *incorporation*. Political control was important to him, and commerce was not to be neglected, but more than that he (and his Belgian successors) sought to have a direct impact on economic production in the colony, and to draw it tightly into the world economy.

These were some of the concepts which Europeans brought with them as they established control over their African colonies. With the passage of time, new concepts and new visions arose. As will be shown below, the French policy of assimilation in West Africa was replaced by that of association; meanwhile, the French policy of association in Central Africa was followed by that of incorporation, borrowed from the Congo Independent State. The missionary vision of religious tutelage led to the development of an administrative vision of secular tutelage. The administration in the Belgian mandate of Ruanda–Urundi, in fact, was generally known by its subjects as "la tutelle."

Out of all the European beliefs about colonization, however, one gradually emerged to become supreme: the belief that Africans must submit to Europeans and to European rule. As the colonial system emerged, the demand for unquestioning submission became more and more prominent. In many areas, Africans were expected to stop and salute any passing Europeans.

Further reasons for the changes in European concepts of colonization came because of the influence of African ideas. These ideas varied at least as widely as European ideas, but certain lines of thinking stand out clearly. Many Africans conceived of colonization as an alliance with the Europeans, rather than as an occupation. The kingdoms of the Tio, or Porto-Novo and of Douala all had signed treaties, and their leaders complained when the treaties were violated.

On the other hand, the rights of the conqueror were acknowledged in other cases. The princes of Dahomey claimed that, since France had conquered Dahomey, France could dispose of lands and wealth as she chose. In precolonial Africa the welfare of the king was often thought to be related to the welfare of the whole of his realm; in the colonial period, African subjects might wish the government prosperity in hopes that it would spread to the whole colony.

Many African peoples denied the legitimacy of colonial rule. The Arabs of Mauritania killed the French governor Coppolani in 1905, and managed to avoid subjugation until 1934. In other cases, great rebellions against colonial rule broke out, only to be suppressed ferociously by the government. These included revolts by the Bariba and the Somba of Dahomey during World War I, by the Gbaya of French Congo and Ubangi-Shari from 1928 to 1931, and by the Pende of the Belgian Congo in 1931. Generally speaking, such revolts ceased in West Africa by 1920 and they ceased in Central Africa by 1935.

As the legitimacy and the permanence of French and Belgian rule became established, all Africans were forced to accommodate to it. They faced three alternatives with regard to their political rights. First, they could accept their lack of political rights, and work within the system as subjects. Secondly, they could seek to become citizens. While France allowed a certain number of its subjects to become citizens on an individual basis, Belgium did not. In the Belgian Congo one could hope to become a Congolese *évolué* but not a Belgian citizen. Thirdly, they could seek to establish their own nationhood. Few Africans dared speak of this possibility in the years before 1940, but the march of events made it a steadily more appealing alternative. For instance, the "tribal" law codes drawn up in the 1930s by the governments of French West Africa and the Belgian Congo (but not in French Equatorial Africa) were intended to maintain Africans as subjects within tribal units. Yet these codes helped ironically to pave the way for the definition of African nations and for their separation from France and Belgium, because they defined a written code of law different from European law.

IMPERIAL DIPLOMACY AND CONQUEST

In the scramble for Africa, beginning in 1880, the character of diplomacy in Africa changed fundamentally. Previously, diplomacy had consisted of relations between European and African governments, with a local focus. After 1880, diplomacy centered on relations among European powers in Africa, and the continental and strategic aspects of diplomacy became dominant. Disputes continue among scholars as to what set off the race. Perhaps it was the British invasion of Egypt in 1880, perhaps it was the French parliament's acceptance of the Makoko treaty in Congo, perhaps it was the French forward movement on the upper Niger. But in any case, after 1880, European adventurers raced across African territory in search of treaties.

In 1884 Chancellor Bismarck of Germany convened the nations of Europe in Berlin for a conference intended to reduce the tensions among them. The effect of the conference was mainly to establish a set of rules for colonization, which enabled the powers to continue the race for colonization. King Leopold's International African Association was recognized by the European powers at this meeting. Leopold quickly relabelled it as the Congo Independent State, with himself as sovereign, and sent expeditions to its frontiers to expand his territories at the expense of the French in the north, the Portuguese in the south, and in an attempt to reach the valley of the Nile in the east.

This European partition of Africa on paper had ultimately to be followed by a partition on the ground. To turn their theoretical protectorates into real colonies, the European powers needed African armies. The officers, arms, and techniques of these armies were European, but the fighting men were African. In the French territories of West Africa, they were known as the *tirailleurs sénégalais*, the Senegalese Rifles. This force, first founded in 1820, grew from 2,000 soldiers in 1888 to over 8,000 in 1900. These soldiers were initially recruited from Senegal, and later from all the territories under French influence. Battalions of *tirailleurs* were moved from Senegal down the coast to participate in the 1892–4 conquest of Dahomey (a major war which the French won only by careful planning and skilled execution), in border disputes in Guinea, and to put down the 1910 rebellion in Ivory Coast.

The main work of the *tirailleurs*, however, was in the long campaigns against Ahmadu, son of al-hajj Umar and leader of the Tokolor state, and against the *almamy* Samori Touré. These French African soldiers, commanded first by Joseph Gallieni and then by Louis Archinard, succeeded by 1893 in conquering Ahmadu's state and in forcing Samori to move his state eastward. Samori, who was a merchant in his early life, had by 1880 become head of a major state on the upper Niger, to the southwest of Umar's Tokolor state. After a decade of uneasy truce and occasional skirmish, Samori lost his original state to Archinard's attacks. Refusing to give in, Samori moved his armies and his state several hundred kilometers to the east, into modern Ivory Coast, and he there continued his battles against the French until his capture in 1898. While he was an immensely resourceful leader, using mobile tactics and producing guns and artillery in his foundries, he also relied heavily on the capture and sale of slaves in order to purchase arms and horses and continue his fight.

In the Congo Independent State, the government established the *Force publique* in 1885. It was based initially on soldiers recruited from other parts of Africa, then from recruits known as Bangala from the middle Zaire valley, and it later came to include many soldiers from the Tetela ethnic group of the Kasai and Kwango valleys. Soldiers in the *Force publique* were very powerful because of their monopoly on modern firearms, but were held in strict submission to their officers. Many of the Tetela soldiers mutinied in 1895 and wandered uncontrolled all across the eastern half of the CIS, collecting other rebel groups, until they were finally defeated and dispersed in 1900. By 1900 the reconstituted *Force publique* included some 14,000 soldiers, the largest army in Africa.

The French advance in equatorial Africa, by contrast, involved almost no military force in the early days. One exception was the remarkable expedition of the French officer Marchand, who led the French attempt to claim the headwaters of the Nile. In 1897 Marchand began with a band of *tirailleurs sénégalais* from Brazzaville. They steamed up the Zaire and the Ubangi, and then marched overland until they reached the Nile at Fashoda, in modern Sudan Republic. But they also met a British expedition which had come to occupy the same area. The two European forces stood eye to eye while a major diplomatic incident brewed. The French hoped to link their Central African territories to Djibouti on the Red Sea; the British wanted to link their Sudan to Uganda. In the end, the French withdrew, and Marchand retreated back the way he had come.

Completion of the French conquests of major African states required a series of expeditions into the area of Lake Chad. There an adventurer from the Nile valley, Rabeh ibn Abdullah, had arrived with an army which had swept across the northern savanna and which seized control of the kingdom of Borno. Urged to accept French sovereignty and to renounce slave trading, Rabeh refused both, and defeated two French columns sent against him. Finally the French, determined to subdue him but constrained by very long supply lines, sent three expeditions against him at once. One came up the Zaire from Brazzaville, one came across the savanna from the Niger, and the third crossed the desert from Tunisia. The three columns met in 1900 and finally killed Rabeh and destroyed his army.

Wars of conquest also took place on a much smaller scale. These small wars were known under the term of "pacification." but they resulted in at least as much death and destruction, in the aggregate, as the larger wars. The pacification of the Ivory Coast is an instructive case, not because it was unusual, but because of the prominence of its executor, Gabriel Angoulvant.

Angoulvant came to Ivory Coast as governor in 1908. The colony had been nominally under French control for over a decade, yet many inhabitants were reluctant to acknowledge French authority. Angoulvant set about achieving full authority, but was short of the military means to do so. The Dan people of the west had embargoed a French post for some months. At first the post captain was able to do no more than arrest some village leaders, but Angoulvant sent reinforcements which permitted him to burn five main villages and confiscate the villagers' rice. Elsewhere, the lagoon village of Osrou, which had failed to pay 15,000 francs in taxes, was occupied in 1909 and ordered to pay a war fine of 100,000 francs in silver, payable within a week. The village was able to comply only be mortgaging its next harvest. Angoulvant set forth the principles of his approach:

> What has to be established above all is the indisputable principle of our authority
> . . . the acceptance of this principle must be expressed in a deferential welcome
> and absolute respect for our representatives whoever they may be, in full pay-
> ment of taxes . . ., in serious cooperation in the construction of tracks and roads,
> [and] in the acceptance of paid porterage . . . Signs of impatience or disrespect
> towards our authority, and the deliberate lack of goodwill are to be repressed
> without delay.

Angoulvant's methods soon brought the situation to a head. The Abe people of eastern Ivory Coast, in addition to paying taxes and performing unpaid road work, had seen their guns taxed and then confiscated in the year 1909, and they now felt threatened by the railway line running through their lands. On 6 January 1910 they rose as one in rebellion. They attacked railway stations and cut the track at 25 points. Such a revolt was a serious threat to Angoulvant's position, but the governor-general in Dakar was alarmed enough to back him up and send nearly 1,400 troops. The revolt was put down with pitiless severity. The government troops burned villages, executed prisoners, and displayed the heads of rebels on pikes at railway stations and in villages.

Thereafter tax payments were regular, and the villages provided the number of laborers demanded of them. Angoulvant, the theorist of pacification, later became governor-general of French West Africa and of French Equatorial Africa, and a deputy in the French parliament.

Widespread as war was in the French and Belgian takeover of African territories, diplomacy was never forgotten. When the representatives of King Leopold reached Katanga, the mineral-rich, southeastern corner of their new realm, they sought in 1891 to enter cordial relations with Msiri, the immigrant from East Africa who had built a large kingdom there. Msiri refused to make his submission to the Congo Independent State, hoping instead to gain an alliance with Britain; Leopold's representatives persisted in urging Msiri to ally with them. After repeated meetings in and near Msiri's capital, an altercation broke out in which Captain Bodson of the CIS shot and killed Msiri with his revolver, and was himself killed by Msiri's son. Msiri's allies hesitated, and the Congo Independent State forces moved quickly to take control of his state.

The alliance between Leopold's state and Tippu Tip was more successful, but it too ended in failure. Tippu Tip, the merchant from Zanzibar who had gained power over a large region of the Lualaba and Lomami valleys, from which he sent ivory and slaves to the east, had accompanied Henry Morton Stanley part way on his voyage down the Congo River in 1878. In 1887 he accepted the title of governor of the northeastern provinces of the Congo Independent State, and worked for some years in alliance with the Independent State administration. This alliance brought large quantities of ivory and many recruits to the Congo State. Tippu Tip could see, however, that the Europeans were determined to subdue him ultimately, so in 1891 he led one final, enormous trading expedition east to the Indian Ocean coast, and retired with his fortune. In 1892 the Congo Independent State forces launched a war on their former Arab allies, labelling it as an anti-slavery campaign, and took direct control of northern and eastern Zaire.

In the years between 1910 and 1920, diplomacy and war among the European powers took center stage again. Just as the confrontation between France and Britain at Fahoda in 1898 had threatened war between those two countries, tensions between France and Germany were revealed in 1905 when Kaiser Wilhelm spoke out in Tangier to defend the independence of Morocco against French colonial designs. This Franco–German tension continued until 1911, when the Germans agreed to give the French a free hand in Morocco in return for territory in Central Africa. France gave portions of four Central African colonies to German Kamerun, and gave some small pieces of Dahomey to German Togoland. In the course of these disputes, the French and Germans each charged the other with being unfit for colonization, on the grounds that they did not know how to bring about proper African development. The stage was now set for a larger conflict.

When World War I broke out in August 1914, German troops spilled across neutral Belgium in execution of the Schlieffen Plan. They drove deep into France and nearly achieved a repeat of their quick victory in 1870. This invasion ended forever the neutrality of Belgium. The Belgians joined France,

Britain, and other Allied Powers in the war. Meanwhile, French forces halted the German advance,and the opposing armies dug in for four years of murderous trench warfare.

The war spread immediately to Africa. In Dahomey, French officials and many prominent Africans became filled with patriotic zeal for conquest. An army was rapidly pulled together and within two weeks of the declaration of war it had obtained the surrender of the tiny German force in Togoland. Kamerun, however, was a different matter. There a more substantial German presence was able to fight for two years against British invaders from the west, and French invaders from the south and east. The Dahomeans who had shown such enthusiasm for the conquest of Togoland lost interest rapidly when they were asked to serve for two years in the Kamerun campaign. Ultimately, however, the French and British prevailed, and they divided Kamerun among themselves much as they had with Togoland. The larger eastern portion became French Cameroon; the small western portion became British Cameroons.

The Germans fought longest and most effectively in Tanganyika. General Von Lettow-Vorbeck held out against British forces in a four-year campaign that covered the whole of German East Africa. The Belgians entered the African war from their base in the Congo. Leopold II had disputed the German claim to the highlands near Lake Tanganyika since 1885, and it was this portion of German East Africa which the Belgian-led *Force publique* occupied in 1916. This territory became Ruanda-Urundi, while the larger British portion became Tanganyika.

These territories – French Togo, French Cameroon, and Belgian Ruanda-Urundi – now became part of francophone sub-Saharan Africa. Administration and schooling began to take place in the French language and a substantial effort was made to remove evidence of the previous German presence. The French and Belgian administrations were sanctioned by the League of Nations in 1921; these African colonies were made Class C Mandates. They were to be governed by France and Belgium, but these powers had to report annually to the League of Nations. The Mandates underwent occasional inspection by League officials to ensure that they were receiving humanitarian government.

World War I in Africa, meanwhile, went far beyond the conquest of German colonies. The Belgian Congo became a central focus of the Belgian war effort, since the mother country was occupied by Germany in the early days of the war. The colonial government called upon the inhabitants to produce and contribute foodstuffs, palm oil, rubber, and cotton for the war effort. The government of French Equatorial Africa tried to do the same, but with meager results. The mining companies responded to the demands of war more effectively than government. Union Minière, with its headquarters moved to London and with the British investors in leadership, expanded its copper exports from 10,000 tons in 1914 to 27,000 tons in 1917.

In French West Africa, participation in the war went as far as recruitment of some 175,000 soldiers, most of whom went to Europe as combat and support troops. Blaise Diagne of Senegal, the first African member of the French

National Assembly, led in urging the recruitment of these troops, for reasons discussed later in this chapter. With support from Prime Minister Clemenceau, Diagne toured the West African colonies beginning in 1917 in search of volunteers for an expanded *tirailleurs sénégalais*, the army of West African subjects. Diagne faced opposition from many quarters – some refused to serve at all, others sought permission to join the citizen army (and thereby become citizens) rather than the subject army, and Governor-General Joost Van Vollenhoven resigned in protest, fearing that further recruitment would cause rebellion. (Van Vollenhoven died in combat soon thereafter.) But Diagne found more recruits than anticipated: 60,000 in the first year. Once in Europe the Senegalese, as these soldiers from all over West Africa came to be known, fought in many of the major engagements, and suffered a relatively high rate of illness as a result of the change in climate. After the war some demobilized soldiers managed to stay on in France, where some of them became involved in political activities.

This subject army was enough of a success that the French administration decided to maintain it in peacetime. Every year from 1919 to the end of the colonial era, young men were called up for physical exams, and many of those found to be fit were drafted for three years' military service. This army served again in World War II, as well as in Vietnam and Algeria in the 1950s.

THE DAWN OF COLONIAL ADMINISTRATION

French and Belgian colonizers set up administrations as soon as they gained control of African territories. For the years from 1880 to 1905, however, completing the conquest had a higher priority than governing the conquered areas. As a result, the early steps in administration were tentative, experimental, and incomplete. Yet it was these rudimentary first steps in administration which set many of the important trends in modern African government.

In King Leopold's Congo Independent State, the central government resided in Brussels, and consisted originally of Leopold as head of state and a cabinet of four ministers appointed by him. In the earliest days Leopold's officials were drawn from all over Europe, as the legacy of his International African Association, but from 1885 almost all his officials were Belgian. The provincial government was headquartered in Boma, on the lower Zaire River, and was headed by a governor-general with a cabinet parallel to that in Brussels. The territory of the Congo Independent State was divided into several provinces, but only the portions near the rivers were actually governed by the new regime.

A unique feature of the Congo Independent State was the heavy investment by its sovereign, King Leopold, in the cost of administration in the early days. Leopold hoped for a rapid rise in exports (particularly ivory) from this colony which would repay his investment. But trade grew slowly, and import duties were prohibited by the international agreements which had brought the Independent State into existence. By 1891, Leopold had used up so much of his fortune that a new policy was necessary. It was then that the Independent State turned to the regime of concessions. In 1891 the government decreed a state monopoly over purchase of rubber and ivory in areas it labelled the Private Domain, roughly half of the colony's territory. At the same time, Leopold turned the other half of the colony over to concessionary companies which, with a tiny amount of capital, undertook to guarantee the commercial and mineral exploitation of these areas. Since these concessions coincided with the world-wide boom in rubber, they focused on the forced collection of rubber by the inhabitants of the concessions. Thus the early administration of the Congo Independent State was a combination of several approaches: allowing African governments to continue much as before, allying with African governments, intervening directly to collect commodities, and turning administration over to private European companies.

In French West Africa, early administration was dominated more by military than by commercial motivation. Especially in the savanna regions, it was large-scale military force which brought France to power, and military forces directed colonial administration for years. The colony of Niger remained under military administration until the end of World War I. The impact of the military was also felt in the coastal colonies, especially Dahomey. The conquering army under Gen. Alfred Dodds destroyed the old kingdom of Dahomey, set a new king on the throne and otherwise did much to set the course of colonial rule before turning power over to a civilian government in 1894. The civilian governments in each of the colonies gradually set about building administrative posts and collecting taxes.

From 1882 to 1897, Savorgnan de Brazza governed France's Central African colonies from his capital in Libreville, usually with the title of commissioner-general. Until 1888, he had to share power with the governor of Gabon, whose capital was also in Libreville, and he reported to two ministries, the naval and foreign affairs ministries. In 1888 Gabon, Congo, and the interior areas were combined into one immense colony, known as French Congo. But in fact the French presence in this great territory was so modest that local communities were hardly disturbed, except along major waterways and along the 400-kilometer porterage route from Loango on the coast to Brazzaville. The small size of political units in the western and southern portions of French Congo meant that large military forces were not necessary, and a civilian administration dominated from the first. The larger political units – Bagirmi and Rabeh's domains in the north, the Zande kingdoms in the east, and realms such as Dar al-Kuti in between – were left on their own until the turn of the century.

Colonel Marchand's 1897–98 expedition up the Zaire of the Nile was as important for its impact on the internal politics of the French Congo as for its diplomatic impact. Marchand objected to being placed under civilian authority, and thus challenged commissioner-general de Brazza's tradition of civilian dominance in equatorial Africa. Paris hesitated but overruled Marchand's plea. Meanwhile, Marchand's heavy demands for porterage caused a revolt even before he reached Brazzaville. He sent 100 tons of trade goods and military equipment overland from Loango to Brazzaville, and the Sundi people refused to provide porters. The revolt, in turn, brought disgrace to Brazza. He was replaced as commissioner-general, and in 1897 he left Libreville and retired. He had supported for years the granting of concessions to bring French capital to Africa, and he was removed from office just as this system was being adopted.

In 1898 the administration of French Congo moved to imitate the Congo Independent State system of granting large land concessions to private firms, and by 1900 it had given concessions to most of the land in the colony. Just as these concessions were being granted in the French Congo, scandal was breaking out of the concessions in Leopold's Congo across the river. These same scandals struck the French Congo. In 1905 two French officials, Gaud and Toque, were put on trial in Brazzaville for having dynamited a porter from the lower Congo while on a mission in the upper Shari valley.

Brazza was called out of retirement in Algeria and returned to Central Africa on an official inspection tour. He prepared a report which was sharply critical of the expanding system of concessions in French Congo, because of low levels of capital investment and the use of repressive measures. But he fell ill and died in Dakar in September 1905, before he reached France. Excerpts of his report were published, but did not lead to significant change. Two decades were to pass before the concessions became a public issue again in France. Meanwhile, the administration of France's Central African territories was almost nonexistent outside of a few towns and major lines of transportation.

As the new colonial regimes set patterns in administration, they also set patterns in property rights and in civil and criminal law. Three general principles characterized the colonial approach to law: the interest of the colonial state was primary, Europeans should be governed by European law, and Africans should be governed by African law. These principles, however, left great room for conflict and contradiction, so that they never evolved into a coherent set of judicial institutions.

The Four Communes of Senegal were ruled under French law. (An interesting exception is that the Muslim citizens of the communes had access to Muslim courts.) French law was based on the Napoleonic Code and on written legislation. It contrasted, therefore, with the English system of justice, in which courts reached decisions based not only on legislation but also on judicial precedent and common law. French courts were also set up in the other French colonial capitals, and French citizens anywhere in the colonies fell under the jurisdiction of those courts. Africans who were not citizens could sometimes get their cases heard in French courts; for example, if they owned land in towns which were governed under French law.

Outside of these tiny jurisdictions, two types of law held sway: the customary law of the Africans (including Muslim law), and the very personal law of the French military or civilian rulers. Customary law continued in force wherever it was able to resolve disputes among Africans. Gradually, however, the colonial governments gained control over customary law; for instance, French administrators became chief judges of the appeals courts.

The personal powers of French officials were narrowed with time, but they were guaranteed by the *indigénat*. The *indigénat* consisted of regulations which allowed administrators to inflict punishments on African subjects without obtaining the judgment of a court. These regulations, first adopted in 1904 and modified periodically in the various colonies, provided formal justification for a fact of colonial life. For specified violations and with specified limits on punishment, the officials were free to act immediately, and to impose fines and prison sentences. The *indigénat* rapidly became one of the most unpopular aspects of French colonial rule with Africans, and it provided one of the main reasons why African subjects sought to become French citizens.

The Congo Independent State adopted a rudimentary version of the French colonial legal system. For the Europeans within its borders, the CIS adopted a code of laws based on Belgian law and the Napoleonic Code. Some Africans were allowed to live under this code, if they were educated or worked permanently for Europeans. These were the *immatriculés*, or registered Africans. Some the *immatriculés* became prosperous, managed to send their children to school in Belgium, and showed other similarities to the *évolué* elites of Senegal and Dahomey. The administration of the Belgian Congo, however, suppressed this opening for African advancement after World War I.

Elsewhere in the Congo Independent State, the law was either the customary law of Africans, itself in rapid flux because of the dramatic changes in the region, or the personal rule of European administrators and company officials. There was no move even to regularize the personal powers of Europeans, as in the French *indigénat*. Instead, the measure of effective work by state officials and company employees was in the quantity of exports they could collect.

The most important legal issues in the early colonial years were matters of property. In 1885 the Congo Independent State decreed itself to be the owner of all vacant and unowned land within its borders. This provided the legal basis for the state's granting control of half its lands to concessionary companies in 1892. In addition, in 1891 the state assumed the monopoly over all rights of commerce. It held on to such rights itself in the Private Domain and the Crown Domain, and passed on its monopoly of commerce to concessionary companies elsewhere. The rights of Africans to their land, even that under cultivation, were precarious under these conditions. Similarly, the government of French Congo decreed itself owner of all vacant lands within its frontiers in 1899, as an accompaniment to the granting of concessions to most of its territory.

In West Africa, on the other hand, the French government did not declare itself to be owner of all vacant land until 1904, and the land concessions granted in West Africa were mostly quite small. The government of Dahomey claimed to have control over all land within the colony by right of conquest, but this claim was repudiated by the courts.

Along with administration and law, the collection of taxes became a growing preoccupation of the new colonial governments. Customs duties, charged on imports to the French territories but on exports from the Congo Independent State, were increased every two or three years from 1885 to 1910, and ended up growing by a factor of ten. The French colonial governments began imposing head taxes by 1900, and collected these taxes from a steadily wider circle of inhabitants. The Congo Independent State had no legislation on individual taxation, and left it to local officials to determine African contributions of labor, commodities, or money. And since the taxpayers did not necessarily stop paying taxes to their precolonial governments, the result was that the burden of taxes in 1910 was much higher than it had been before the colonial era.

As the colonial administrations became more effective, new questions began to demand resolution. Were questions of law, resulting from disputes over land, property, or crimes, to be decided under African law, under European law, or under some combination? Were African chiefs and kings to be left in power, or were they to be replaced by administrators responsible directly to the colonial government? These questions were debated, and the outlines of the answers had become clear by the time of World War I.

THE FATE OF AFRICAN POLITIES

With the beginning of the colonial era in the 1880s, European map-makers drew boundaries on maps of Africa, encircling or dividing African states. But the mere drawing of boundaries did not bring African political life to an end. African rulers could recognize the power of French and Belgian influences without renouncing their own powers; African subjects could provide tax payments and labor for French and Belgian officials without renouncing loyalty to their own governments. The decline and transformation of African governments and polities – and their absorption by the colonial state – was thus a gradual process rather than a sudden step.

The largest states sought recognition within the European-dominated state system. When the French built the Dakar–St.-Louis railway through the kingdom of Kajoor in 1881–85, they did so based on a treaty which recognized the Damel, Lat Dior, as sovereign of Kajoor. (Nevertheless, the French defeated and killed Lat Dior in 1886.) Samori Touré also sought recognition from the French, and coexistence with them, in the 1880s. King Glele of Dahomey had considered treaties with both French and British representatives, and rejected them mainly because they did not provide clear enough recognition of the independence of Dahomey. Glele's successor Behanzin, even after a brief war with the French in 1890, still sought recognition.

When African states could no longer gain recognition of their full sovereignty from the Europeans, many of them sought recognition as allies. Brazza's 1880 treaty with King Iloo I provided (in the French version if not in the Tio version) for the cession of Tio land to France, but it initially involved no interference in internal Tio affairs. The French in the Western Sudan, while their policy was ultimately one of military conquest, accepted uneasy truces with Shaikh Ahmadu, with the rulers of Sikasso, and even with Samori.

Military conquest sometimes caused the destruction of African states, but this was not always the case. Samori's realm was certainly destroyed with its conquest – particularly since Samori himself had moved the state eastward from its original base beginning in 1891. So too was the Masina state of Ahmadu on the middle Niger, and the domain of Rabeh in the Lake Chad basin. But the Muslim theocratic state in Futa Jallon (in the highlands of Guinea) retained its existence, as did the four Mossi kingdoms in what became the colony of Upper Volta – though the French tried to ensure that their favorites became king.

When the French conquered Dahomey in 1894, General Dodds dismembered the kingdom. Only the central province, the area around the capital of Abomey, remained in the kingdom; prince Goutchili, brother of the deposed Behanzin, was appointed king. All the remaining provinces were either placed under direct French rule or made into new kingdoms. These arrangements soon became unsatisfactory to the French, and they deposed three kings in 1900.

Joseph Tovalou Quénum in Dahomey represented a different sort of alliance with the Europeans. As a leader of the most powerful family in the coastal region of the Dahomey kingdom, he rallied to the French at a crucial moment in the French conquest of the area. He provided supplies and recruited boats and boatmen, and helped arrange the surrender of the port town of Ouidah. As a result he was awarded a medal of honor, and became one of three African advisors to the French colony's administrative council. But this close relationship was not destined to last much longer than the others we have discussed. In 1903 he was removed from the administrative council, and by 1908 the French government was seeking actively to break his power over his large family.

In some instances the alliances between Europeans and Africans were more durable. A remarkable example is the case of Mademba Sy, King of Sinsani (or Sansanding), the great Maraka trading city of the middle Niger. Mademba Sy was born in St.-Louis in 1852, the son of a Tokolor aristocrat but also a French citizen. He became a telegraph operator in 1869 and worked his way up in service of the French. The French military commandant Archinard, after taking Sinsani along with the rest of Ahmadu's Tokolor state, appointed Mademba Sy king of the city in 1892. The new king's Maraka subjects, noting his Tokolor birth, tended to see in him a continuation of the Tokolor regime against which they had rebelled, only now with the support of the French as well. Complaints arose on the oppressiveness of his rule, and these were supported by French officials jealous of his power. At one point the administration filed charges to dismiss him, but these were eventually dropped, in part because of Mademba Sy's ties to the military. For instance, his son Abdel Kader Mademba rose to the rank of captain in World War I, but was disabled by poison gas at Ypres; he then accompanied Diagne in the West African recruiting campaign of 1917. Mademba Sy, meanwhile, continued to be successful in collecting taxes, and in recruiting large numbers of soldiers. He remained in power until his death in 1919. Later generations of this family rose to high military and diplomatic positions in independent Senegal and Mali.

African states, in one way or another, lost the diplomatic recognition they had earlier enjoyed in the earliest years of the colonial period, and they were thereafter treated as protected states. French and Belgian overlords felt free to interfere in selection of the leaders of their protected states. Then, at the turn of the twentieth century, the French and Belgian governments removed any legal taxing power from the African states and substituted their own tax systems. Many rulers were deposed at this time, and all who remained were put in the position of becoming agents of the colonial state rather than rulers in their own right. Titles were changed to make this point clear; those who had been known as "king" in earlier times were now labelled "chief" or, at best, "superior chief."

Yet even where the old states lost their formal political power, they continued to exist, and the kings and chiefs could act as representatives of their constituents, not simply as tools of the administration. The Mogho Naba (king) of the Mossi kingdom of Ouagadougou, placed in office by the French in 1905 at age 16, gained the trust of his people. He was known during World War II as an opponent of the collaborationist Vichy regime, and his death in 1942 was widely thought to have been a suicide in response to pressures from the Vichy administration.

In the remains of the old Dahomey kingdom itself, the monarchy survived in a strange fashion. When the last king was deposed, the old central province was divided into several cantons. The canton chiefs were members of the royal family, so each had himself installed with the ceremonies appropriate to a king, and they disputed among themselves who was the legitimate heir to the throne. The prize in this dispute was control of the old palaces, which had now become a museum. Ultimately the agreement was that one person be recognized as caretaker of the museum and master of ceremonies for the royal ancestors; this man, Sagbaju, died in 1977 at an age of roughly 100 years.

ADMINISTRATIVE CONSOLIDATION

The administrations of francophone sub-Saharan Africa underwent revision and consolidation in the first two decades of the twentieth century, and took the form they were to retain with little change for the rest of the colonial era. Three great central governments developed, in Dakar, Brazzaville, and Leopoldville; separate governments developed after World War I in the mandates, with capitals in Lomé, Yaoundé, and Bujumbura.

The federation of French West Africa was formally decreed in 1895, but in fact the idea did not take practical form until ten years later. In 1904 France's eight West African colonies, which had been administered under a variety of conditions, were amalgamated into a single federation, with its capital in Dakar. The governor-general was the chief officer of the federation, and he reported directly to the Minister of Colonies in Paris, The Dakar government consisted of a set of ministers – of finances, justice, army – and of federation-wide services for health, agriculture, and education. A consultative council, with some elective but mostly appointive members, proposed and discussed legislation. Each of the nine colonies was headed by a lieutenant governor, who reported to the governor-general. The capital of each colony was a miniature of the government-general, with departments of finance, public

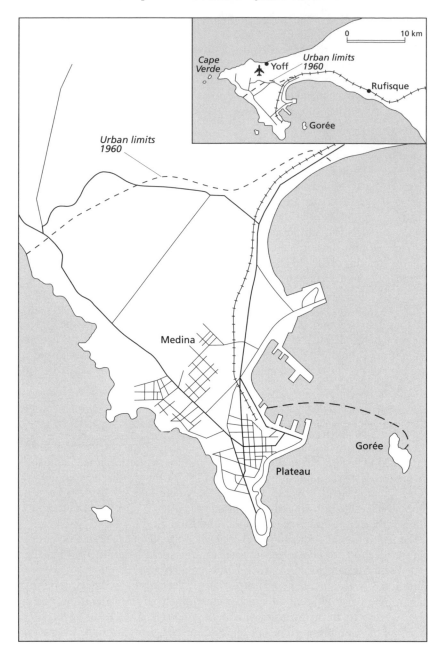

Map 8   Dakar, 1940

works, policy, health, agriculture, and education. Each colony was then divided into a set of districts, known as *cercles*, presided over by a French administrator or commandant. Various territorial modifications took place over the years; Upper Senegal-Niger was divided into Sudan and Upper Volta in 1918, and Niger remained under military government until 1922.

The glue which held the federation together was its financial system. Customs duties, by far the greatest source of government revenue, were collected in each of the colonies (but especially in the coastal colonies) and were all sent to Dakar. The government-general kept what it needed, and allocated the rest among the colonies in what were known as "subsidies." The colonies, on the other hand, were permitted to raise revenues for their own use through head taxes. Whenever finances got tight, the colonies and the government-general would seek either to raise tax rates or to establish new taxes or fees. Fees were levied on commercial licenses, on market stalls, on fishing permits, on livestock, on registration of property, and so forth.

The government-general and each of the colonies had a reserve fund. Since revenues generally exceeded expenditures, several million francs were placed in reserve funds each year. These reserve funds were invested in bonds in France, and thus drew some interest. Their purpose was as a reserve for contingencies, and they were used in this fashion during years of shortage, but they represented an excessively conservative fiscal policy. Large amounts of tax money were drawn out of African hands and placed idly in banks, usable only as capital by French bond sellers. Worse still, when prices inflated dramatically, as they did during World War I and in the 1920s, the value of these massive savings dropped precipitously.

The government-general of French West Africa also put out a bond issue as it was formed in 1905, borrowing 100 million francs on the French financial market. Most of this money went for purchase of the railroads in Senegal, Sudan, Guinea, and Dahomey from the private companies which had initially undertaken to build and operate them. The purchase prices for the railroads were high, so that the railroad companies were able to achieve, through their liquidation, profits that they had not been able to gain in building or operating the railroad lines. The bonds were paid off with African tax receipts.

French West Africa thus became the model for a central colonial government in Africa. Other central governments were formed not only in francophone territories, but also in the Dominion of South Africa (1910) and in the amalgamation of northern and southern Nigeria (1914).

French Equatorial Africa was created in 1910, very much on the model of French West Africa. What had been known as French Congo was now clearly divided into three colonies: one retained the name of French Congo (or Middle Congo); Gabon regained its identity as a separate colony, and the interior territory was named Ubangi-Shari. (In 1920, the northern portion of Ubangi-Shari became the separate colony of Chad, and the southern portion retained the name Ubangi-Shari.) The government-general was established at Brazzaville, and each of the colonies was led by a lieutenant governor who reported to the governor-general. As in French West Africa, customs duties went to the government-general, which returned a portion of them to the colonies as "subsidies"; head taxes and other local fees went to the individual colonies.

In contrast to French West Africa, however, the level of international commerce in French Equatorial Africa was too small to provide the tax revenue necessary to support a government of such an ambitious scale. As a result, the metropolitan government of France provided occasional subsidies to Brazzaville. In another contrast, establishment of the government-general did not mean buying out all the private European investors. In particular, some of the large agricultural and commercial concessions which had been granted at the turn of the century remained in force until 1930.

When the Belgian parliament asserted its control over King Leopold II's African territory and created the Belgian Congo in 1908, it set up a government even more centralized than those of the French federations. This was partly because the Congo had always been a single colony, rather than several colonies as in French West Africa. But it was also because the Belgians decided that the government must have firm control over affairs in the colony in order to be certain of easing the heritage of scandal. What developed instead was a system of paternalistic rule which was in many ways the most complete in Africa.

The colonial capital remained at Boma; only in 1929 did it move inland to Leopoldville. The government-general grew in size, and the provinces were reorganized slightly. Large numbers of missionaries were sent out to work in schools and missions, Belgian settlers began to take up farming in the eastern highlands of the colony, and Belgian banks and industrial firms increased their investment in the colony's mineral potential. What emerged as a result was a trinity in the structure of Belgian control in the Congo; a secular trinity in which government, the church, and industry worked very closely together.

The colonial government imposed a regular head tax (which was intended to replace the irregular demands made in earlier days) and levied taxes on both imports and exports. In addition, the colonial state received revenue from taxes on the income of mining and other industrial ventures, and earned dividends on its holdings of corporate stock. The government of the Belgian Congo was far better funded than that of French West Africa, which in turn was far wealthier than that of French Equatorial Africa.

The final stage in the consolidation of government in francophone sub-Saharan Africa came with the conquest of German territories during World War I. The French and Belgians, after dividing up their conquests with the British, immediately set up their own administrations to Togo, Cameroon, and Ruanda–Urundi, but they had to await the conclusion of the peace treaty before they could set up permanent administrations. The settlement of the war prevented the victors from absorbing their conquests into existing colonies or federations, and required that they be governed as Mandates from the League of Nations. (In practice, the Mandates were governed almost as part of the adjoining governments-general.) Reports to the League and occasional visits of League delegations had the results of additional protections for the inhabitants of the Mandates. In addition, tax moneys raised in the Mandates had to be spent there, so that the colonial financial system was less restrictive in the Mandates than in other francophone colonies.

The expanded colonial governments, while small and short of resources in comparison to European governments of the time, were the most powerful governments that had ever existed in the lands of francophone Africa, and they were able to carry out new activities. They set up expanded systems of courts, department of agriculture and forestry, and departments of education. The departments of agriculture and forestry included some very well-trained officials, but they were often no more than one per colony in the French territories, so that agricultural experiments proceeded at a very slow rate. The Belgians, in contrast, conducted a more energetic and successful program of agricultural research. In education, the Belgian Congo encouraged primary education, but followed in its Catholic tradition by giving most of the work of education to missions, most of which were Catholic (although American, British, and Swedish Protestant missions were important in the colony). The French governments, in contrast, preferred to set up state schools, and in some cases drew on France's anticlerical tradition to undermine mission education actively.

Two energetic and far-seeing colonial ministers, Louis Franck in Belgium and Albert Sarraut in France, laid out influential plans for colonial development in the years following World War I. Franck, Colonial Minister from 1918 to 1924, proposed a reorganization of the system of chiefdoms and tribunals, hoping to provide more autonomy for such peoples as the Luba and the Mongo. He established the Colonial University in Antwerp to train Belgian colonial officials. He was a liberal and a free-thinker, yet he strengthened the role of the Catholic Church in what was known as the Colonial Pact – the arrangement by which state, church, and corporations shared responsibility for the Belgian Congo. His enthusiasm for the colonial venture provided energy for many of the Belgian innovations of the interwar years. His proposals for administrative decentralization, however, were to be reversed.

Sarraut, a radical republican, became Minister of Colonies of France in 1921. His particular focus was on plans of massive public works for economic development, though he expressed interest in administrative decentralization and in African education. He published his plan in a 1923 book entitled *La Mise en valeur des colonies françaises*. The book focused on the need for France to become economically self-sufficient after the experience of World War I. He too created great enthusiasm for the colonial venture, but most of his projects were never implemented. The Sarraut Plan called for the investment of hundreds of millions of francs in railroad projects, including a trans-Saharan railroad and lines linking all the French colonies to each other, as well as heavy investment in ports and in agricultural development. The collapse of the post-war economic boom in 1922 put an end to hopes of funding such a project, but the idea lived on. Late in the 1920s a new construction campaign did begin, though it was financed far more by African taxes than by French loans.

But the greatest effort of this construction campaign went into a railroad whose rationale was more political than economic, and whose construction brought disaster and death to thousands of African workers. The railroad from Pointe Noire on the Atlantic to Brazzaville, built from 1921 to 1934, was constructed so that the French could avoid using the Belgian railroad from Leopoldville to Matadi for the trade of inland areas in Equatorial Africa. It would be an improvement over recruiting porters to carry goods by head for 400 kilometers. But the Congo–Ocean railway was long and difficult to construct. Nearly 130,000 workers were recruited from sparsely populated French Equatorial Africa to build the railroad. Nearly 10,000 died on the job, and many others deserted and sought to return home on their own.

Despite disappointments and scandals such as the death rate in construction of the Congo–Ocean railroad, and despite the economic problems brought by the depression of the 1930s, the colonial regimes entered their second half-century stronger than ever before. In the eyes of the colonizers, the strengthening of their administrative structure, their tutelage of African subjects, and their replacement of African ways with European ways, seemed to be progressing at a good rate, and seemed to be slowed only by the inherent difficulty of African conditions, and perhaps by the continued unwillingness of some Africans to accept the new order.

DEMOCRACY: THE RISE OF A POLITICAL CLASS

As the colonial order became steadily more entrenched, and as the precolonial political systems declined in importance, a new group of African political leaders emerged, who accepted the legitimacy of the French and Belgian national frameworks, and who sought to achieve their own political goals by moving up within the colonial political system.

The first major breakthrough by an African in the French political system – the 1914 election of Blaise Diagne as Senegal's deputy in the National Assembly – remained in many ways the most spectacular. In Senegal, the *originaires* (the inhabitants of the four communes of St. Louis, Gorée, Rufisque, and Dakar) held citizenship and the vote. They elected representatives to municipal councils, to the General Council of Senegal, and one delegate to the National Assembly. But they generally voted as instructed by the French merchants and the French-speaking creoles (many of them mulattos) who dominated local politics; the few *originaires* elected to office remained close to these patrons. Then in 1908 French administrators and French settlers began calling systematically for restrictions on the citizenship rights of the *originaires*. They were illiterate in French (through some knew Arabic), and they did not rely on French law in civil matters of marriage and inheritance, but only for criminal matters. This threat to their citizenship began to galvanize the *originaires*. They elected Galandou Diouf of St.-Louis to the General Council, and he spoke actively for their interests.

In 1912 the government of French West Africa promulgated a naturalization decree. It permitted African subjects to become citizens of France, but only under very strict conditions, including literacy and high recommendations of personal character. (By 1922, less than 100 persons in all of French West Africa had qualified for citizenship.) The Senegalese citizens of France feared more than ever that they would lose their citizenship. In the 1914 elections for the National Assembly, they supported Blaise Diagne, who won over a field of white and creole candidates. Diagne had only recently returned to Senegal after years of work as a customs agent in several French colonies. His status as a successful civil servant gave him prestige which was important in his victory.

Once elected, Diagne ably achieved the principal goals of his constituents. When war broke out in the fall of 1914, Diagne insisted on the right of the *originaires* to serve in the *troupes coloniales*, the citizen army, rather than in the subject army, the *tirailleurs sénégalais*. As the war went on, he launched his campaign to recruit thousands of troops from across West Africa to participate in the French war effort. In exchange for his efforts, the National Assembly adopted in 1916 a citizenship law which confirmed the status of the *originaires* and of their descendants. They could retain their personal status before customary courts, vote, and also go before French courts. In 1917, Diagne gained the gratitude of the French central government by touring West Africa and leading a campaign which recruited 60,000 subjects into the *tirailleurs sénégalais*. He came to represent the identification of some African leaders with the French empire.

A more radical style of political action was exemplified by Louis Hunkanrin, a school teacher trained as part of the first class at the William Ponty school in Dakar, who returned to his native Dahomey to begin teaching in 1907. By 1910 Hunkanrin had been fired for criticizing the local administrator, and he left teaching for a lifetime of journalism, political activism, and imprisonment. During World War I he edited a clandestine newspaper criticizing the French government of Dahomey. He came out of hiding only when Blaise Diagne arranged for him to volunteer for the army. But at the end of the war Hunkanrin broke with Diagne, accusing him of having accepted bribes for recruiting soldiers, and turned again to critical journalism.

Hunkanrin represented a radical republican line of political action. His loyalty to France was unquestioned and unbending, but he was loyal to a very particular vision of France; the France of 1789 and 1848, which emphasized the universal rights of man, regardless of race or national origin. Hunkanrin was not born a citizen and never became one. Throughout his life he criticized the notion that some French should have more rights than other French.

Hunkanrin was indirectly involved with the Porto-Novo incidents of 1923, in which two types of rebellion – French republican protest against the restrictions of the French empire, and African protest against the imposition of French rule – were combined. (Hunkanrin was in jail throughout the events, but was nevertheless influential.) The outbreak, which included demonstrations in favor of an excluded candidate for the throne of Porto-Novo and strikes by dockworkers in Porto-Novo and Cotonou, as well as peasant protests against taxes, was suppressed firmly by the French, and Hunkanrin was sent off to ten years' exile in Mauritania, along with ten other leaders of the affair.

Dahomey was the home of a number of other figures who became active in early colonial politics, and who took a republican approach. The greatest manifestation of this outlook was during World War I, when hundreds of ambitious Dahomeans sought to join the citizen army, hoping that service in Europe would be sufficient to gain them French citizenship and the full political and economic rights that went with it. The administration refused to grant their requests, and only a handful were able actually to achieve citizenship.

Two among these were Jean Adjovi and Marc Tovalou Quénum (later known as Kojo Tovalou-Houénou). The latter was the son of Joseph Tovalou Quénum, who had been so important in assisting the French conquest of Dahomey. Marc Tovalou Quénum achieved his citizenship after 13 years of education in France, during which he received degrees in law and medicine; he then served in the medical corps in the war. Jean Adjovi achieved his citizenship by volunteering for military service in the subject army and collecting an imposing set of letters of recommendation from his French superiors (including one from Henri Poincaré, soon to become President of France). Adjovi had already become head of a family of several thousand persons, probably the second richest family in the colony, when he went off to war. His gamble that military service would bring him citizenship was linked to his family's need for full status in French courts in order to defend its land holdings. When he returned to Dahomey he found that the administration treated him as an upstart and a rebel. He, in turn, became involved in journalistic and political activity in attempt to change the government's policy which, in his view, was restricting the economic growth of the colony.

Two new types of political activity surfaced after World War I, both of which accepted the new national framework, but contested French leadership. The first of these was black nationalism, especially under the leadership of Marcus Garvey. This outlook was inspired by the range of business opportunities, and was symbolized by Garvey's shipping line, the Black Star Line. Garvey, a Jamaican political activist, brought his Universal Negro Improvement Association to New York in 1916, where it grew rapidly in an atmosphere of black anger against white-led lynchings and race riots. Garvey argued that blacks should form a nation of their own rather than be subordinated to white nations. His newspaper, the *Negro World*, was circulated throughout the black world, and began to reach West Africa in 1919 and 1920. In Senegal, a small group of immigrants from Sierra Leone became supporters of Garvey, and accepted his message that Africans too could build businesses and nations which would achieve greatness on the order of the Europeans. Because of the mobility of the African merchants, telegraphers, and other minor professions based in Senegal, the message spread among this community as far along the African coast as Boma and Leopoldville in the Belgian Congo. But the European administrations saw this sort of nationalism as revolutionary and anti-European, and the police in Senegal were able to arrest and deport the small clique of Garveyists before they could expand their influence.

The second new sort of politics was inspired by Marxism and the Russian

Revolution, and by the growth of an African working class, especially in railroad and shipping work. The number of African communists in the 1920s and 1930s was small indeed, but they were to have an important formative influence. The key figure was Tiemoko Garan Kouyaté born in 1902 in French Sudan. He graduated from the William Ponty School in 1921, taught for two years in Ivory Coast, and was sent on a scholarship to continue his eduction in France. There he was expelled from school, and he rapidly became involved in African politics, and became a member of the French Communist Party.

Kouyaté, along with Lamine Senghor from Senegal and a few others, combined to produce newspapers, organize trade unions, and campaign in any way possible for the recognition that Africans were a subject nation, and that African workers provided the hope for Africa's future. Kouyaté corresponded with Marcus Garvey from time to time, but their perspectives were too different for any permanent alliance. He was more closely allied to George Padmore, the Trinidadian activist who became the leader of the African section of the Comintern in Moscow in 1927, and who later became the political advisor to Kwame Nkrumah of Ghana. Like Padmore, Kouyaté was devoted to African nationalism as well as to the rise of the proletariat. This view was reflected in his decision to break with the Communist Party in 1933 when he concluded that the party had sacrificed the interests of Africans to the needs of the French nation. He continued to publish newsletters and to correspond with activists. Kouyaté was the single most influential figure in the interwar politics of the French colonies, because of his tireless work in maintaining contacts among a wide range of other activists. He remained in France to the end of his life – he was killed by the Germans in Paris during World War II – but the men with whom he corresponded were among the main leaders of post-war nationalism in the French colonies.

These three African approaches to politics – assimilation, black nationalism, and revolutionary nationalism – contended for recognition in the interwar years, and struggled to survive under the suspicions and pressures of the colonial governments. The assimilationist approach remained the safest and the most influential, but it too was dangerous, as the case of André Matswa demonstrates. Matswa was born in Brazzaville in 1899, obtained a mission education, became a clerk, and worked his way to France in 1923. There, after military service, he became a bookkeeper and obtained French citizenship. In the course of obtaining citizenship he met Garan Kouyaté and other activists. Then in 1926 he founded a regional fellowship, the *Société amicale des originaires de l'Afrique équatoriale française*. Such organizations were common enough; Kojo Tovalou-Houénou had formed an *amicale* for Dahomeans, and it ultimately became absorbed into his newspaper.

But Matswa's *amicale* developed in a new direction. In 1928 delegates of the association began collecting subscriptions in French Congo. As many as 13,000 had joined by 1929, most of them from the Bakongo, Matswa's own ethnic group. As membership grew, the local organization raised the demand that Africans be granted French citizenship, that they be freed from the *indigénat* and that the administration invest in economic growth for French

Equatorial Africa, which had become very poor in comparison to the Belgian Congo. The government of French Congo, fearful of the movement, brought Matswa back from France. It tried and convicted him on charges of mishandling funds of the *amicale*, and sent him into exile; the Congo was left in an atmosphere of confrontation. Matswa, meanwhile, made his escape from exile in Chad and returned to France.

The closest resemblance to an actual campaign for colonial independence was in the demands of the Douala people of Cameroon. The Douala had petitioned the German Reichstag in 1909 on compensation for lost land. In the years from 1927 through 1939, various Douala groups submitted petitions to the Permanent Mandates Commission of the League of Nations, calling variously for the re-establishment of the Douala kingdom and for creation of a Cameroon Republic, as well as for more specific reforms.

In the Belgian Congo, meanwhile, Africans lost the ability to act politically in the aftermath of World War I. The *immatriculés* of the previous generation had prospered in some cases, and had sent their children to school in Belgium. One of the latter, Mfumu Paul Panda Farnana, spoke out in Belgium as a critic of colonial policies of forced labor and restrictions on political rights, until his death in 1930. Such commentary served only to confirm Belgian fears of the seditious nature of any African *évolué* class. No further Africans were allowed to live under Belgian law, and education in the French language was halted at all but the highest level. African political participation was restricted to that within the missions and at local levels of government, except when it took the form of demonstrations, strikes, or revolts.

THE ZENITH OF COLONIAL RULE

Paradoxically, the high point of French and Belgian colonial rule was the decade of the Great Depression, 1929–1939. The authority of colonial governments went almost unchallenged within their borders and without. Governments were of course forced to carry out some economies. Nevertheless, government's share of the domestic product rose dramatically during this decade, since the private incomes of African subjects fell much more rapidly than the tax revenues of the state.

Even economy measures, such as territorial reorganization, tended to serve the purposes of the state. In French West Africa, the colony of Upper Volta was annexed to Ivory Coast, since the abolition of a colonial government saved some expenditure. But this measure also served another purpose, since it unified politically the lower Ivory Coast, where white planters owned a growing set of cocoa and coffee plantations, with the source of their migrant labor in Upper Volta. Similarly, the provinces of the Belgian Congo were reorganized in the 1930s as an economy measure, which further centralized the government in Leopoldville while at the same time the government sought to provide additional support for Belgian planters in northeast Congo.

In both French West Africa and the Belgian Congo (but not in French Equatorial Africa), the colonial regimes sought to strengthen their legal foundations by drawing up formal codes of African law. For various ethnic groups or for whole colonies, government officials drew up written codes based on traditional law, on decisions made in the Native Courts, and on the needs of the colonial state. Their idea was to strengthen the Native Courts, to base decisions on a formal code and no longer on common law and judicial precedent, and to reduce the number of cases going before courts of French or Belgian law. For Dahomey, the political activist Louis Hunkanrin did much of the work of drawing up the manual of customary law.

Colonial regimes sought also to strengthen and broaden their administrations. This meant establishing a reliable set of African chiefs. In the French colonies, these were the canton chiefs. There were usually from five to 15 cantons and canton chiefs for each *cercle* and each *cercle* had a European administrator. By the 1930s the canton chiefs were often literate in French, and many of them built significant fortunes. Although they had standing in the traditional hierarchy, their wealth and power came mainly from their position in the French government. One of the most famous canton chiefs was Justin Aho Glele, a descendant of king Glele of Dahomey who ruled Ounbégamé canton near the old Dahomean capital of Abomey. His wealth, his power in the old royal family, and his close ties to the French administration made him a target for constant political attacks by Dahomean critics of the administration.

Another influential canton chief was Félix Houphouët-Boigny of Ivory Coast. His was the rare case of a man who became a canton chief despite administrative opposition. He was born in 1905 to a chiefly family. After graduating from the William Ponty Normal School on the island of Gorée and from the School of Medicine in Dakar, Houphouët-Boigny returned to Ivory Coast in 1925 as a medical auxiliary, and served there for 13 years. Meanwhile his younger brother, who had become canton chief, died in 1938. The administration felt bound to appoint Félix as his successor, but was reluctant to do so because he had been critical of poor health conditions which the administration tolerated in the colony. Once Houphouët-Boigny became canton chief, he gave up his medical practice and became a planter, as was typical for such chiefs. And part of his job, as canton chief, was to recruit labor for European planters at the same time as he was seeking labor for his own fields. Thus was the stage set for one of the most important political careers in postwar Africa. Houphouët was highly educated, widely respected, a traditional chief, a successful businessman, and a government official, whose conflicts with European planters were to become crucial in the postwar nationalist movement.

The postwar collapse of colonialism seemed inconceivable from the vantage point of the 1930s. It is true that there were major reforms in colonial administration during the 1930s, but these were carried out with the confident intention of making colonialism function more efficiently, and not out of the fear that it might collapse. The greatest reforms were those carried out by the Popular Front government of France, an alliance of moderate, socialist, and communist parties which governed France in 1936 and 1937. Under Colonial Minister Marius Moutet, the French administration softened the requirements for forced labor and narrowed the scope of the *indigénat*, and it expressed increased concern for African workers and peasants. But political rights remained as restricted as ever, and those suspected of disloyalty to France were jailed as they had been before.

<h2 style="text-align:center">ABSOLUTISM</h2>

Absolutism was a political theory which enjoyed great favor in Europe during the seventeenth and eighteenth centuries. This theory recognized that society was divided into contending groups, and that their interests might not be resolved peacefully. Theorists of absolutism argued that the groups without property had no interest or stake in the future of society, and concluded that only the sovereign could rule in the interest of all. In Europe, while the aristocracy was still the leading class, the expanding classes of merchants, artisans, and peasants demanded satisfaction of their needs. France's most powerful sovereign, Louis XIV, argued that only he could represent the interests of the kingdom as a whole. Under the theory of absolutism, he and his successors ruled and reformed France with minimal interference from the people.

In opposition to absolutism there grew up the theory of representative democracy. According to this view, the differences among contending social groups could be harmonized through give-and-take. Theorists of representative government also believed that government could not function effectively unless all social groups were represented in it. The sovereign, in this view, was not a lone figure with power to decide on the interest of all; the sovereign, instead, was the sum total of all the people working out decisions in the common interest. (Later on, theorists of socialism argued that the working class should dominate government.)

In Europe the theorists of representative democracy won out over the theorists of absolutism. This is the history of the French Revolution and of many other political changes which followed. But in Africa, the European conquerors set up absolutist governments, based on reasoning similar to that of Louis XIV. African society was made up of contending groups whose differences could not be resolved peaceably. Most Africans had neither the property nor the level of civilization to give them a stake in the future. The leading class in Africa was that of the European merchants and settlers, but even they could not be trusted to govern, because they would exploit the Africans. Therefore it was necessary to maintain an absolutist colonial government which made all decisions, and which ruled in the interest of the colony as a whole. For these reasons, colonial officials favored democracy in Europe, but absolutism in the African colonies.

Pierre Ryckmans, an energetic and reforming Belgian administrator who served as governor of Ruanda–Urundi and then as governor-general of the Belgian Congo, expressed this view forcefully in a little book on Ruanda–Urundi: *Dominate to Serve*. His mission, as he expressed it, was to serve the people of the colony by civilizing them and by making them "better, happier, more manful." The details of his book include a sensitive discussion of famine in Ruanda–Urundi, and a well-informed explanation of the crisis brought about by labor recruitment. But the resolution of these and other problems was to be carried out through domination by the Belgian colonial government.

The French colonial official Robert Delavignette developed a more sophisticated defense for absolutism. Delavignette, who taught in the Colonial School in Paris after serving as an administrator in French West Africa, wrote a handbook for *commandants de cercle* in 1940. In it he presented, for French West Africa, three great social objectives which he related to the protection of humanity and the dignity of the individual: the freeing of slaves, education, and the fight against epidemics. To achieve these objectives, it was necessary to introduce agricultural machinery, and to recruit and train teachers and doctors. But these required money, and money could only come from trade. Therefore it was necessary to draw Africans into wage labor, and even compulsory labor. Thus did the colonial regime advance the welfare of its African subjects: "The colony has proletarianized them in order to free them, educate them, care for them." Delavignette went on to argue that the local French administrators, working as they did under difficult conditions, qualified as heroic leaders. *The True Chiefs of the Empire,* as he titled the book, celebrated the work of these administrators.

Publication of Delavignette's book was prevented during World War II, in part because he was considered too close to the socialists. It was published in 1946 under the title *Service africain* (African service) and was translated into English in 1950 as *Freedom and Authority in French West Africa.* It remains a classic of enlightened colonial administration.

Yet Delavignette's outlook clearly represented despotism as well as enlightenment. For Africans to gain access to the freedom which went with full exercise of French citizenship, they had first to submit to the authority of the French empire, until it was established that they were worthy of elevation to citizenship. As it was for those individuals who obtained French citizenship, such as Jean Adjovi, so it was for the African subjects of France collectively; they had to serve generations of tutelage, demonstrating their willingness to accept unquestioningly the decisions of the authorities, before they could be admitted to citizenship. And, as it worked out, the inhabitants of France's African colonies never qualified for French citizenship. The choice was that posed in 1924 by Kojo Tovalou-Houénou:

> *We wish to be citizens of some country.* For this reason, if France rejects us, we must have autonomy. If she embraces us, it must be total and integral assimilation.

4

Culture and religion, 1880–1940

The clash of cultures which accompanied the colonization of Africa was very real. The outlooks of European rulers and of their African subjects were so distinct that communication across the cultural boundary was often impossible. For much of the colonial period, French and Belgian observers felt free to dismiss African culture as savage, while Africans in turn labelled their European rulers as destroyers of civilization. Yet within a century a remarkable synthesis of previously antagonistic cultures has emerged. The synthesis is neither complete nor fully comfortable, but there does exist an identifiable francophone African culture, expressed through a mixture of African and European concepts in the French language, and also expressed through the use of French words and concepts in African languages.

The clash of cultures, then, was not an irreconcilable conflict of alien traditions. It was a confrontation of European and African ways, but one in which enough similarities and mutual benefits of the two cultural traditions emerged for them to be combined usefully, though only after debate and transformation. Neither Europe nor Africa had a unified culture. Europe was divided into Catholic, Protestant, and atheist, into elite and popular culture, into radical and conservative political traditions. Africa was divided into Muslim, Christian, and many other religions, into hierarchical and communitarian political traditions, and into many local cultures. The possibilities for combining these elements into a culture to meet the needs of twentieth-century Africa were greater than they first seemed.

The debates on the culture of francophone sub-Saharan Africa, however, were not debates among equals. French and Belgian colonial rulers, the Christian religion, and the French language were backed by military power and a belief in European cultural superiority. So the cultural transformation of francophone Africa began as the imposition of European ways, and it therefore began with the division of Africans into those who submitted and those who resisted.

The French were more successful in imprinting their national culture on Africa than were the British. The Belgians, since they were so divided on the meaning of their nation, made a smaller cultural impact on Africa than either the French or the British. On the other hand, the Belgians were more successful in transmitting their religion to Africa than were the French, British, or

Portuguese. The French, though ambiguous about Christianity, were more fearful of Islam than the British. In both North and West Africa, French administrations studied Islam carefully, concerned that it would become a focus of anti-colonial resistance. The British, in contrast, found it relatively easy to ally with Muslim rulers. In education, each colonial power left a unique legacy for the territories under its rule. The French developed a French-speaking elite, the British permitted African languages to become literary languages, and the Belgians emphasized widespread elementary education in African languages. The developments in African culture in the early colonial years varied in response to the specific nature of the colonial regime, but also according to local conditions. Literary and intellectual movements sprang up in both British and French Africa, but the francophone writers focused on literature and philosophy while the anglophone writers focused on history and law. In the plastic arts, the colonial period brought an outpouring of both traditional and innovative work from the French and Belgian colonies. Meanwhile Arab Africa, though greatly changed by colonial rule, retained the Arabic language and reaffirmed its Islamic heritage and its cultural links to the Middle East.

This chapter begins with a brief survey of the European francophone culture which was imposed on Africa through colonialism, and turns then to the European and African debates on the validity and the viability of African culture. We turn next to the impact of Christian and Muslim missionaries on African religious institutions and beliefs, and then to art and literature in the colonial situation. Overall, this chapter traces the expansion of European culture (but also Muslim culture) in francophone Africa, and it also traces the beginnings of a new African culture.

FRANCOPHONE CULTURE

By the term "francophone culture" we refer to the culture of the French-speaking peoples of Europe, who live mostly in France, but who also populate half of Belgium and a portion of Switzerland. By the nineteenth century, francophone culture had spread further than these countries. This was not only because of colonies and former colonies in the West Indies, Canada, and the Indian Ocean, but also because French was widely used as a language of diplomacy and culture throughout Western and Eastern Europe, and to a lesser degree in Latin America and the Middle East. In one sense, our story is simply the extension of this international francophone culture to sub-Saharan Africa.

The heritage of francophone culture goes back to the Middle Ages. With the Renaissance a literature in the French language grew up, touching on literature, drama, philosophy, and political theory. The central tradition in francophone culture was that dominated by the French kings, with their capital in Paris. Throughout the Middle Ages these kings gradually expanded the area of their effective power to include most of modern France. Louis XIV suppressed and expelled the Protestants (or Huguenots) and he expanded the kingdom eastward to the Rhine. The power and wealth of the French kings was such that they attracted the best writers and artists to their court. Under the French kings, music, cuisine, art, and architecture thrived. With the power and effectiveness of the French state, French became the language of diplomacy, and French terms such as parliament, minister, and portfolio became common in governments throughout Europe.

With the growth of the French kingdom, the French language came to dominate in many peripheral areas of the kingdom: Gaelic-speaking Brittany in the northwest, the Occitanian-speaking south, and German-speaking Alsace and Lorraine. The local traditions of these areas survived, though now under French domination, both in their own languages and in translation into French. Equivalent examples of acculturation were later to take place in Africa.

The French Revolution, beginning in 1789, brought dramatic change to some aspects of French culture, yet reinforced others. The principle of the absolute monarchy was overthrown with the execution of the king in 1793, and in its place rose the principle of the nation, in which all inhabitants were citizens who were equal before the law. The Catholic Church was overthrown, and in its place (for a brief time) there arose the worship of Reason. French armies moved all across Europe, not initially for conquest, but to liberate all Europe from monarchies and feudal aristocracies as had been done in France.

Many of these revolutionary changes were soon limited. The most radical of the revolutionaries lost power in division among themselves, and the tide of change slowed in the later 1790s. Then Napoleon Bonaparte, the most effective of the revolutionary generals, seized power in order to provide stability, and by 1801 he had made himself emperor. There followed the establishment of a new aristocracy, a realignment with the Catholic Church, and conquests of territory in which the French came as oppressors rather than liberators. The other European powers finally united to defeat and exile Napoleon in 1815. They made France a kingdom again, but kept her under close watch. France would never be the same as before the revolution. Many new elements – republicanism, the celebration of popular culture, and a devotion to the universal rights of man – had been added to French culture.

Belgian culture, as a much smaller national tradition within the francophone world, is less imposing and less easy to identify than that of France. This is partly because of the small size of the country, partly because it is divided between speakers of French and Flemish, and partly because Belgium has only had a national existence since 1830. The Belgian cultural tradition, nevertheless, runs very deep. Belgian culture reaches back to the Medieval communes, those towns which were able to separate themselves from feudal landholders, and which began to grow as centers of commerce and manufacturing. These Belgian towns, of which Antwerp, Liège, and Brussels became the largest, were the earliest centers of capitalist economic growth in northern Europe. Their textiles – ranging from delicate lace to great wall panels – were traded far and wide.

But Belgium, for all its economic importance, never had political independence. The area which today includes Belgium, the Netherlands, Luxembourg and northern France was, in the Middle Ages, a mixture of Dutch-speaking people (mostly in the north) and French-speaking people (mostly in the south) ruled by a group of counts and dukes who themselves were part of the Holy Roman Empire. Of these, the dukes of Burgundy unified the Netherlands in the fifteenth century, and unsuccessfully sought the title of king. By the sixteenth century, this area had come to be ruled by the Habsburg family, which ruled Spain and then Austria.

The Protestant Reformation brought the next stage in the definition of modern Belgium. Beginning in 1517, Martin Luther declared the Pope to be the antichrist, and led large numbers of believers in northern Europe out of the Catholic Church. By mid century, most of the Dutch-speaking people of the Netherlands had become Calvinist. At the same time, the northern Netherlands had become very powerful in shipping and banking, and sought independence from Spain. Spain fought to defend her Netherlands territories in a war which was both economic and religious. The result of a century of bitter fighting was a line drawn roughly at the modern frontier between Belgium and the Netherlands. To the north lay the independent republic of the Netherlands, dominantly Protestant, and to the south lay the Spanish (later Austrian) Netherlands, dominantly Catholic, and including a substantial French-speaking (or Walloon) population.

Thus it was that, after the Napoleonic wars, when the powers of Europe combined Belgium with the northern Netherlands in a Kingdom of the Netherlands, the result was not satisfactory to the Belgians. In a moment of national fervor which coincided with the French July Revolution of 1830, the Belgians seceded from the Netherlands and gained their national recognition, and a king. The new Belgian kingdom was strongly Catholic, and the French-speaking Walloons were again, as they had been under Napoleon, politically dominant over the Flemings. Put in other terms, the Belgians were a group at the edge of France who managed to avoid incorporation into the French nation. While they have partaken of the culture of France, they have also emphasized their own national identity. Meanwhile the Belgian tradition of industrial leadership continued throughout the nineteenth century.

The industrial transformations of Belgium and France brought new developments in their national cultures. The newly affluent bourgeoisie provided support for remarkable achievements in architecture in the expanding cities, in literature, and in painting. Supporters of bourgeois interests defended the philosophical merits of individualism and competition in the economic arena. At the same time a wage-earning class of industrial and service workers grew in large and small towns. It demanded education for its children, and gave support to a popular press, to sports, and other entertainments. Leading speakers for this class supported an ideology of collectivism, and succeeded in building powerful socialist parties in both countries after 1890 and an influential communist party in France after 1920. Class conflict, however, usually remained within limits; in the unity of the nation or of the church, the contending influences in French and Belgian culture were able to coexist.

These well-developed national cultures established new and intensive relations with Africa in the nineteenth century. They defended their accomplishments as representing "civilization," and considered themselves to be bringing its benefits to Africa. The French, who were content to be missionaries if it did not implicate them in being religious, sought to carry out a "civilizing mission." The Belgians, while they were unable to agree on a superior culture because of their ethnic bickering, confidently presented themselves as sources of economic progress.

Since the French and Belgian rulers of Africa saw themselves as bringing civilization to Africa, they measured Africans according to their willingness to accept these imported ways. It was not just that Africans were expected to emulate francophone culture, they were expected to express their loyalty to France and Belgium, and to demonstrate that loyalty in their every act. In the French colonies, French was not only the language of communication, but within that language it was necessary for Africans to speak the correct phrases affirming their loyalty, before any discussion could begin. In the Belgian colonies, obeisance could be expressed in a wider range of languages. Whenever African individuals sought to register their land, or African groups sought to protect tax increases, they began by declaring their loyalty to France or their love for Belgium, and they attempted to show that their requests were within the best tradition of loyalty to the mother country.

THE DEBATE ON AFRICAN CULTURE

Two debates on the nature and future of African culture – one among Europeans and the other among Africans – were joined in the early colonial years. Francophone culture, vibrant, innovative and backed by the military and economic power of those who carried the culture, seemed so imposing as to bring into doubt the survival of African culture, even among African thinkers. Only gradually did the underlying strengths and adaptability of African cultures come to be recognized by both sides. In the meantime, the power and repetition of European rejections of African culture had become a factor itself, one which slowed and biased the integration of European elements into a new francophone African culture.

The more enthusiastic and dogmatic French and Belgian writers portrayed Africans as lacking in history, as bound in a timeless and primitive culture, and as children on the evolutionary scale on which Europeans had reached maturity. The writings of missionaries, travellers, and ethnographers were filled with descriptions of strange rituals among primitive tribes, and conveyed the assumption that these African tribes had lived isolated and unchanging lives for centuries. The falseness of such assumptions of African changelessness has been discussed above, as in the section on slavery in chapter 2. But African slavery provided, in the eyes of the colonizers, not an example of African social change but a justification for conquest and a demonstration that Africans needed to be protected against themselves by colonial masters.

The involvement of Europeans in African life also brought out another side of the debate. Certain of the French and Belgian officials and missionaries learned African languages and steeped themselves in African culture. By describing the languages and customs they learned, and by collecting histories and translating them, these writers provided ample evidence of the substance, the variety, and the evolution of African societies. Maurice Delafosse was perhaps the most distinguished of these early writers. He edited and translated the major Arabic-language histories of the Niger bend region, and collected traditions in Mande languages which he worked into a three-volume study of geography, ethnography, and history of the upper Niger region entitled *Haut-Sénégal-Niger*. In Dahomey, administrator Auguste Le Herissé entered into a common-law marriage with a princess of the royal family, interviewed the elders of the old kingdom, and wrote a study of Dahomey which became a classic.

These writers, while defenders of African culture, were not critics of colonialism. On the contrary, they were colonial officials, they believed in the justice of colonial rule, and in the superiority of European culture. They saw the African past as important, and hoped to preserve its memory. For the African future, however, they saw no alternative but in submission to the tutelage of Europe. In this sense their views, though far better informed, were little different from those of the popular writers who called for the abolition of old African customs.

Another area of the debate over African culture was that of art. European visitors to Africa had been collecting sculptures, textiles, and other artistic and handicraft work for centuries. In the late nineteenth century a growing number of European shops began selling African art work as curios. In addition, museums began to expand their collections of African art – the Ethnographic Museum in Paris (now the Musée de l'Homme) was an outstanding example. Finally, in the early years of the twentieth century, some of Europe's leading artists – Vlaminck, Bracque, Picasso, Kirchner, and Nolde – began collecting African art and incorporating its motifs and its principles into their work. This strong response to African art represented a clear approval of the skill and imagination of African sculpture. Beyond this, however, the reaction was more complex. Europeans responded to African art precisely because it was so different – so alien – from what they were used to. At the same time, Europeans found meaning in this art, and felt able to recognize the emotional and aesthetic values it conveyed. But the European consumers of African art did not, with few exceptions, seek to understand the cultures which produced the art they admired.

As the case of African sculpture suggests, the European debate about the *past* of African culture had two sides, in that some defended the achievements of African culture in the face of those who rejected it as changeless primitive superstition. The debate about the *future* of African culture also had two sides, but neither side suggested that African culture would be useful in the construction of that future. On one side were the *assimilationists*, those who sought to assimilate Africa to European culture. They believed that an African elite would first adopt French language and European culture, and that Africans generally would more gradually learn to fit into French or Belgian society. Ultimately, Africans might become full citizens of the mother country. On the other side were the *associationists*, those who wished to preserve the connection between European and African societies, but without the culture of one permeating the other. According to this view, Africans would not be able to assimilate the full range of francophone culture, and should remain within their own culture; African culture, in turn, should not be adulterated and confused by the introduction of French and Belgian ways. The functioning of an associationist system did require, however, a sizeable number of translators between the two systems: an African elite knowledgeable in both cultures. Yet this elite group of translators was, in the associationist view, unstable and dangerous group; in the assimilationist view, on the other hand, the African elite represented the most progressive and advanced African element.

Among the Europeans in this debate, little thought was given to the possibility that Africans might transform their own ancestral culture to respond to their new situation. The Europeans gave this possibility little thought because they saw African society as being too technically inferior to provide a basis for a twentieth-century existence, and because they accepted the vision of African culture as unchanging and incapable of change.

At the opposite limit of the European debate were those who became so taken with African society, that they simply joined it. This was the case of at least one French administrator in Guinea, who learned the Fulbe language and became deeply involved in Fulbe culture. With time, his dispatches to the capital began including more and more Fulbe phrases, and he ultimately left the service of France as a relatively successful Fulbe poet. In so doing he left the European debate on African culture and joined the African debate.

The second debate on African culture, that among the Africans, is less well documented, but it was no less important for the actual course of history. For Africans under French and Belgian rule, many of whom were profoundly respectful of European technology and power, the question was whether the European conquest had discredited African culture. To place the question in religious terms: had the old gods been killed? In many cases the French and Belgian invaders had desecrated shrines, violated sacred groves, and halted the performance of important rituals, yet they had not been struck down by the gods. Should families and kings still consult the ancestors in times of difficulty, as they had done in the past? For those Africans who had become Christian, were they now cut off from their ancestors, and would they become fully European? Was it possible to accept certain European ideas without destroying the fabric of their own society?

The best-recorded part of this debate is that published in French by members of the African elite who served as translators and intermediaries for Europeans and Africans. What one sees in their writings is a determination to synthesize francophone and African culture. They proclaimed complete loyalty to their colonial masters, yet they sought to dignify the past traditions of their colonies and to translate them into French, and they sought to combine African with French elements into a new culture. No doubt they were arguing against others, who expressed themselves in African languages, who rejected francophone culture, and who sought to meet new problems by working within the confines of their past culture. But even then, another element of the argument had to be faced; were the cultural traditions of Africa changeable enough to meet the challenges of life under colonialism?

MISSIONARIES

Missionary work directed by Portuguese and Italians from the fifteenth to the nineteenth centuries led to the growth of Catholic communities in some areas along the Atlantic coast. The largest of these communities was among the Kongo people of Angola and Zaire; smaller communities clustered along the coasts of modern Senegal, Bénin, Gabon and Congo. In the nineteenth century, Christian missionary efforts in Africa became far more intensive, and these efforts were rewarded with millions of conversions in the twentieth century.

The new wave of Christian missionary work began in the late eighteenth century, especially among British and German evangelical Protestants. Wesleyans, Methodists, and Moravians, all opposed to slavery and all convinced that the salvation of their own souls depended on bringing the good news of the Bible to the heathens who had not heard it, sent missions to African territories, most of which eventually fell under British rule. American Congregationalist missionaries, to give a further example, arrived in Gabon in 1842.

The Catholic anti-slavery movement in France and other Catholic countries became influential only in the 1830s, but from that point on a steadily growing Catholic missionary movement worked until, eventually, its African converts came to outnumber those of the Protestants. The Vatican worked out a partition of the African continent among the missionary orders of both men and women. Cardinal Lavigerie, leader of the White Fathers missionary society, began his work in Algeria during the French conquest, and later turned the focus of his work to East Africa, including Rwanda, Burundi, and the upper Zaire valley. The SMA Fathers of Lyon, founded in the mid nineteenth century, focused their work on the western coast of Africa, in Ivory Coast, Dahomey, and Nigeria. German Catholic missions established stations in Togo and Kamerun; these remained in place after the French and Belgian conquest. Belgian Catholic missionaries began work in Leopold's Congo Independent State, and increased greatly in number under the Belgian Congo. Leopold was able to renegotiate with Cardinal Lavigerie, so that Belgian White Fathers replaced French White Fathers in the eastern Congo.

The Christian missionaries tended to leave alone those areas which had already become Muslim. They focused on setting up schools as a way of recruiting young converts, and trained African cathechists who would be able to lead in prayer and study. The Christian missionaries wrote home regularly and traveled occasionally, seeking contributions from the European church members to continue their mission in Africa. These mission reports were perhaps the main source of public information in Europe about African affairs in the early colonial period.

The experience of Muslim missionaries in Africa was in many ways parallel to that of the Christians. Centuries of missionary work had led to the development of some significant Muslim communities. The earliest conversions to Islam in the northern savanna were in the third century of Islam (the tenth century AD) and by 1800 a large minority of the inhabitants of the Senegal and Niger valleys, as well as the Lake Chad basin, were Muslim. Then an energetic campaign beginning in the nineteenth century led to the conversion of millions, so that francophone sub-Saharan Africa was nearly 30% Muslim by 1940, and nearly 50% Muslim by 1985. The Muslims, like the Christians, were "people of the book," and Muslim missionaries emphasized indoctrination, education, and literacy just as the Christians did.

The contrasts between Christian and Muslim missionaries were as important as the similarities. Almost all the Muslim missionaries were African, while the leading Christian missionaries were European. (Even among the Christians, however, and especially among the Protestant Christians, African catechists, ministers, and missionaries were very important in spreading the word.) Christian missionaries were usually specialized and professional servants of the church. Muslim missionaries were sometimes specialized as religious leaders – as with the shaykhs of the Kunta tribe in the desert north of Timbuktu – but at least as often they were merchants, political figures, or had other positions in addition to their work in spreading the faith.

Muslim missionaries made their twentieth-century converts under fundamentally different conditions from those of the nineteenth century. In precolonial years, Muslim missionaries were often associated with an actual or potential political power. This is not to suggest that their efforts were backed up by political power alone, for in fact a more important factor was the religious and scholarly prestige of these missionaries. But the prestige of Muslim religious figures was almost always linked to the idea that a Muslim society should be run according to Qur'anic principles from top to bottom. Thus the states of Shaikh Ahmadu in Masina on the middle Niger, of al-hajj Umar on the upper Niger, and of Futa Jallon in Guinea were all based on Muslim theocratic principles. On the other hand, the conversions of people in Dar al-Kuti (in modern Central African Republic) under the sultan of that kingdom were reflections of political power more than moral reform.

The other way Islam spread in precolonial years was through trade contacts. Juula merchants in the Western Sudan and the adjoining forest, and Hausa and Yoruba Muslim merchants in Bénin, Togo, and Niger were among the leading merchant groups who created Muslim colonies wherever they went, and gradually spread the religion to local people in each area.

In the colonial period, however, Muslims no longer had state power, nor did they dare appear as alternatives to the French or Belgian authorities. Any militant Muslim movement immediately found its leadership arrested. Nonetheless, and perhaps because they were more clearly distinct from the colonial authorities than the Christian missionaries, Muslim missionaries had more success with peaceful methods in the twentieth century than with the threat of *jihad* or holy war in the nineteenth century. Qur'anic schools sprang up in large towns and small. Mosques were constructed not only in the northern savanna but in coastal towns of Ivory Coast and Bénin, and even in Brazzaville and Kinshasa. Pilgrimages to Mecca swelled each year in numbers.

A key decision faced by every missionary was how to approach other religions. Should a Muslim preacher attempt to discredit and destroy the old religion and its symbols, or simply argue for the validity of Islam, or seek actively to combine Islam with other religious beliefs? Believers in African religions facing Christian or Muslim missionaries faced the same question: was this new religion a threat to the old gods, or could the Christian or Muslim god be fitted into their existing beliefs? Christian missionaries tended to focus on issues of morality and on the sacraments, insisting that Africans become monogamous and eliminate superstitions before they could be accepted into the church. As a result, Christian missions in the early days tended to win as converts people of low status in African society – slaves and women, for instance – as they had the most to gain from changes in social patterns. Muslim missionaries during the colonial era were able to win many onverts by their emphasis on the strength of the Muslim community.

Catholic missionaries gave strong emphasis to doctrinal training among their converts. This training tended initially to invalidate African systems of thought. In the longer run, this focus on theology, and on the mystical and contemplative aspects of religion, contributed to a renewed tradition of African philosophy. The Protestant dominations, in contrast, put relatively great effort into medical facilities. These hospitals and dispensaries served a humanitarian purpose, but they were also intended to show the superiority of Western medicine, and to undermine African religion by invalidating African medicine. Medical stations did improve the health of those few people able to benefit from them, but they did not end the work of traditional healers. Perhaps the most famous medical facility in francophone sub-Saharan Africa was the hospital at Lambaréné in Gabon operated by Albert Schweitzer. Schweitzer, who achieved great fame in Europe as an organist and as a medical doctor, moved to Gabon after World War I and lived out his life as a medical missionary.

NEW RELIGIOUS INSTITUTIONS

The church and the mosque, the Christian denomination and the Sufi order, the mission school and the Qur'anic school – these were the institutions which diffused throughout francophone sub-Saharan Africa along with the spread of Christianity and Islam. These were new centers of power, sources of a new culture, and anchors for new ideas.

There were never more than 2,000 European and American missionaries in francophone Africa. Each mission station tended its small flock, and conversions grew slowly. In the Belgian Congo this process of conversion was speeded up in part because of strong state support for missionary efforts, which gave the missionaries more resources than in the French territories. But in the Belgian Congo as in the French territories, much of the work of converting Africans to Christianity was done by African rather than European missionaries, many of them in conflict with the Europeans.

Along the lower Zaire River, Simon Kimbangu began preaching in 1921, saying that the angel Gabriel had appeared to him in a vision. Kimbangu, who had been baptized by Baptists in 1915, preached a straightforward New Testament doctrine, and he helped thousands of people in his village of Nkamba for several months. His preaching reached slaves and wage workers, frustrated by the limits of the colonial system, yet he did not promote rebellion. He preached self-improvement, and urged his disciples to accept the state and the will of God. The Belgian government, however, after mis-translating his statements from Kikongo to French, chose to treat his movement as seditious. The administration put the region under military occupation and arrested Kimbangu. He spent the remaining 30 years of his life in prison in Elisabeth-ville. While his movement was banned, it survived underground, and burst into the open on occasion. Thus, when the Salvation Army arrived in the region of 1934, supporters of Kimbangu flocked to its meetings, accepting the flags and the prominent "S" as a symbol of Simon Kimbangu. Two decades later, on the eve of independence, the movement became a church, with the formation of the Church of Jesus Christ on Earth by Simon Kimbangu. By 1985 the church had a membership of about four million.

Eight years before Kimbangu's preaching, William Wade Harris left his native Liberia and carried out a brief but highly successful campaign of evangelism in Ivory Coast. Harris, walking from village to village clothed in white and carrying a Bible and a long staff, preached that all must give up their previous religion, accept Jesus Christ as their savior, and prepare to be baptized. Harris preached that others would follow him with Bibles, and asked his audiences to follow them. French officials, frightened by Harris's mass appeal, arrested him in 1913, and he was not able to preach again. Yet as missionaries came to the areas where he had preached, they found whole villages awaiting baptism and instruction in Christianity.

With the 1920s and 1930s, some Africans had begun to work their way into positions of responsibility in Christian churches. The first African priest ordained in the Belgian Congo was Stefane Kaoze in 1917. The first African priest ordained in Dahomey was François Mouléro in 1928, but no further African priests were ordained in that country for another 20 years.

Muslim missionaries worked within the Muslim equivalent to Christian denominations, the Sufi orders. While African Islam was not divided by a great theological schism such as that which separated Catholics from Protestants, it was divided into the followings of Muslim saints, living and dead, who by their piety and their scholarship had set a pattern which others followed in an organized manner. All Muslims shared the Qur'an, the traditions of the prophet Muhammad, and such duties as prayer, alms-giving, and pilgrimage. In addition to these formal duties, Sufism added a mystical, popular form for the celebration of God which attempted to put each person into closer contact with God through the performance of ritual. The various Sufi orders, named after their founders, represented different rituals – "ways" – for achieving contact with God, especially through the high personal qualities of the founders and leaders of the orders.

The Qadiriyya order, for instance, originated among the followers of the great mystic Abd al-Qadir in Iraq during the thirteenth century AD, and it was disseminated in sub-Saharan Africa particularly by the shaykhs of the Kunta, an Arab tribe which lived in the desert north of the Niger bend, and by the leaders of the great savanna Muslim states of Sokoto and Masina. The prestige of this order as one able to hold forth the Muslim way against European incursions was reinforced by the Algerian resistance struggle of Abd al-Qadir, a namesake of the founder of the Qadiriyya order. A second major order in West Africa was the Tijaniyya, founded by Shaykh al-Tijani in Morocco in the eighteenth century, and brought to prominence in West Africa by al-hajj Umar, who preached and conquered to spread this interpretation of Islamic belief and ritual. Remarkably, as important as conquest was in the initial spread of the Tijaniyya order, it spread far more widely in the colonial era, when Muslims dared not use force in conversion.

Another Sufi order is of more recent origin, but has won the loyalty of much of the population of Senegal. The Mouride order, founded by the Senegalese cleric Ahmadu Bamba (c. 1850–1927), was based on an ethic of piety and subservience to God through work, and especially through the cultivation of peanuts. Ahmadu Bamba was known early in life as a holy man; he blessed Lat Dior of Kajoor as he went into his final battle against the French in 1886. In about 1891 he had a prophetic revelation, and began to gather followers. His teaching was sometimes condensed to a simple expression: "go and work." His followers specialized in the cultivation of peanuts, and the *marabouts* (religious notables) surrounding him came to control great tracts of land and a large-scale commerce. The French, fearful of his influence, exiled him to Gabon in 1895, and them to Mauritania in 1902. By the time of his return to Senegal in 1912, however, he had some 70,000 followers. The French administration finally set up close ties with the Mouride *marabouts* on the basis of shared interest in peanut commerce. The order became part of the political and economic establishment of Senegal.

Conversion to Islam led to new social customs. Islam permitted and even encouraged polygyny, but limited the number of wives to four. In Middle Eastern countries, Muslim women were often secluded after marriage, and very commonly wore the veil when in public. In sub-Saharan African Islam, conversion did often lead in the direction of secluding wives, but use of the veil never spread as it had in the north.

The institutions of church, mosque, and Sufi order were key elements in the religious transformation of francophone sub-Saharan Africa. In addition to these, the school was a key religious institution. But since schooling involved instruction in social behavior and technical skills as well as religious practice, we shall discuss it in a separate section.

EDUCATION

The education of most children in early colonial Africa was performed informally in the home and village. Children learned household, farming, and herding tasks by working alongside their parents and their siblings. They learned their values and traditions by listening as their elders spoke. Their formal education, while of great importance, was generally of brief duration. It took the form of rites of initiation, such as circumcision for boys and, sometimes, clitoridectomy for girls. Before such rites, children received intensive instruction in history, philosophy, and religion, to impress on them the importance of becoming upstanding members of their society.

The colonial era brought expansion of three formal systems of education in francophone sub-Saharan Africa: Muslim, Christian, and Western secular systems. These systems challenged, supplemented, and ultimately transformed the information systems of African education and child rearing.

Qur'anic schools had existed for centuries in some parts of francophone Africa, but they expanded rapidly during the early twentieth century. This expansion was linked primarily to the spread of Muslim religious beliefs, but it also provided parents with a way of providing formal education for their children without sending them to European schools. The first level of Qur'anic school was for boys and girls (though mostly boys) aged six through 12. Schools included up to 50 pupils, instructed by a family or village leader who received contributions from the parents. The pupils were to learn to recite the Qur'an by heart, in Arabic, although many pupils learned only a few of the best known *suras* or verses. In addition, however, students learned the Arabic alphabet and some arithmetic. Those who went on to advanced work went to study with a learned scholar (known as a *marabout* in the Western Sudan and a *mallam* in the Central Sudan). Once they had mastered Arabic, they undertook the study of Islamic law and theology. Timbuktu and Jenne were two great West African centers of Islamic scholarship, and from there the best of the students went on to study at the universities of al-Azhar in Cairo and Qayrawan in Tunisia.

Christian mission schools also focused heavily on rote learning and on language instruction. Students in Protestant schools learned the Bible, those in Catholic schools learned catechism. Protestant missionaries often sought to reduce African languages to writing and to translate the Bible; Catholics wrote catechisms in local languages, but were bound by Latin for the mass. In French West Africa the mission schools fell under the shadow of government schools, but elsewhere they remained the mainstay of primary education. In French Equatorial Africa the mission schools received small government subsidies; in Togo and Cameroon the mission schools received rather larger subsidies. In the Belgian colonies, Catholic (but generally not Protestant) missions received substantial subsidies for providing primary education.

Government primary schools were established with the idea of training an African elite to serve as clerks, as teachers, or to govern the masses. This elite would have to be literate, able to perform bureaucratic tasks, and loyal to the colonial state and its policies. The Congo Independent State established School Colonies at Boma and Nouvelle-Anvers, training young wards of the state for such a purpose. The latter trained soldiers for the *Force publique* and was important in the spread of the Lingala language. In the French colonies, this desire for African apprentices was reinforced by an anti-clerical heritage, so that vocational skills and Western secular culture were presented with ideological overtones. The schools taught the belief that the French language, literacy, and francophone culture were the means to individual social advance and aggregate social renovation. In boarding schools, children were brought up under the care of the church or the colonial state, which instilled values and loyalties quite different to those the parents had in mind. School children often worked on garden plots for the schoolmaster. This work was supposed to instill discipline and regular work habits; it also made life easier for the schoolmaster.

The total number of children in school was not large. It would be difficult to estimate the number of children in Qur'anic schools, though it was certainly larger than the number in Christian or government schools. By the 1920s the total number of children enrolled in Christian and government primary schools came to no more than 3% of school-age children in French West Africa; the proportion in French Equatorial Africa was similar. Primary education reached a much larger 15% of school-age children in the French mandate of Cameroon. The French system was based on a six-year course of primary study. In the Belgian Congo, where primary education was a four-year course of study, roughly 15% of school-age children received primary education in the 1920s.

In French West Africa, most primary school students attended government schools; in French Equatorial Africa most primary school students were in mission schools. In Cameroon, mission schools taught many more students than government schools, and in the Belgian colonies virtually all primary education was in mission schools. In French West Africa the government actively undermined mission schools; in French Equatorial Africa the government forced mission schools to follow a French curriculum, but provided small subsidies for mission schools. In Cameroon the French government provided more substantial subsidies for mission schools, and in the Belgian colonies the state gave significant subsidies to the Catholic mission schools.

By the 1920s, higher primary schools (for the seventh through ninth years of schooling) had been established in France's West African colonies (except Niger and Mauritania) and in Cameroon. In French Equatorial Africa virtually no public education beyond the first six years was available until the Renaud School of Brazzaville, a higher primary school with a teacher training course, was established in the 1930s.

Some secondary instruction was available to African students through mission seminaries, particularly in the Belgian Congo. Otherwise, education at the secondary level was found only in French West Africa. The William Ponty School was established in 1903, admitting students by examination from the higher primary schools, and providing a three-year teacher training program. By 1945 it had granted 2,800 certificates to men who became teachers and functionaries. Its graduates constituted the real elite of francophone Africa, and many of them later assumed positions of political leadership. The African Medical School opened in Dakar in 1918, training doctors and midwives, and was followed by schools of pharmacy and veterinary medicine. In 1938, a Girls' Normal School opened at Rufisque, training teachers and midwives. Two secondary schools were founded in Senegal, primarily for European students: a government school in St.-Louis, and a private school in Dakar. The first secular secondary education came to the Belgian Congo during the 1930s, primarily for Europeans, though a few Congolese were admitted.

Finally, a small number of students from the French and Belgian colonies were able to obtain secondary or university education in Europe, either through support of their families or through successful competition on exams. Those mentioned elsewhere in these pages include Léopold Senghor and Mamadou Dia of Senegal, Garan Kouyaté of Mali, Kojo Tovalou-Houénou of Bénin, and Mfumu Farnana of Zaire.

BELIEFS

The religious and philosophical views of the people of francophone sub-Saharan Africa appear to have undergone great changes in the early colonial years, in that many had converted to Islam and Christianity by the end of that time, and many appeared to have accepted the legitimacy of the colonial order. But what, in religious terms, is the meaning of a conversion from a local African religion to a world religion? The missionaries tended to exaggerate the magnitude of the change, first because they saw conversion as a change from false beliefs to truth, secondly because they saw conversion as a change from polytheism to monotheism, and thirdly because they portrayed African religion as no more than magic and superstition.

On the third point, African belief in magic was widespread. That is, humans were believed to be able to manipulate supernatural powers through charms, spells, prayers, and sacrifices. Many Africans also believed that the future could be foretold, and they consulted diviners to learn of future events. But to present these beliefs as the sum total of African religious beliefs, as so many missionaries did, is to neglect the main elements of African moral, philosophical, and cosmological thought. The religions of the Dogon in Mali, of the Fon in Bénin, and of the Rwanda all began with the one creator god; this god created other high gods, and the high gods created nature spirits which controlled sacred forests and waterways. At the same time the Fang of Gabon, for instance, devoted most of their actual worship to cults of the ancestors and of initiation. That is, the Fang creator god, while ultimately more important, had retired from active direction of the world. The need to maintain contact with the ancestors and to ensure proper initiation of the young provided the most immediate, though not the most fundamental, aspect of Fang religious belief. The interactions among gods and angels and the links between god and man are as complex and as subtle in African religions as in Christianity, Islam, and Judaism.

Why then should Africans have found any advantage in Christianity and Islam? One difference which may have been important is that African religions, while they included all the elements of Islam and Christianity, did not have these elements integrated into a structural whole. An individual might be devoted to one deity or to another, but there was no single form of worship required of all believers. In Christianity and especially in Islam, God has provided instructions on how man should worship Him. (But through mysticism – as in Sufism and certain Protestant sects – the individual worshipper can regain the initiative and reach out for contact with God.)

Another sort of reasoning that may have influenced Africans is that they were now in a world-wide political system, that of colonies and their European mother countries, so their beliefs should extend to a world-wide frame of reference. In this sense, conversions to Islam and Christianity may not have been renunciation of the old religions, but translation of the old religions into new terms. The world-wide vision of Islam and Christianity did provide Africans with certain advantages. In both Islam and Christianity, all men are equal in the sight of God. Thus, even though French and Belgian officials treated Africans as subjects and inferiors, they professed a religion which denied the validity of such inequality in God's eyes. Within this frame of reference, one could either become a Christian, and link one's beliefs to those of the dominant colonial rulers or to leading figures in Europe, or one could become a Muslim, and link one's beliefs to a world community which was distinct from that of the colonizer.

Most religious conversions were not based on such theoretical considerations, but on personal experience within the limits of a community. In practical terms, when the leaders of a community converted to a new religion, their followers soon converted as well. Yet these questions of philosophy and world view cannot have been absent from these village-level decisions. Africans clearly needed an organized set of beliefs to make sense of the tumultuous changes which imperialism and colonialism had brought to them.

The Kongo of Zaire and the Wolof of Senegal were two peoples whose societies underwent great change in early colonial years. As all were now required to work for the colonizer in one way or another, new cleavages grew up among them. A few successful entrepreneurs were now distinct from the mass of peasants and wage laborers. Disappointed men took frustrations out on their women. Under these conditions Simon Kimbangu's re-enactment of the Jesus story, the story of God's sacrifice for man, was attractive in bringing hope and principle to the Kongo as it has been elsewhere. Similarly, the story of God's messages to Muhammad and the establishment of a rightly-guided community on earth, as restated by Ahmadu Bamba – as well as the threat of enternal punishment – have brought comfort and guidance to the Wolof.

Meanwhile, the belief in Western secular culture spread at the same time, though it was restricted to an elite of educated Africans and to others seeking to enter that elite. More than religious salvation, it was material and cultural progress which these believers sought. Those who sought to achieve the grace of recognition within European culture took on French names, they perfected their use of the French language, they developed flawless handwriting, and they drank deeply of European and classical history. Among the most outstanding of these believers was Marc Tovalou Quénum of Dahomey.

Marc was born in 1887, the son of Joseph Tovalou Quénum, the great merchant and planter who had supported the French conquest of Dahomey. Marc was sent to Europe in 1900 for his education. He was a brilliant student, and by 1911 had completed a law degree plus some medical work in Bordeaux. Tall, handsome, and aristocratic in his bearing, he developed an impeccable style in French. He returned to Dahomey for the first time in 1920, where he was welcomed by the elite for his accomplishments. But during this visit he began to become disillusioned with the reality of colonial rule, in contrast to the vision he had maintained in France. Soon he started using his African name, Kojo, and he changed the spelling of his family name from the Portuguese form, Quénum, to the more phonetically correct Houénou. He also began to claim descent from royalty; he was now Prince Kojo Tovalou-Houénou. As such he became, in the mid 1920s, the most prominent and most devastating African critic of the French colonial order, as well as a prominent cultural figure. He was an enthusiast of vocal music and dance, and he published a small book of philosophical maxims. He founded a newspaper, *Les Continents* (1924) and traveled to America to visit Marcus Garvey and black American leaders; he later married a West Indian singer he met in Chicago. The French government response was to harass him and seek to discredit him on all sides. In 1925 he was disbarred; he was held in jail without charges in Dahomey for several months in 1926, after which he lost his former influence and contacts. He died while in prison at Dakar in 1936; he was serving a sentence for contempt of court, and succumbed to typhoid fever.

Just as the philosophy of the Western-educated elite was distorted under the pressures it had to bear, so was the philosophy of African societies generally distorted and hidden in the early colonial years. Francophone Africa's universities were limited to the Muslim schools of the Sahara fringe. There Islamic learning continued to thrive, though now under watchful French eyes. But philosophers elsewhere in Africa did not have the advantage of universities and the written word to pass on their ideas. African philosophy has been transmitted to the present indirectly, incompletely, and with many changes in the process. Three main statements of African philosophy have come to us from francophone sub-Saharan Africa in the colonial period: *Bantu Philosophy*, a work by the Flemish priest Placied Tempels based on the beliefs of the Baluba of the Belgian Congo, *Bantu-Rwandese Philosophy of Existence*, by the Rwandese priest Alexis Kagamé, and *Conversations with Ogotommeli*, recorded from a Dogon elder in Sudan by the anthropologist Marcel Griaule. Tempels centered on the idea of the Life Force as the central concept in African philosophy. Kagame, focusing on the logic inherent in the Bantu languages which dominate Central Africa, emphasized their thorough system of classification on the basis of philosophy, and discussed categories of being and the logic of causation. Griaule, reflecting the arguments of Ogotemmeli, gave primacy of place to the *word*, the particular form of the life force which, through consciousness, influences the material reality of the world.

Modern African philosophy at the university level relies heavily on these three texts as points of departure, though often disagreeing with them. For the practical philosophy by which Africans generally live their lives, we can gain some insight from these philosophical statements, but little detail. As a principle, though, one can say that African thought, while it has doubtless changed dramatically during the colonial era, retains a distinct identity in contrast to the European thought with which it has been in such close interaction.

ART AND LITERATURE IN THE COLONIAL SITUATION

European art collectors began gathering large numbers of African sculptures in the late nineteenth century, treating them as curios or as trophies of imperial conquest. The most intensive collection of sculpture was carried out by French and Belgian collectors, partly because of the proclivities of the French and Belgian curio markets, and partly because of the large quantities of sculpture produced in Sudan, Guinea, Ivory Coast, Dahomey, Gabon, French Congo, and the Congo Independent State. These sculptures were sold in shops, and they were also exhibited in museums throughout Europe and in North America.

The German ethnographer Leo Frobenius carried out work beginning in 1904 in the Congo Independent State, Nigeria, Cameroon, and the Western Sudan, collecting and studying sculpture and other art work, in which he attempted to develop a theory of the origin and development of African arts. Thus the first major work on African art history began at the opening of the twentieth century.

Quite a different response to African sculpture came from working artists in Europe, particularly in France and Germany. Shortly after 1900, some of the experimentally-minded painters and sculptors of Paris began buying African masks in curio shops, and began studying them for aesthetic content. The greatest of these, Pablo Picasso, has described the revelation he received during a visit (now dated in mid 1907) to the Ethnographic Museum in Paris. He had gone to look at Romanesque sculpture, but entered the African gallery on impulse. There, poorly displayed in dank and musty halls, he found sculptures from West and Central Africa whose visual power left him shocked and yet charged with new energy. He had in fact seen African sculpture before, but now the simplified lines, the abstract and symbolic representations conveyed to him the idea of a "conceptual art," in contrast to the more explicit representational art against which he was rebelling. The influences of African sculpture are clear in Picasso's great work, "Les Demoiselles d'Avignon," which marks his transition into more than a decade of work in "primitivist" work. In the years from 1915 to 1930, a group of German Expressionist painters also drew heavily on African sculpture for inspiration.

Picasso never showed any interest in African societies, nor in the African context of the sculpture on which he relied. He took the sculptures as pure forms, or as examples of techniques. But he also believed that these forms conveyed meanings, and he sought to use both the techniques and the meanings in his work. He called the African work "primitive," but his use of the term was different from that of those who were celebrating the conquest of Africa. Picasso was interested in the psychologically primitive, in the deep and fundamental emotions of fear, love, anger, and peace which are conveyed by sculptures which are aimed at use in ceremonies renewing the land or celebrating the ancestors. It was in these areas that he and other European artists saw the work of African sculptors as an improvement on the overly realistic, rationalistic European art previously dominant in Europe.

To the degree that African artists changed their work and began to incorporate European motifs and techniques, the European artists and collectors lost interest in their work. From the viewpoint of the European artists, and especially of the collectors, the colonial period meant the destruction of African tradition, the adulteration of African culture, and the loss of the best creative work by African artists. (The African artists, meanwhile, had their own reasons for continuity and change in their style.)

With this admiration of precolonial African culture, and with this fear of the demise of African art and culture, European colonial governments and museums put considerable effort into acquiring African art for permanent collections. At the turn of the century, King Leopold II established the Royal Museum of Central Africa at Tervuren, outside Brussels, and built a large collection of art work from the Congo. In 1935 the French anthropologist Marcel Griaule led a great expedition across the continent from Dakar to Djibouti, purchasing quantities of sculpture wherever he could find it. His collection is housed at the Paris Ethnographic Museum, now known as the Musée de l'Homme.

The African area of wood sculpture corresponds very neatly to the area of francophone sub-Saharan Africa (plus the English-speaking territories of West Africa). Thus it was not only the interest of French and Belgian collectors that brought the art of francophone Africa to prominence, but the quantity and inherent quality of the work from this region. Specialized sculptors tended to congregate in workshops, where they created works under the direction or inspiration of a master. Their work was generally for sale, to African or European purchasers. Kongo sculpture began to be exported to Europe in the 1830s, and its volume had grown considerably by the 1880s. Among other works which became well known outside Africa were the Kota funeral statues of Gabon, which were abstract representations of the deceased, Nimba masks from Guinea, which were used in dances celebrating the return of the rains and renewal of the earth, Gelede masks from Dahomey, used in social dances, and sculptures of Kuba kings from the Belgian Congo. That is, these works were used within the society in which they were created, and it was only within that society that their ritual or symbolic meaning would be fully comprehended. But they could also be sold to African collectors – political leaders, for instance – who wished to show that they had wide contacts.

Sometimes the commerce in art objects reflected the contradiction between the colonial world and African society. Such was the case of young men among the Dogon of Mali who stole ritual statuary from their elders as they ran away to the city. At a single stroke, they provided themselves with some money for city life and made clear their rejection to traditional ways.

For the reasons above, selling sculpture to European buyers was neither inconceivable nor, usually, inappropriate for African sculptors. In some cases, the European market consumed an important portion of the artists' work. For the Gelede masks of Dahomey, for Fang masks of all sorts from Gabon, and especially for the Kuba sculptors of the Congo, exports of sculpture became quite important. Especially in the case of the latter, one can see from the quality of work done for export that this tourist market has caused work to be done more hurriedly and with less feeling. In some cases the work became simpler as a result, but in other cases the opposite was the result. Bamum sculptors of the Cameroon found that outsiders could not understand their simplified but beautiful representation of frogs, and had to carve their frogs in more detail for the export market.

Did the experience of colonialism bring an end to the great days of African art? This question is similar to one which might be posed for art in the modern world as a whole, where simplification, abstraction, discontinuity, and the stresses brought by a growing market for art objects have done much to undermine high quality work. But in francophone Africa there were signs from the first that artists would respond to their new conditions with a high level of creativity.

First, they introduced European motifs and colonizers themselves into their work; guns, bicycles, automobiles, books, and Europeans showed up in sculptures. Secondly, African artists began experimenting with new materials and new media: new fabrics in textiles, imported goods worked into sculptures, and painting on walls and canvases. Thirdly, African artists learned European techniques and canons: perspective and portraiture.

In literature the gap between the old and the new was greater than in the plastic arts, because of the barrier of language. African oral literature could be translated into French, and in fact many translations of narratives, tales, poems and songs were completed in the early colonial years. Most of these translations were performed by Europeans, however, since the Africans who knew this literature gained nothing by its translation. They were not seeking a wider audience.

To the degree that African languages became written, the existing oral literature could be reduced to print, and new writings could be linked to the old. But here the policies of the French and Belgians interfered to prevent much development. In the French colonies, instruction was only in French and writing of other languages was actively discouraged. This policy was not sufficient to prevent widespread literacy in Arabic, though there were virtually no Arabic-language newspapers in French colonial Africa. In the Belgian colonies, literacy in French was actively discouraged, and instead the development of several local languages was encouraged: Kikongo, Kiswahili, Tshiluba, and Lingala. But it was the missionaries who wrote the grammars of these languages, and most writings were restricted to the missionary press. In

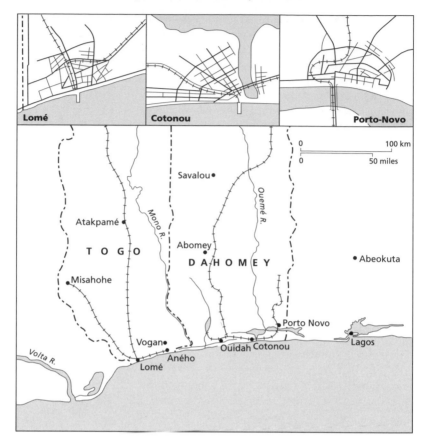

Map 9   Coastal Togo and Dahomey, 1940

addition, the restriction of students in the Belgian territories to elementary education further hindered the development of these as literary languages.

Literature in colonial francophone Africa had therefore to be written in French, and it had to enter print in the face of the formidable standards of literary criticism in the French-speaking world. African writers had to choose between seeking an audience in the main line of French literature, and expect rejection, or seek an audience in their own region alone, and expect to be considered marginal.

An early example of the latter approach was that of the little magazine, *La Reconnaissance africaine*, which appeared in Dahomey from 1923 to 1927. It was directed by Fr. Francis Aupiais, a Breton priest who had been a leading mission educator in the country for 20 years already. In this magazine, Catholic Dahomeans wrote stories telling of the history and culture of their country, giving an appreciation of their past yet expressing enthusiasm about their future under French and Catholic leadership.

The most energetic and talented of the writers in this magazine was Paul Hazoumé, a school teacher who went on to write two major books. One of these, *The Blood Pact in Dahomey*, gave a detailed analysis of the use of blood pacts over two centuries of Dahomean history, and won him a degree in ethnology. The other, *Doguicimi*, is a long novel which portrays all the ambiguities of the author's social and ideological position. The heroine, Doguicimi, is a slave woman who has become wife of a leading prince in the kingdom of Dahomey. The prince is captured on a raid into the country in which Doguicimi was born. The long negotiations for his ransom ultimately fail, and he is executed. Hazoumé used his powers of description to give an imposing image of the strength and complexity of the Dahomean monarchy, but he also exposed its cruelty and criticized its moral weakness. As the novel continues, he has his heroine express the wish that the French would conquer Dahomey and bring it up to a higher level of civilization. The author expressed pride in the old regime but also criticism of its flaws, and he expressed obeisance toward the French colonial regime. As it happens, Hazoumé completed this novel in 1936, and he was involved in a major political dispute with other Dahomeans, in which he was closely allied with the French government.

French literature on Africa was dominated by writers in France. Popular literature at the turn of the twentieth century was dominated by romantic stories of conquest, and by stories of mission work. Then in the 1920s, two major works focused French literary criticism and social criticism on Central Africa. René Maran's novel *Batouala* was the first of these works. It is the story of an energetic head of family, Batouala, who lived in Ubangi-Shari. Maran gave almost no direct role in the story to French colonial officials, yet the plot implies that colonial rule brought ruin to the area, and underlay the tragic collapse of the hero's family, accompanied by his own death. In a forcefully written preface, however, Maran was quite explicit in stating that the conditions of Africans had worsened since the arrival of the French. The novel won the prestigious Goncourt Prize in Paris in 1921, and it was all the more remarkable because the author was a black man. René Maran was born in 1887 in Martinique, in the French West Indies, the son of a minor administrator. He was sent to school in Paris and Bordeaux. At Bordeaux he came to know both Félix Eboué and Marc Tovalou Quénum, and was associated with each of them in the 1920s. Maran studied administration, but writing was always his passion. He served several years in the administration of French Equatorial Africa, and wrote *Batouala* and two other novels while there.

His prize created a scandal, not so much because he was black but because he was a black writer criticizing French administration. For Maran, however, his critique of French administration was not intended to be anti-colonial, but rather to demand that France in the colonies live up to the standard of the French republic at home. Maran, a French citizen from birth, believed that France could accept all her African subjects as citizens, once they met minimal tests. Many white Frenchmen did not agree.

In 1927, the leading French writer André Gide added to the debate with a travel narrative, *Travels in the Congo*. Gide had traveled up the Zaire River and across wide stretches of French Equatorial Africa and Cameroon. His description of the countryside and of the people he encountered portrayed the results of the forced labor on roads and railroads for the government, and also portrayed the continuing influence of the private concessionary companies. His report, written in a powerful journalistic style, startled many French readers and brought about demands for reforms. No one should have been startled, for the oppression Gide described had been a matter of policy for over two decades, and had been criticized before. This time, however, the result was the final abolition of the concessionary companies. Gide's narrative was more widely accepted by French readers than Maran's novel, perhaps because it elicited pity for the Africans rather than the identification with African protagonists which a reading of *Batouala* requires.

Now that some major issues in the values of French culture had been joined with first-rate prose in an African context, the stage was set for a new type of writer. Léopold Sédar Senghor of Senegal and Aimé Césaire of Martinique, two young poets and essayists, published their first works at the end of the 1930s, and received wide acclaim among African and West Indian audiences, and also among audiences in France. Senghor and Césaire celebrated *Négritude* ("blackness" or "Negro-ness") in such a way that it reaffirmed African culture and yet translated it into memorable French. Césaire became best known for *Return to my Native Land*, a poetic account of a voyage back to Martinique after years of schooling in France, in which he expresses a critique of colonial rule at the same time as he offers beautiful images of blackness and the survival of African traditions. Senghor's poems praised African women, sculpture, land, and drums in concise language full of complex allusions. Senghor and Césaire reveal in their work the same ambiguity as that in the work of Paul Hazoumé – an attachment both to African tradition and to metropolitan French culture – but Senghor and Césaire were at least able to do so on a far grander stage, attracting wide attention from both white and black audiences.

THE NEW AFRICAN CULTURE

African culture was bombarded on all sides in the early colonial years. Africans lost the independent political power which is so important in protecting cultural traditions from outside influence. African languages were no longer the languages of official expression. African religious traditions were criticized as savage and superstitious, and lost many believers to Islam and Christianity. In these and many other ways, African culture was criticized, weakened, and undermined.

Many of the old ways have in fact disappeared and many Africans did in fact come to doubt the validity of their own culture. But the history of the culture of francophone sub-Saharan Africa has yielded none of the simple results which might have been predicted a century ago. African culture was not rigid; it did not shatter under the impact of Western culture, nor did it stand unyielding in refusal to recognize or respond to changes around it. Africa was transformed, but it did not mock every European move, nor become transformed into a new France or Belgium.

We have already seen some examples of the originality of the African cultural response. Ahmadu Bamba and Simon Kimbangu, though leaders of religious renovation, saw themselves as no less African than those around them. They preached peace and submission to European governments, not renunciation of their heritage. Kojo Tovalou-Houénou, who proclaimed his love for France in brilliant prose, used his literary skill to justify the African past and to create an image of African destiny. Even Blaise Diagne, the Senegalese politician who became a minister in Paris, relied on close ties with the *marabouts* to stay in office.

During the 1930s, at the height of the colonial regimes and their power, the first outlines of a new African culture had begun to emerge. This new culture owes most of its roots to the old African culture, but also owes a great deal to the culture of Europe and to the experience of dealing with the conflicts of the past century. Jahnheinz Jahn, an eminent student of African culture, made this argument forcefully in *Muntu*, a book published in 1958 (just as African nations were gaining their independence) which drew heavily on examples from francophone sub-Saharan Africa. In religion, dance, philosophy, medicine, art, and literature, he demonstrated the clash of cultures which came with the New World system of slavery and the later European subjugation of Africa. He then demonstrated the way African cultural traditions reasserted themselves – in different forms and with different purposes, to be sure – after a long and painful period of reassessment.

For the case of francophone sub-Saharan Africa, we can say that the French and Belgian rulers imposed francophone culture very firmly on their African territories. These colonial rulers imposed francophone culture as the elite culture – a culture made attractive yet inaccessible to all but a few Africans. The later African cultural response bore the clear marks of that colonial imprint. Yet the literary works which began to emerge in the interwar years, though obviously in the francophone tradition, were clearly African works, and were oriented at least in part toward an African audience. In religious terms, the conversions to Islam and Christianity were clearly a step away from other African religions, but the result of these conversions was that Islam and Christianity ceased to be foreign religions and became African religions. Perhaps the most difficult area of expression for the new African culture was in philosophy. African philosophers had to face the negation of African philosophy and culture by European critics. Further, at the same time as they had to defend their Africanity, these philosophers had also to defend their humanity. The new African philosophy thus has the difficult task of explaining, on the one hand, the specifically African patterns of culture and thought and, on the other hand, the ways in which the African experience is a good example of the human experience in general.

5

Economy and society, 1940–1985

Between 1939 and 1942 Europe and Asia were engulfed in a war which extended to all the oceans of the world and to North Africa. Africa had undergone a foretaste of the war with the Italian conquest of Ethiopia in 1935–36. This was the last colonial conquest, but it was also a stepping stone to World War II. The course of the war resulted, in part, in the isolation of francophone sub-Saharan Africa, as the main battles and supply lines lay elsewhere. In another sense, the war and its aftermath resulted in a deeper integration of francophone Africa into the world community. The Allied victory over the Axis powers of Germany, Italy, Japan and their allies was widely interpreted as a victory for democracy and human rights, and as a rejection of fascism, of racial discrimination and persecution, and of the conquest of territory by military might. Africans came to the end of the war with hopes that they might gain equality with other peoples in political rights, in social standing, and in economic conditions. The formation of the United Nations in 1945 and its adoption of a Declaration of Human Rights in 1947 gave further reason for such hope, as did the 1947 achievement of independence from British colonial rule by India and Pakistan.

In the French colonies, the aftermath of the war led to the granting of new political rights. African voters were enabled to elect representatives to territorial councils and to the French National Assembly. These representatives led in the 1946 abolition of forced labor in France's African colonies, and fueled the hope for a new and better colonial system. Then, after a brief postwar economic depression, francophone sub-Saharan Africa experienced a great economic boom for nearly 20 years. Prices for export goods rose to high levels and provided Africans with income to import growing quantities of industrial goods, to pay for a great expansion in such social services as schools and health facilities, and to pay for investment in roads, harbors, and government buildings.

In the midst of this boom, francophone sub-Saharan African countries gained independence, in the years from 1958 to 1962. The transition to independence involved some bitterness, as in Guinea's 1958 declaration of independence from France, and it involved some severe civil conflict, as in Zaire and in Cameroon. But these initial difficulties did little to reverse the dominant feeling of optimism among Africans. Perhaps most important was the feeling among many Africans that, after generations of colonial rule and racial discrimination, they had regained control over their own destiny.

The two decades from 1965 to 1985 were to provide sobering commentary on this belief. World prices, which had provided African producers with growing incomes for two decades, now turned in the other direction for two decades. The markets for agricultural commodities became glutted, and their prices fell in contrast to the prices of industrial goods that Africans purchased, which continued to rise. This trend was already well established when the oil crisis of 1974 signalled a round of inflation that left African economies at an even worse disadvantage.

Changing climate brought reverses every bit as serious as changing prices. Two great droughts parched the soils of the northern savanna, the first from 1967 to 1974, and the second from 1979 to 1985. The effects of the drought were compounded by the social policies of the colonial period and by the political decisions of the new governments; as a result many lives were lost to famine, and large areas of land fell out of cultivation.

Despite the reverses after 1965, francophone sub-Saharan Africa experienced overall economic growth in the years after 1940 and by 1985 many of the francophone countries had caught up to anglophone African countries in per capita income. South Africa and the nations of Arab Africa, however, retained a significant economic lead over francophone Africa. Continuing links to France made the former French colonies economically dependent, but provided them with monetary and economic stability. Francophone African cities grew rapidly after 1940, and caught up with the anglophone cities in size, in glitter, and in urban unrest. The governments of francophone Africa have intervened in the economy more systematically than in anglophone Africa, and more successfully than in lusophone Africa. The former Belgian territories, however, experienced slow economic growth after independence, largely because of their outbursts of civil war and class war following independence. This civil strife was comparable to the long anti-colonial wars followed by civil war in lusophone Africa, and to the civil wars of Nigeria, Uganda, Sudan, and Zimbabwe in anglophone Africa. Nor were former French nations free from civil strife. Police repression was severe in the Central African Empire and in the last years of Touré's Guinea, and Chad entered into a long civil war. Meanwhile, by the mid 1980s most of the nations of francophone Africa had slipped deeply in debt to foreign banks and to the International Monetary Fund.

The control which Africans sought over their own affairs escaped them for three reasons. First, the continuing economic influence of powerful outside forces over Africa set limits on African economies at every turn. Secondly, the hand of the past was still upon them; the decisions made and policies implemented during 50 to 80 years of colonial rule had set limits and conditions on African societies which could not easily be overcome. Thirdly, there had emerged significant conflicts in interests and actions among the people of francophone sub-Saharan Africa, which prevented them from acting in unity. In sum, colonialism had given way to neocolonialism.

Yet for all the frustrations felt at the end of this period, there could be no denying the tremendous advances which had taken place. In this chapter we will focus on the social and economic conflicts and changes of francophone sub-Saharan Africa after 1940. We begin with a review of changing conditions in the rural areas where the great majority of the people made their lives. We turn next to the cities, which grew with extraordinary rapidity; the greatest of them, Kinshasa, reached to a population of over three million in 1985. Two further sections then focus on the international economy and on the role of government in the economy. Then, based on this background of economic conflict and change, we discuss the social and ethnic conflicts of the period. Finally, a summary of the chapter focuses on changes in the physical landscape, showing how the landscape reflects the economic and social changes of the period.

RURAL LIFE

The majority of the people of francophone sub-Saharan Africa continue today to live in rural areas and most rural inhabitants live and work on small farms. Most of their villages are still without electricity or running water, and without good links to main roads. The crops, the livestock, and the farming techniques are in many cases similar to those a century ago. Yet despite the poverty and the isolation of the countryside, the rural areas have undergone substantial changes in recent decades. Villages are linked to each other and to national centers by roads, by radio, and by school systems. Travel, both in short visits to sell crops and in long stays for employment, has given the rural people wide experience with other regions and with city life.

One of the greatest changes in the countryside has been brought about by the declining rate of death. In Ivory Coast, the expectation of life at birth rose from under 40 years in 1940 to 50 years in 1980. The reasons for this declining mortality rate are diverse and are not entirely understood. Western medicine has made some contribution to improved health, but the decline in mortality began before the number of doctors and medical clinics increased significantly. Improved nutrition is another possibility, though in some cases the impact of colonial rule was actually to worsen African nutrition, in particular by drawing men away from farming and into forced labor for the government or into production of cash crops for export. Public health measures against some diseases were successful. A Belgian campaign against sleeping sickness in the Congo, conducted through the clearing of the brush in which the tsetse fly thrives, reduced the incidence of sleeping sickness sharply. (During the civil wars of the 1960s, sleeping sickness came back to areas from which it had been cleared because the bush grew back.)

Since women continued to have the same number of children as before, and since less of them died, average family size rose significantly in postwar francophone Africa. Parents had the joy of keeping more of the children born to them, but they also had the additional responsibility of providing for them.

For certain areas of francophone Africa, however, population did not grow significantly. In the Central African countries of Gabon, Congo, Central African Republic, and in northern areas of Zaire, the rate of fertility remained very low. While the decline in death rates was sufficient to end population decline, the birth rate remained too low to bring about population increase. Many of the men and women in this region were infertile. Contributing factors included the number of parasites in this particularly humid environment, widespread incidence of venereal disease, and the heritage of relatively op-pressive regimes which have sought to extract wealth from a small and poor population.

Modern medicine had at least one unambiguous victory, as smallpox was eliminated from the African continent during the 1970s; an internationally supported team of doctors vaccinated a large enough proportion of the population that the virus simply died out. With this, a disease which had scourged Africa for nearly 500 years was eliminated.

The growth in population brought implications for the ecology of franco-phone Africa. Higher population meant more intensive use of land, and this in turn meant exhaustion of the land's fertility, which in turn brought increasing need for improved farming techniques. Overfarming and overgrazing ex-ceeded the limits of the sahel lands from Senegal to Chad. Sheer increase in population was one factor which exhausted this marginal soil; another was government policy which favored agriculture over herding, and which restric-ted the movements of farming families through tax policies and political boundaries.

As a result, when the rains failed for several years beginning in about 1967, famine and disaster struck. Perhaps millions of cattle died, and scores of thousands of people (especially children) died as well. By the time resources were drawn together to address this issue, the land and the population had each suffered so much that it was much harder to make the necessary changes. With this disaster, the independent nations of the sahel zone became drawn into the politics of international famine relief. International donor organiz-ations, which controlled relief funds, became constituents of African govern-ments. Governments were under pressure to meet the requirements of these organizations even when to do so brought them into conflict with the demands of their own citizens. Drought returned in the early 1980s, and by 1985 Senegal had lost so much land to advancing desert that peanut production and exports declined dramatically.

While the savanna and sahel lands were being subjected to increased use by a growing population, and then devastated by drought, the forested areas of Central Africa and of the West African coast were being attacked by different users. Increased population of forested areas resulted in cutting out of signifi-cant amounts of timber, especially in Ivory Coast where commercial agricul-ture had expanded so steadily. International logging firms were a far more significant cause of deforestation. From the 1920s, Gabon's main export was *okoumé* or gaboon mahogany wood; the volume of exports grew rapidly in the booming economy after World War II.

Rural families, now larger in size, also changed in structure and organization. With the expansion of schooling, children were no longer brought up solely under the guidance of their parents and neighbors, but were away at school during the days or, as was the case for many, away at boarding school. Family patterns also changed in response to religious change. For those areas which became Christian, polygyny fell into disfavor; for areas which became Muslim, polygyny was reinforced or reinterpreted. As new legal codes were established, particularly with independence, divorce became permissible in every country within francophone sub-Saharan Africa. The rate of divorce increased sharply, particularly in Central Africa, with women initiating a growing number of the proceedings.

The family became the primary unit of agricultural production, and the methods of agricultural production changed along with the structure of the family. With increasing pressure on the land, farmers sought to find more productive food crops. Particularly in Central Africa, manioc cultivation continued to expand (displacing the beans, bananas, and millet which were grown before) often on the recommendation of Belgian colonial officials. From the viewpoint of the farmer, manioc is an excellent crop; its roots will grow to good-sized tubers in almost any soil, they require only a minimum of care, and they can be left in the ground for as much as 18 months before being harvested, thus reducing problems of storage. From the consumer's viewpoint, however, manioc has severe disadvantages. It must be processed slowly and carefully, or else it can be poisonous, it is less tasty than other starchy staples, and it is almost entirely starch, with little other nutritional value except in the leaves.

The actions of market forces combined with those of colonial administrations to encourage Africans to sell crops for export. During the 1930s, unprecedented quantities of palm oil, palm kernels, cocoa, peanuts, coffee, cotton, and timber had been exported, even in the depths of the depression. In addition, mineral exports from the Belgian Congo hit a new peak as the mechanization of the mines advanced. With World War II, however, the experiences of the three blocs of colonies diverged. In French West Africa, which remained loyal to the Vichy regime until 1943, foreign trade came almost to a halt; imports and exports dropped to one-eighth of their pre-war level. French Equatorial Africa and Cameroon, on the other hand, contributed to the Free French war effort without interruption; foreign trade declined, but to one-third of the prewar level. In the immediate postwar years, the level of foreign trade remained very low in the French colonies; France's economy was in collapse, and French currency then underwent a substantial inflation which distorted African prices. For the years from 1940 through 1947, therefore, the French colonies in Africa lived a relatively autonomous economic life. During these years, small-scale domestic industry sprang back into life to produce textiles, hardware, and to distill alcohol to drink and as fuel.

The Belgian Congo, in contrast, experienced continual growth in its agricultural and mineral exports throughout the war years; imports declined, but only modestly. The Belgian administration insisted on full support for the war effort, and demanded extra labor from Africans in agriculture and in industry.

The resulting output contributed significantly to the Allied war effort, but it also caused thousands of overworked Congolese to flee to neighboring colonies. Union Minière's stock of uranium had already been transferred from Belgium to New York as war broke out, and was used in the development of the atomic bomb. Further shipments of uranium, copper, tin, platinum, and diamonds flowed from Central Africa to the factories of Britain and America. The revenue generated by these African exports was so great that the Belgian economy recovered from the war much more rapidly than did that of France. For the Belgian colonies, therefore, World War II was not a time of autonomy, but a time of increasing incorporation into the world economy.

From 1948 through the 1960s, an economic boom brought continued economic growth and expansion to the Belgian Congo, and a reversal of the wartime economic contraction in the French colonies. World prices for primary products rose rapidly, and exports of peanuts, cocoa, coffee, and timber grew in response. The profits from this expanded trade led, for instance, to the purchase of many trucks by African transporters, who were then able to extend the boom by reaching new areas. Some African planters were able to move beyond the level of family farming to develop numerous farms producing cocoa (in Ivory Coast and Cameroon) or peanuts (in Senegal) and employing migrant wage laborers. In later years large, highly capitalized farms emerged at the outskirts of such major cities as Abidjan and Kinshasa, providing food for the urban populations. Most farms, however, were limited to several hectares worked by a single family.

The profits of the agricultural boom were also diverted by the governments, which set up marketing boards with the official objective of providing farmers with a fair and level price. Farmers were required to sell their crops to the marketing board at a price set each year; the marketing board then sold the crops on the world market, pocketed the difference, and applied these profits to development projects.

Most of the increase in exports resulted from the work of peasant farmers. But governments also tried to set up big projects for large-scale agricultural output. In French Sudan, the government had begun in the 1930s to construct a set of dams and barrages on the Niger, with the objective of producing cotton on irrigated land. Investment in this project expanded greatly in postwar years. The results, however, were not what the French expected. Cotton exports never grew to significance. Instead, farmers used the irrigated lands to produce rice and sugar, and sold these crops on the growing domestic market.

A somewhat more successful project was that of the *Paysannats indigènes* in the Belgian Congo. Huge strips of forest and savanna land were cleared, and farmers were assigned to work them, producing crops under exact instructions from colonial authorities. Then, when the land had reached the limit of its fertility, adjoining strips of land were cleared, and the process repeated. This system, while physically productive, was not popular with the nearly one million farmers drawn into it, since many lost ownership of their land. When independence came in 1960, the end to coercive power over the peasants meant the end to this system of farming.

Forced labor continued to the end of the colonial era in the Belgian colonies. In the French territories, the participation of Africans in the effort of World War II helped bring an end to forced labor at the end of the war, and thus marked a major advance in the status of Africans within the colonial system. Félix Houphouët-Boigny of Ivory Coast sponsored the 1946 legislation which abolished forced labor in the French colonies, and this association earned him recognition in Ivory Coast and in other French colonies. Houphouët-Boigny was himself a wealthy planter, a producer of cocoa and coffee, and leader of the planters' association. It was in support of African planters' interests that he came to prominence and opposed forced labor. European planters in Ivory Coast were able to benefit preferentially from forced labor, and the African planters sought to have the benefit of a free labor market in order to be able to hire workers for their planters.

This example provides a reminder of the differences in the social order of rural francophone Africa. At the top of this order, for as long as the colonial period lasted, were the government officials, the white staff of the big companies, and (in countries such as Ivory Coast) white planters. Next were the African officials and chiefs. Chiefs might claim membership in the traditional aristocracy (such as the Mossi royal families of Upper Volta) but their real legitimacy came from the colonial government which appointed them and paid them. Next in the social hierarchy were the wealthy merchants and planters, who often found themselves lacking in political power. The great mass of the rural population came next, and was itself divided into those with land and those without.

During the late colonial years, the chiefs in French colonies tended to lose power and status, and were able to retain their position only if they were able to win elections. We will discuss in chapter 6 the bewildering set of elections which took place in French colonies between 1945 and 1960. Here it is sufficient to say that the government-supported chiefs tended to lose their positions of rural leadership to men who were the economic leaders of the countryside. The growing capitalist sector of the rural economy tended to develop a reflection in rural politics. In the Belgian Colonies, where elections began late and then only in cities, the chiefs retained their influence to the end of the colonial era.

TOWN AND INDUSTRIAL LIFE

Francophone African towns grew rapidly from 1880 to 1940, but even in 1940 the urban population of francophone Africa was no more than 3% of the total. With the continued rapid growth of towns, francophone sub-Saharan Africa as a whole was roughly 30% urban in 1985, and two countries, Congo and Gabon, were over 50% urban, with most of the urban population focused in their capitals. In 1985 Kinshasa, with a population of roughly three million, claimed to be the second largest francophone city in the world.

These cities grew as governmental centers and transportation centers, rather than as industrial centers. In much of francophone Africa, the capital cities also doubled as ports or transportation centers: Dakar, Conakry, Abidjan, Lomé, Cotonou, Libreville. (St.-Louis in Senegal remained capital of Mauritania until 1954. The new capital, Nouakchott, grew from the 1950s both as capital of a new republic and as entrepôt for the export of the newly opened iron-ore mines.) Kinshasa, Brazzaville, and Bangui are major river transit centers. Bamako and Ouagadougou are rail centers. Several countries developed more than one large city; Cameroon has the port of Douala and the inland capital of Yaoundé, and Congo has the port of Pointe-Noire and the capital of Brazzaville. Zaire developed major urban centers at Kananga, Lubumbashi, Kisangani, Mbuji-Mayi, and Bukavu. Of all of these, only Lubumbashi grew primarily as an industrial town; it grew up as a center of copper processing and transport.

In good times the towns grew because work was to be found there. While civil service jobs were open only to those with education, the existence of government service created the need for many service jobs – cooks, drivers, guards, hairdressers – and the growth of cities provided employment for construction workers. Quite aside from the attraction of jobs and good pay, the city offered other benefits. It was easier to gain entry for one's children to school in the town and health conditions and health services were better there. In bad times, other forces served to draw people to the towns, as refugees from the countryside. Peasants who had lost their land or who found taxes too onerous, migrant workers seeking to find wage income with which to pay their taxes – these and others settled in cities in increasing numbers. Conakry grew from 50,000 inhabitants in 1958 to 600,000 in 1980, largely because independent Guinea's economic isolation brought depression to the countryside.

From the earliest days of colonial rule, African towns imported food from beyond Africa. With the growth of towns, shortages of domestic food appeared (because of limits on land productivity and the emphasis on producing export crops) so that urban Africans came to purchase steadily larger quantities of imported food. Rice and wheat were the main imported staples, followed by alcoholic beverages, coffee, salt, and a wide range of other food products.

The cities of francophone Africa were not well planned, they did not have adequate municipal governments, and they grew up without a wide range of city services. Transportation, water supply, electricity, fuel, fire protection, and medical care – all these tended to be handled on an *ad hoc* and private basis, rather than by municipal authorities whose efforts were supported by collection of local taxes.

In the colonial period, modern facilities were set up in the European centers, in the areas of town devoted to government offices, and in areas where Europeans were resident. Electricity, paved roads, even sewers and running water were to be found in the downtown areas of the cities from the early twentieth century. But the populations in outlying areas were often squatters rather than owners, and they were often outside city jurisdictions. In addition, the African inhabitants did not generally have political rights with which to demand city services. The efforts of colonial and post-colonial governments to

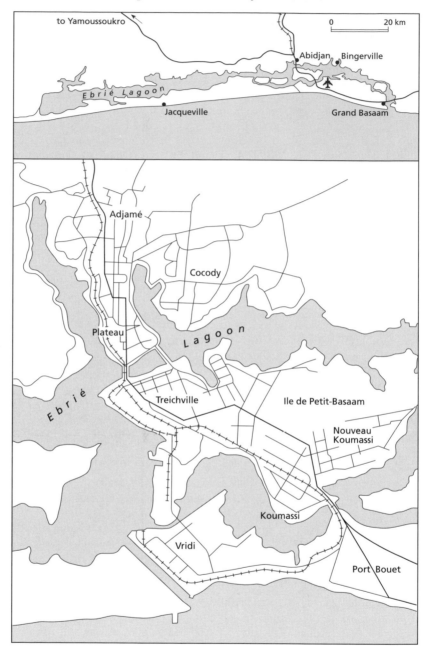

Map 10   Abidjan, 1980

plan – as in the cities of Zaire – were overcome by the massive urbanization upon independence.

Since the public sector of the cities was devoted to serving the government and large-scale commerce, most of the urban population had to depend on the private sector for city services. Indeed, a remarkably flexible private-sector response sprang up. Private taxis, jitneys, and trucks developed in place of public transit. These conveyances did have to purchase licenses. Wells and latrines were dug at many compounds, but private water services and private night-soil services also grew up. Since cooking was still done largely by wood stoves, immense networks for collection and transport of firewood came to surround each city.

Most work in the cities was commercial and service work: transportation and commerce at all levels, personal service for those who were wealthy enough to afford it. Work in government service was usually the best work to get, because of its stability, its relatively high rate of pay, and the relatively good working conditions. Government workers included postal employees, clerical and maintenance employees in government offices, police work, and teachers, and other employees of government schools. Other government workers were employees of government enterprises: port workers, railroad workers, and employees of government print shops and electrical power plants.

Industrial workers were concentrated in a few areas of colonial francophone Africa. The majority of them were in the Belgian Congo, where the copper mines of Union Minière du Haut Katanga employed some 30,000 workers in the 1950s. The mines, which had expanded to a large scale by the 1920s, had rapidly concluded that a permanent rather than a migrant work force would bring much higher productivity. As a result the town of Elisabethville (now Lubumbashi) grew up, populated by miners, their families, and others whose work provided service to the mining community. Similarly, Luluabourg (now Kananga) grew up because of the diamond industry. After independence, Abidjan, Douala and Dakar became significant centers of industry.

The cities developed an informal social structure in the course of their rapid growth. New quarters formed and took on names as new arrivals built their homes. Quarters often developed an ethnic unity, as the initial settlers invited their friends and relatives to join them. Churches and mosques grew up according to the denominations of the settlers.

Communication between town and countryside was regular and frequent, as relatives traveled to visit each other for weddings and funerals, and as those came from the countryside to seek work in town. As a result, ethnic associations formed in the towns, gathering all those who spoke the same language or bore the same identity into organizations of mutual support. One of the most prominent such urban ethnic associations was ABAKO (*Association des Bakongo*), which formed in Leopoldville in 1950 as a successor to earlier Bakongo organizations. The Bakongo people inhabited the lower Zaire Valley, the area surrounding the city, and also areas of northern Angola and southern Congo-Brazzaville. This urban ethnic association not only served to unite the Bakongo people of the Belgian Congo into a single ethnic identity, it also became a powerful political movement. As a result its leader, Joseph Kasavubu, became the first president of the independent Congo.

THE INTERNATIONAL ECONOMY

Involvement in the international economy was not new to francophone Africa. Centuries of commerce during the slave-trade era, plus participation in the nineteenth-century boom in industrial products, had drawn most African regions into close contact with outside economic forces. Commercial ties were unequal, because of Africa's relative poverty, but African domestic economies retained their autonomy. During the twentieth century the world economy became far more formidable, not only in its growth and productivity, but also in the depth of its occasional crises. African economies, further, had now to confront the world economy under conditions of colonialism. Colonial governments intervened in domestic African economies, and exposed them to the most direct impact of changing outside forces.

By 1940 the African colonies had become independent on imported industrial and consumer goods in many areas, and the virtual inability to get such goods after the opening of World War II brought widespread deprivation. At the same time, this situation permitted African industry to grow. Handicraft textile production, particularly strong in Sudan, was able to provide substitutes for the imported textiles no longer available. The absence of gasoline for motor vehicles was a serious hindrance to transportation, but entrepreneurs in many localities learned to distill methanol and use it as fuel.

The return of the world economy at war's end undermined these local industries. As had been the case at the end of World War I, the colonial powers determined that their colonies should be tied more tightly than ever to the economy of the metropole. The French were especially firm in their determination that the trade of their African colonies should be directed toward France. This was accomplished, on the one hand, by French investment in the colonial economies and, on the other hand, by arranging currency rates so that the colonies were induced to buy goods from France.

Among the important governmental arrangements affecting African economies at the end of the war were the Bretton Woods currency reform of 1947, and the Marshall Plan of 1948. The Bretton Woods agreement set the relative rates of European currencies and in it the Americans recognized the continued right of France and Belgium to control the currencies of their African colonies. The Marshall Plan was conceived as a plan of major United States economic assistance to the countries of Western Europe, to enable them to recover economically from the effects of war, and to prevent the communist parties from coming to power in those countries. Included in the generous American investments in France was the stipulation that a certain portion of the funds should be spent in France's African colonies, in the hope of discovering and developing new mineral resources. The French investments in Africa thus included a certain amount of American money.

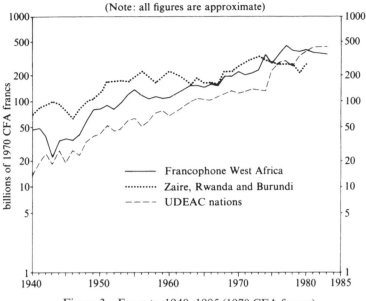

Figure 3   Exports, 1940–1985 (1970 CFA francs)

The French and Belgian firms investing in Africa became significant within the national economies of the metropolis. For the Belgians, Union Minière and the many other firms active in the Belgian Congo provided major sources of profits for the great holding company, Société Générale. The rapid recovery of the Belgian economy after World War II was a reflection, in part, of the high levels of wartime output and profitability in the Congo. Two main French commercial firms had grown up in Africa: SCOA (Société Commerciale de l'Ouest Africain) and CFAO (Compagnie française d'Afrique Occidentale). These firms purchased African crops for export to Europe, and sold imported goods at outlets throughout West and Central Africa. In the years after World War II, both SCOA and CFAO began investing significant portions of their African profits in France, in supermarket and department store chains. SCOA developed Monoprix and CFAO developed Prisunic, which became the two largest such chains in France (with branches of each in African cities). The African market thus contributed significantly to the development of modern French merchandizing.

Terms of trade for Africans were very favorable in world markets from 1948 to 1965; which is to say that African purchasers had to pay a great deal in 1947 to purchase imported goods, but that purchases of imports became relatively easier for almost 20 years. The volume of African exports rose rapidly in those postwar years, and the volume of imports to Africa rose even faster, as would be expected from the improving terms of trade. This was the case despite a rather drastic inflation in prices from 1948 to 1965.

Prices inflated again at a drastic rate from 1970 to 1980, but this time the terms of trade went seriously against African countries – the prices of imports (especially oil) rose much more rapidly than the prices of exports. The oil crisis of the mid 1970s was perhaps more severe for Africans than for those elsewhere in the world. Low African incomes meant that they were simply unable to pay the higher prices for petroleum, and some people had to go back to head transport.

Under these circumstances, transnational firms came to have growing significance. In earlier times the main expatriate firms had been trading companies such as the French firms SCOA and CFAO, and the British firm United Africa Company (a subsidiary of Unilever) plus mining firms. Now a wider range of transnational firms became prominent in francophone Africa: petroleum companies (Mobile and Texaco from the US, Shell from Britain and the Netherlands, and Total from France); automobile companies (Peugeot and Renault from France, Volkswagen and Mercedes from Germany, and later Toyota and Nissan from Japan); Nestlé in chocolate and coffee. French and Belgian airlines expanded their flights to Africa, and Air France set up Air Afrique as a subsidiary with many flights in Africa.

Faced with this growing array of transnational firms, African entrepreneurs were restricted to a few areas in their efforts to develop domestic industry. Most such local industries were for production of consumer goods intended to substitute for imports; breweries, soft drink bottleries, and textile factories were the most common. With independence, some new national governments established nationalized firms to show the flag abroad; Air Zaire and Air Mali are examples. Several other countries set up domestic airlines.

In order to participate more equitably in the international economy, francophone African countries have joined in several attempts at African economic integration. The first such attempt, of course, was that of the colonial empires; the federations of French West Africa and French Equatorial Africa acted as units in the world economy. But they were ruled strictly by France, and had no independent negotiating power. The federations themselves broke up after 1956, in part because their governments were seen as representative of metropolitan French interests rather than of African interests.

In the immediate aftermath of independence, most of the francophone nations joined in the African and Malagasay Union (UAM) which linked former French and Belgian colonies to France, Belgium and the European Economic Community (or Common Market.) It was succeeded in 1965 by the African and Malagasay Common Organization (OCAM). These organizations provided in practice for little economic integration, though they did give the ex-colonies some special trading ties to their former mother countries.

More significant were the smaller regional organizations. In 1965 Congo, Gabon, Central African Republic, Chad and Cameroon joined to form a Customs Union of Central African States (UDEAC). This remained one of Africa's most successful regional organizations, though it was shaken by its brief association with Zaire in the late 1960s, and by the 1969 seizure of the common ports and railroads by President Marien Ngouabi of Congo. The central bank of the Central African states, established in 1959 at Brazzaville to govern the flow of CFA francs in the region, worked closely with the customs union. Economic integration was less successful in West Africa. In 1975 the West African francophone countries joined with the other countries of West Africa to form the Economic Community of West African States (ECOWAS). With Nigeria as the wealthiest and most influential participant, this community appeared for a time to have the potential to link the economies of its member states for common benefit. Disputes among the member countries, however, reduced the effectiveness of the community to almost nothing.

While the francophone African nations had partial success in linking their economies more closely to each other, they had another partial success in breaking away from their heavy dependence on France and Belgium. The proportion of foreign trade with France and Belgium declined sharply during the 1970s, and the United States became a major trading partner for many francophone African nations. Trade ties also increased with West Germany, the Soviet Union, Japan, and China.

In the terms of the economist Samir Amin (of Egyptian birth, but who worked from a base in Dakar beginning in the 1960s) the economies of the francophone African countries were 'extraverted', oriented toward foreign economies rather than toward domestic economic growth. He predicted (in 1969) that these countries, by relying on tax breaks for foreign investors and by continuing to emphasize exports rather than production for the domestic market, would not only increase their dependence on foreign economic interests, but would also end up in debt and without economic growth. The prediction came true in many ways, though Ivory Coast (which relied most heavily on foreign investment) remained in 1985 the wealthiest of the francophone African nations.

PUBLIC FINANCE AND PUBLIC ENTERPRISE

Tax levels in French and Belgian colonies roughly doubled in the 1930s from their previous levels, as levels of government intervention in the economy increased beyond those set in the first decade of the century. In the 1950s tax levels again increased sharply, again because of increased public investment in transportation infrastructure, but also in response to widespread demands for social services. Government had been a formidable power in the economy of the colonies since the formation of francophone Africa, but it now took on even greater powers.

The most widely known aspect of this growth of government was the postwar development plans of the French and Belgians. These involved huge expenditures on public works: ports, airports, roads, public buildings, dams. The French program was known as FIDES. The acronym was chosen to fit the Latin word for "faith" or "fidelity," and thus to reinforce the bond between France and her colonies. In the remarkably successful propaganda supporting this project, the French government explained that it was investing large amounts of French capital in Africa in a campaign to bring about economic growth.

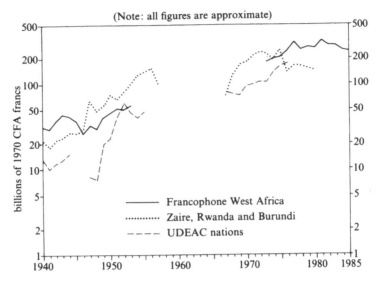

Figure 4   Tax revenue, 1940–1985 (1970 CFA francs)

In fact, the FIDES program did not bring about dramatic growth as a result of the investment, and this is not surprising. The largest amount of the funds invested came not from France, but from African taxes. That is, the amount of public investment was increased only by reducing the amount of private African investment. Such a transfer of investment funds should have and did result in increased economic efficiency. But the most creative part of this endeavor was the myth of huge French investments rather than the actual nature of the investments. In addition, as noted above, a significant portion of the funds sent from France to Africa were American Marshall Plan funds. The Belgian campaign of public investment in its colonies, formally adopted in the 1952 Ten-Year Plan, may well have involved larger net investments of capital in Africa than the French campaign.

Along with the growth of public works projects, the central state apparatus grew as well. This growth in colonial central government paralleled the growth of government in postwar France and Belgium. In France, a huge technocratic apparatus known as ORSTOM was set up: the Office of Overseas Scientific and Technical Research. ORSTOM and its affiliates in Dakar, Yaoundé, Brazzaville, and Lomé conducted research, prepared statistical surveys, and produced large numbers of publications. In one sense, these new state bureaucracies represented the first real attempt by colonial governments to perform proper studies of the countries they ruled. In another sense, the growing bureaucracy made government still more distant from the people.

At the same time, Africans were permitted to elect officials to local governments in the 1950s and, in the French territories, to colonial governments. The newly elected officials, seeking to maintain their support, were sensitive to the demands of African civil servants for higher salaries (equal to those of Europeans) and to the demands of the general population for higher government expenditures on education and social welfare. In the French colonies, the base salaries for European and African civil servants had long been equal; the difference was that Europeans received travel and family allowances which roughly doubled their salaries. Africans pressed successfully for passage of the Second Lamine Guèye Law in 1950, and thereby gained equality in fringes as well as salary for all civil servants. (The First Lamine Guèye Law, adopted in 1946 and named after the Senegalese deputy who proposed it, granted citizenship to inhabitants of France's colonies.) Salaries of African civil servants were then raised to the level of European officials – whose salaries had been artificially inflated with "hardship pay" and allowances for travel to Europe. This was the origin of the great difference in post-colonial years between the high salaries of government officials and the low wages of Africans in the private sector.

Government, in the late colonial years, not only carried out great expenditures in public works and increased its spending in social services, but opened up a great deal of new public enterprise. This government intervention in areas which might have been left to the private sector was a heritage of the early colonial years, when French colonial governments took over the railroads. Now colonial governments built new ports, founded development corporations to expand agriculture, and established marketing boards to direct commerce in export crops.

For the whole colonial period, governments in francophone Africa (and particularly in French West Africa) had managed to collect taxes far in excess of the amounts they spent. The rise of African political power ended all that, and opened an era of deficit spending by African governments. Such deficit spending was, according to the new economic theories of John Maynard Keynes, the correct approach to stimulating economic growth in these poor territories. On the other hand, the existence of government debt opened up questions of how to finance that debt. Ultimately, the debts of African governments became a point of great vulnerability, in which the domestic benefits of the debts threatened to be overshadowed by their international liabilities.

For a decade immediately following independence, France granted subsidies to many of her former African colonies, which helped to cover the recent increases in government expenditures. These subsidies might be seen as compensation for the earlier years in which France collected revenue surpluses from the same colonies. More practically, the subsidies were part of a broader program which included placing many French civil servants in African governments, and also included arrangements on trade which served the interests of France by guaranteeing the African countries as markets for French goods. The French Ministry of Cooperation handled these arrangements. The radical regimes of Congo and Bénin led in revising the cooperation agreements with France in the years 1973–75, and achieved more control over central banks and investment projects. At the same time, the French subsidies declined in these years.

The early 1970s also brought oil crisis and drought. African countries began appealing for aid through the United Nations and through bilateral arrangements with governments and with private philanthropic organizations. Upper Volta, a country whose main source of income was the remittance of its workers who had gone to Ivory Coast and other countries, and a country especially hard-hit by the drought, became a particular focus for such aid. By 1984, Captain Thomas Sankara led a military coup and formed a new government which attempted to reject international aid as a solution, arguing that a decade of aid had failed to make a dent in the country's poverty and dependence. The name of the country was changed to Burkina Faso, and Sankara launched it on an aggressive, populist program of self-help. But while recipients of *grants* could seek simply to cut off the flow of aid, recipients of international *loans* were caught in entanglements which could not simply be renounced.

Virtually all the francophone African nations contracted large loans from consortiums of banks in the late 1960s and early 1970s, when interest rates were very low, and when it seemed that their export earnings would make it easy to repay the loans. But when interest rates jumped in five years from 3% to nearly 20%, the borrowers suddenly found that they were responsible for immense interest payments, and they threatened default. At this point the International Monetary Fund (IMF) provided these nations with loans (or arranged for loans from consortiums of banks) to pay off their immediate obligations, in return for promises to cut back sharply the level of government expenditures at home. Togo, Senegal, and especially Zaire had to arrange repeated rescheduling of their debt payments, and even Ivory Coast and Gabon found themselves overextended. Thus did francophone Africa's wealthiest countries end up losing substantial control over the direction of their own economies. (Cameroon, a significant exception, grew fast enough to pay its debt readily.)

The problem of graft and corruption further compounded an already difficult situation. Money allocated for development projects was diverted into the pockets of officials; loans which would not have been made were arranged through bribery of officials. In these and many other instances, economic calculations in modern francophone Africa have had to account for the factor of bribery. For Zaire in particular but also for other countries, it is a major issue in public discussion to understand what caused corruption and what keeps it going. Some argue that the problem goes back to the conditions of precolonial Africa in which people were required to pay to get a desired decision in court; others argue that the colonial system, which set up the Europeans as absolute rulers, created a situation in which only through bribery could one hope to obtain a fair decision.

Under these conditions, the hopes of several African governments to establish socialist economic systems, with state ownership and state control, brought stability but not prosperity. In Guinea, a state-dominated socialist economy was set up beginning with independence in 1958, in Congo-Brazzaville, a similar decision was taken in 1967, and in Bénin, a socialist state was proclaimed in 1975. The shortages of resources, the problems of heavy debt, and the compounding factor of corruption prevented any of these economies from growing rapidly. At the same time, the economy of Ivory Coast, which may be labelled one of state capitalism (since it draws in private investment funds, but invests them under state control) is in some ways very similar. Ivory Coast's growth rate was very high in the years 1965–80, but this was mainly a reflection of the high levels of foreign investment. The country had levels of debt and problems of corruption as serious as those of the poorer nations following socialist policies.

As a result, the "second economy" grew steadily in importance in modern francophone Africa. Wages in Zaire fell to such a level by 1980 that the main advantage to keeping a wage-earning job was such housing and medical benefits as came with it. Participants in the economy learned to avoid taxes when possible, to pay bribes whenever necessary, and to steal when the opportunity arose. On Lake Mobutu in Zaire, for instance, the output of industrial fisheries declined sharply from 1976 to 1979, while the output of artisanal fisheries rose in the same period; the independent fishers had benefitted from the theft of nets and spare parts from the big fisheries. In Dakar, the international business trips of *marabouts* were arranged by writing up stolen airline tickets. The "second economy" made it possible for many people to survive and for a few to profit greatly, but it brought waste and inequitable distribution of income. As a response to grasping and ineffective government policy, the second economy rendered the policy even less effective, and made official statistics nearly worthless.

SOCIAL AND ETHNIC CONFLICTS

The economic transformations of francophone sub-Saharan Africa made themselves felt in social conflicts and changes which ranged from migrations to strikes and to ethnic massacres. Certain social classes gained in strength and identity, while others declined in influence. New ethnic groups formed and existing groups redefined themselves.

With the end of World War II, and with the extension of new political rights and the hopes for more such rights, a wave of strikes broke out across francophone Africa, especially among transport workers. The most dramatic of these strikes was the 1947–48 railroad strike in French West Africa. The workers, after reforming a union which had first been permitted as a result of an earlier 1938 strike, demanded a major wage increase (at a time when prices were inflating rapidly) and also demanded allowances for health and for the education of their children (in order to gain equality in these areas with European railroad workers). When the demands were rejected, several thousand workers ceased working on four separate railway lines: the Dakar-Niger line, the Guinea railroad, the Abidjan-Ouagadougou line, and the Dahomey railroads. For months the workers held out, and the trains were virtually halted. Finally the union in Ivory Coast gave in and its members returned to work, but the workers in Senegal were still able to win a portion of their demands. Ousmane Sembène wrote a successful novel, *God's Bits of Wood*, based on the strike in Senegal, but the full story of the coordinated strike remains to be told. This and other acts of labor militancy made it clear that a wage-labor class had become an important part of the social scenery in francophone Africa.

An African bourgeoisie emerged with equal clarity, but only in a few areas. The strongest example of a bourgeoisie was that of Ivory Coast, where African owners of cocoa and coffee plantations, who had enjoyed economic success since the 1930s, rose to challenge European planters and the French government in the late 1940s, demanding government support for their enterprise. Félix Houphouët-Boigny led the planters' association and used this platform to become a minister in the government of France and later president of Ivory Coast. These bourgeois planters made unusual alliances. They allied with their workers (mostly migrants from Upper Volta) against the European planters and the government, and Houphouët's political party allied with the French Communist Party in the years 1946–51. The strategy worked. In 1951 the colonial government changed its policy, and gave African planters equality of treatment with European planters. Houphouët became closely associated with French officials, and the planter class has since prospered. In Cameroon as well, a successful bourgeoisie arose, based on urban industry as well as on plantations of cocoa and coffee. On the other hand, the repeated failure of the bourgeoisie of Congo and Bénin to make profits in the private sector was reflected in those nations' turns to socialist policies, where enterprise was dominated by the public sector.

The petty bourgeoisie grew steadily with the urbanization and economic diversification of the years after 1940. Transporters, photographers, tailors, mechanics, launderers, merchants of all descriptions – these and other such occupations provided hope but rarely prosperity for those who undertook them. Over the long run, the growth of large-scale industry and of the wage-earning class threatened to cause the petty bourgeoisie to shrink. But by the 1980s the slow growth of industry and the high levels of unemployment tended instead to force more people into developing their own small businesses.

The largest class, however, remained that of the peasantry; those who worked the African land. While many moved to the cities in hopes of escaping taxes, and while the expansion of education made new generations reluctant to stay on the land, the peasantry continued to comprise the bulk of African population. This peasantry found a theorist and propagandist in Frantz Fanon. Fanon, born in Martinque and trained as a psychiatrist in France, was one of few blacks in the medical profession. Sent to Algeria to work in French hospitals during the Algerian war of liberation (1954–62) Fanon decided to join the Algerians, and he became a theorist of peasant revolution. In this view the colonial situation led necessarily to a violent revolution, and he saw the peasants as those who would provide its best fighters and steadiest supporters. Fanon thought that the wage laborers in the cities were a "labor aristocracy," who benefitted from high wages and were compromised by the colonial system. The "lumpen-proletariat," however, those who hung at the edges of city life without regular employment, were those on whom Fanon relied for essential support of the revolutionary movement. As for the "national bourgeoisie," the African capitalists, Fanon saw them as figures who had made no real economic contribution, who were false and narrow leaders, and who would ultimately fall before the demands of the peasantry for a revolutionary nationalist government.

Fanon's analysis has remained controversial since it first appeared in the years leading up to his death in 1961. His view of the proletariat as a labor aristocracy has turned out to be overstated, but his critique of the bourgeoisie has served as a prediction of the weakness of most African parliamentary regimes, as most of then were replaced within a few years by military regimes. For our purposes here, though, the main strength of Fanon's analysis is that it identifies and characterizes the social classes of modern francophone Africa.

Important as social class is to the understanding of modern social conflict in Africa, it is usually overshadowed by ethnicity. Hausa against Zerma in Niger, Luba against Lulua in Zaire, Kanuri against Gbaya in Chad; these are but a few examples of major ethnic disputes. From the 1950s on, ethnic groups have fought each other with a fierceness which demands explanation.

The simplest possible explanation, that these ethnic groups have carried forth ancient hatreds from the past into the present, is not sufficient, for ethnic conflict was at a low level during much of the colonial era. Instead, ethnic conflict was primarily a phenomenon of decolonization. In the Belgian Congo, where every individual was given a tribal label which was inscribed on his or her pass, these artificially reinforced ethnic divisions provided clear lines of social fissure once independence brought the pressures of civil war. In the French colonies, the first decade of electoral politics, from 1945 to 1955, reveals the process by which ethnic factionalism arose. With the first elections in the postwar era, political figures in each of the African colonies put forth colony-wide slates of candidates, without regard for ethnic origin. But as the number of elections grew, and as the number of voters was expanded, the basis for campaigning changed. Some candidates, rather than campaigning based on a platform of ideas, found that they could win votes by campaigning based on ethnic identity, and by promising to improve government services in their home area. The formation of one ethnic political party tended to cause the formation of others, and by 1955 most of the political parties of francophone Africa were based primarily (but never entirely) on ethnic organizations. To this degree, "tribalism" in francophone Africa is a recent development.

In some cases, however, what passed for ethnic distinctions reflected class distinctions in reality, and the potential for conflict was greater. In Rwanda and Burundi, the Hutu and Tutsi are the two main social groups. They are often called tribes or ethnic groups, but in fact the Hutu and Tutsi of each country shared the same language and culture. The distinctions between them were those of social class; the Tutsi were the hereditary aristocracy, who dominated the kingdoms, tended cattle, and collected tribute from the Hutu. The Hutu were the majority, a farming population, long subjugated by the Tutsi aristocracy. In Rwanda, independence was the signal for class war. The

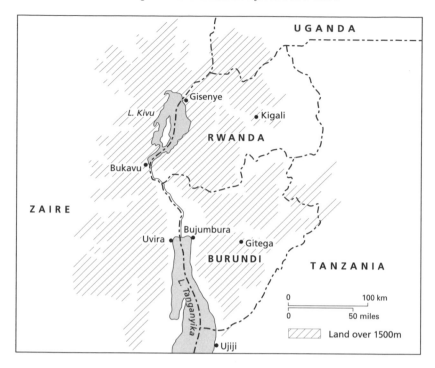

Map 11   Rwanda and Burundi

Belgians, in the last years of colonial rule, had shifted their support from the monarchy to the political party dominated by Hutu *évolués*. The death of the king in 1959 led to Hutu uprisings against Tutsi domination, and the Hutu political party, *Parmehutu*, took power at independence in 1962. The tensions were unresolved, and in 1963–64 both police and private actions caused the death of some 50,000 Rwandese, most of them Tutsi, and to the flight of most other Tutsi to neighboring countries.

In Burundi Prince Louis Rwagasore sought to lead a movement of national unity, but was assassinated before independence. The monarchy, always stronger than that in Rwanda, remained in power until 1965 when, in response to Hutu attempts to gain power, Colonel Michel Micombero established a republic and a Tutsi military government. A 1972 Hutu rising killed 1,000 Tutsi, and the government initiated a massacre which took the lives of an estimated 200,000 Barundi (roughly 5% of the population), mostly Hutu. As in Rwanda, thousands of refugees fled to neighboring countries.

CHANGES IN THE LAND

The social and economic changes of the years since 1940 left their mark not only on the lives of Africans, but on the land itself. These changes in the land are linking African affairs more closely to the rest of the world than ever before, just as social and economic changes are drawing the African people into closer contact with people outside the continent.

The cutting of the equatorial African forest, for instance, is not simply a question of changing African ecology, but is a matter of changing the climate of the whole world. The African forest, along with the larger Amazon valley forest, is the source of a significant portion of the world's supply of oxygen. If these forests disappear, as is rapidly becoming the case, then major droughts are possible not only for the tropics, but for temperate areas as well.

The shrinking forest also illustrates other links between African and external affairs, and between ecological, social, and economic issues. Transnational logging companies have taken out immense stands of African hardwoods and have torn them into sawdust for use in particle board. Their reasoning has been that restrictions on logging in Europe and North America have caused them to look further for their supply of timber. The African countries too have restrictions on logging, intended to protect their own forests. But bribes from the logging companies have been sufficient to circumvent the legal restrictions, and the African countries have been unable to halt bribery or its consequences.

Other changes in the land have less to do with the wills of individual humans. In about 1940 a cutting of water hyacinth, *Eichornia crassipes*, was brought from the Amazon valley to the Zaire River. This plant, which at maturity cuts loose branches which float downstream bearing large and beautiful flowers, soon became an uncontrollable weed which contaminated the whole Zaire river system. No methods for control have been successful so far. In the short run, the water hyacinth appeared to clog waterways and to interfere with fishing; with time, however, fishers learned to benefit from the shelter it gives fish. A more widespread and more devastating change was brought by the succession of droughts which appear to have removed hundreds of square kilometres permanently from cultivation in the northern savanna.

While much of the countryside has come to appear more desolate, the urban areas appear to be thriving. Tall buildings dominate the skyline of the main cities, warehouses and factories line the waterfronts and the railroad lines. Countless trucks, large and small, most of them gaily painted with proverbs and prayers, link the various quarters of the cities; they share the road with even more numerous taxis. Smaller numbers of trucks ply the thin ribbons of two-lane highways between the cities and fewer yet risk the dirt tracks to the villages.

Agriculture generally in francophone Africa declined in the years from 1965 to 1985, but agriculture in areas near to the cities grew. Demand for grains, tubers, vegetables, and fruits in the cities encouraged the development of truck farms near to the major urban markets. Population generally grew, but it grew far more rapidly in the cities. The capitalistic economic order established its dominance more fully in the cities than in the countryside, and did so in countries with both capitalist and socialist governments. The cities thus represented the wave of the future for francophone Africa, but the meaning of that future remained ambiguous. For the cities, vibrant though they might appear from a distance, contained a large proportion of unemployed adults, children of broken homes, and people lacking in the levels of health, education, and welfare which they believed independence from colonial rule would bring them.

The incorporation of francophone Africa into the world economy proceeded rapidly in the years from 1940 to 1985. While capitalism had become fundamental to the African way of life by 1940, there still remained many aspects of family life and working life in which the world economy could be held at arm's length. But the expansion of African exports and the emigration of African labor to 1965 committed Africans far more deeply to involvement in the vortex of world prices, and the sudden debts of the 1970s prevented them from retreating back to an autonomous existence.

6

Government and politics, 1940–1985

By the end of the 1930s, the colonial system of absolute rule had imposed itself forcefully on African peoples. But then, after the cataclysm of World War II, a great modification of the political system of francophone Africa took place. The transformation took place because of pressures from the African subjects, from the world outside the French and Belgian empires, and from critics of colonial rule in the metropoles. As a result, the political system rapidly changed from one based on authoritarian rule to one based on European parliamentary democracy. With that new political structure came an emphasis on nationalism and nation-building in Africa. Nationalism and democracy led to independence: the re-emergence of African sovereignty. But with African sovereignty, politics were no longer constrained within the limits of European structures, be they authoritarian or parliamentary. African politics re-emerged, now at the national level.

Democratization and independence brought much wider political participation in African countries, but they also brought many unresolved conflicts to the surface. The need for solidarity and the fear of outside interference caused many francophone governments to limit politics to a single party. In some cases democracy itself was an early casualty, as military dictators or civilian autocrats took advantage of social conflicts to seize power.

Among the major, unresolved problems in African government were the choice between dictatorship and democracy in political process, and between civilian and military leadership at the national level. In domestic policy, African nations had to choose between industrial and agricultural development, and between free-market capitalist or state-directed socialist economic policy. In social policy, they chose between advancing the standing of an elite and improving the conditions of the masses. In international politics, African nations chose whether to act alone or in a pan-African grouping. They chose among alliances with France and the United States, with the Soviet Union, or with the Third World bloc.

With the exception of civil wars in Zaire and Chad, the nations of francophone sub-Saharan Africa experienced less political disjuncture than most other areas of the continent. By 1980 these nations had one hundred thousand soldiers in uniform for a population of one hundred million, a lower ratio than for the rest of Africa. In colonial times francophone Africa, an area with few

European settlers, was spared the anguish of protracted racial conflict which characterized the postwar politics of Arab, lusophone, and much of anglophone Africa. The nations of francophone Africa obtained independence through political means, rather than through the warfare of lusophone Africa, southern Africa, and Algeria. In government, the francophone African reliance on the Napoleonic tradition in law and on French and Belgian patterns in administration provided continuity in those areas, and set an overall pattern of moderation. On the other hand, such experiments as the Central African Empire and the Dahomean Council of Presidents were as extreme as any on the continent, though less murderous than many. As elsewhere in Africa, the francophone nations face a host of unsolved political problems.

Despite the legacy of conflicts and unresolved issues dominating the recent political scene, the years after 1940 must be seen as a heroic and creative time in francophone African politics. Nations were created, and took their place in a position of legal equality with the great world powers. In this chapter we begin with the impact of World War II on francophone African politics, and then show how the postwar political order, with its introduction of large-scale electoral and participatory politics, resulted from the influences of war. We then turn to the politics of nationalism which led to the independence of francophone Africa. The decolonization of the Belgian Congo included events of such magnitude and such importance for Africa as a whole that we consider it separately. We then turn to domestic politics in the years after independence, where the issues of dictatorship and democracy, capitalism and socialism were struggled out. Next we consider the international politics of independent francophone Africa, and we conclude with a discussion of the strengths and limits of African nationhood.

WORLD WAR

From 1940 to 1945 the world was shaken by a second great war pitting great empires and nations against each other. But beyond the struggle to control land and people, the war pitted structures of fascism against democracy, and principles of racial discrimination against racial equality. The influence of fascism was felt in Africa before the general war broke out, as Italy invaded and conquered Ethiopia. The anti-Semitism which had spread throughout Europe and which the Nazis brought to its height was, to a degree, related to anti-black racism. The Italian state hungered for more African territory; Nazi Germany sought revenge for the loss of an earlier African empire.

The countries which led in the defeat of the Axis powers in Europe and North Africa were the United States, Britain, and the Soviet Union. Of these, Britain and especially the Soviet Union suffered heavily, but they emerged from the war in glorious victory, having defended their national traditions and at the same time having saved the world from threatened conquest.

It was quite different in France and Belgium. These countries lost the war, suffered national humiliation during the war years, and were liberated primarily through the efforts of others. This was particularly true of France, where the government surrendered and then collaborated with the Germans. For the French and those in French colonies, the war years were a time of division and a source of recrimination. To a lesser degree, the same was true for Belgium. Belgium suffered occupation throughout the war, though its government escaped first to France and then to England. But King Leopold III, leading the army, surrendered to Germany and remained in German hands throughout the war; a hot dispute broke out between the king and the Belgian government in exile.

France and Britain declared war on Germany in September of 1939, as the Germans invaded Poland. But virtually no fighting took place in Western Europe until May of 1940, when the German *blitzkrieg* led to the occupation of Belgium. The French mobilized to fight the invaders – Africans were nearly 10% of the French troops at the front in 1940 – but they were overwhelmed, and they surrendered in June to Germany. With the French defeat and surrender, thousands of African troops became prisoners of war, and waited out the war in German prison camps.

There was no government in exile for the French. The National Assembly voted to surrender on June 17 and then voted to dissolve itself. The north-western half of the country was ruled directly by Germany, and the south-eastern portion of France was ruled from the small city of Vichy, under the leadership of Marshal Philippe Pétain, the hero of France's victory over Germany in World War I.

Only a few French officers and soldiers, under the leadership of General Charles de Gaulle, escaped and vowed to continue to fight. On June 18, General de Gaulle broadcast from London a radio plea for the French to join him and continue fighting. This became the Free French movement, and it eventually set up a government in exile. Inside France, a Resistance movement grew up. The strongest influence in the Resistance was the Communist Party, while the Free French outside the country were politically conservative. But they shared a combative spirit and a nationalistic devotion to France, and they cooperated until a year after the war's end.

Outside Europe, colonial governments then had to respond to the conquest of the mother country. For the rulers of the Belgian Congo, the decision was taken rapidly: the Congo declared its loyalty to the Belgian government in exile. Governor-general Ryckmans sought to draw on the colony to provide support for the Allied war effort.

In the French territories, colonial governors had to decide whether to accept orders from the defeated government of Marshal Pétain, or to continue fighting along with de Gaulle. Initially, most French officials in Africa hoped to continue the fight, but they hesitated to break with the Vichy regime. The British dared not wait. In early July they destroyed the French fleet in the Algerian harbor of Mers-el-Kebir, at a cost of 1,300 French lives. With this further humiliation, colonial governors found it harder to break with Vichy and side with de Gaulle and the British. Pierre Boisson, governor-general of French Equatorial Africa, accepted a Vichy appointment as High Commissioner for French Africa, and flew from Brazzaville via Chad to his capital in Dakar.

In the end, only a single governor in all France's colonies declared for the Free French: Félix Eboué in Chad. Eboué was also the only black governor. He remained in contact with de Gaulle and the British from the first, and encouraged other governors to continue to fight. On August 26, Eboué publicly declared his allegiance to the Free French. The same day, de Gaulle's aide Colonel (later General) Leclerc entered Cameroon with 24 men and took control of the colony – African support enabled him to remove the pro-Vichy government of Cameroon. Within a few days the same happened in French Congo and Ubangi–Shari; the conquest of Gabon, however, required several weeks. With the Central African colonies now loyal to the Free French, de Gaulle named Eboué governor-general of French Equatorial Africa. For a time Brazzaville became, in effect, the capital of the French empire.

Eboué was born in French Guinea, and was thus born a French citizen. He was one of few blacks to rise high in the French colonial administration, and most of his service was in Central Africa. His strong support for the Free French reflected his belief in republican values, even though he worked within the French empire. That is, he refused to accept the defeat of France by a new German empire, and he considered France's African subjects as potential citizens who would save the nation.

Meanwhile Boisson, once he arrived in Dakar, was made High Commissioner of French Africa – in effect, governor-general of French West Africa. He had a portion of the French fleet in the harbor at Dakar, and he also had control over a portion of the Bank of France deposits, as well as those of Belgium and Poland. The main objective of his policy was to maintain French sovereignty in Africa, and to keep both British and German forces out. "No anti-British offensive will be tolerated, nor any German or Italian control." Thus, Boisson chose the French empire where Eboué chose the French republic. (De Gaulle's reasoning was not completely different from that of Boisson; he argued that it was necessary for France to fight on, even with a tiny army, in order to be a participant in the eventual war settlement. Otherwise France might lose her borders and her colonies.)

In September of 1940 the small Free French fleet, supported by the British navy, attempted to force the governments of Morocco and French West Africa to abandon Vichy; they bombarded the harbors of Casablanca and Dakar. After a day's fighting in Dakar, however, the Free French saw that their bombardment of French territory was only driving the administration further into the arms of Vichy, and the fleet withdrew. French West Africa was left alone for two years.

Boisson arrested European and African supporters of the Free French. Aside from that, French West Africa was not involved in the war to a great degree. Taxes were low and there were few demands for forced labor, as the government did not wish to provoke social unrest which might bring British or German troops in. An additional levy of 50,000 troops was raised to discourage either the British or Germans from invading.

Meanwhile Leclerc, at the head of troops recruited in French Equatorial Africa, crossed the Sahara to join the fighting in North Africa. He remained the Free French field commander. In 1944, as General Leclerc, he led the Free French army in the liberation of Paris.

In late 1942, after the Allied landing in North Africa and the rapid advance against French troops, High Commissioner Boisson began to feel the pressure to switch his alliance, and in November he rallied to the Free French. His reasoning was that this was necessary in order to preserve French control in West Africa. Boisson himself had to resign, and was later imprisoned on charges of collaboration with the enemy. From the beginning of 1943, the *tirailleurs sénégalais* were sent into the North African campaign. Now that French West Africa had joined the war effort, taxes went up and corvées returned.

For the Africans in French West Africa, the political personalities set before them had changed many times. Albert Teveodjre, a Dahomean writer, noted how he had been taught in primary school to sing the praises of Marshal Pétain each day; then, suddenly, the radio announced a new leader and Marshal Pétain's photograph was removed from his school room. While Tevoedjre experienced this confusion in the classroom, Casimir d'Almeida experienced it in the political arena. As a long-time elected official, he had simply continued to work with the French administration as it turned to Vichy. But with the repudiation of Vichy d'Almeida found that his political reputation had been ruined.

Administrative fear of African activism continued throughout the war. Even before the fall of France, in April of 1940, the government of Middle Congo had Andre Matswa sent to Brazzaville from France on charges as a dangerous agitator. Matswa, who had earlier formed the "Amicalist" movement in which thousands of Bakongo people demanded French citizenship, had re-enlisted in the French army when war broke out in 1939. Many Bakongo volunteered for the subject army. But the administration remained fearful of Matswa's influence and in April 1940 sent him to prison on vague charges of supporting German propaganda. He was not released when Eboué became governor-general six months later. After poor treatment by his captors, he died in prison in 1942. Matswa's supporters in Congo, however, refused to believe that he was dead. For this reason they placed his name on the ballot in two elections at the end of World War II, and in each case he won a majority of votes cast.

Those who worked with the Free French fared little better. Louis Hunkanrin, a political activist in Dahomey since 1910, worked on behalf of the Free French to ferry French administrators to British Nigeria. He was arrested in December of 1940 as a supporter of the Free French, and interned in French Sudan. One might imagine that he would have been freed as a hero in late 1942. But when French West Africa rallied to the Free French, the same officials who had jailed Hunkanrin remained in charge and he was not released. He was not even released in 1945 when the war ended. It took a public campaign to achieve his release, which only came in 1947. The charges against him had never been more than aiding the Free French.

Toward the end of the war, West African soldiers who had been prisoners of war in Europe demanded to receive the back pay and premiums they were due before demobilization at Thiaroye near Dakar in December 1944. They briefly held the commanding general hostage. French officials labelled their demonstration a mutiny, and fired on the demonstrators, killing 35 and wounding 35 more. This incident became the source of widespread bitterness among African soldiers who felt they had contributed significantly to the liberation of France, only to be rewarded with denial of their back pay. Bitter rumors spread of de Gaulle's "whitening" of Free French troops as they came into view in French cities. Perhaps it was the depth of wartime division among the metropolitan French that caused them to lash out occasionally against Africans. In French West Africa as in France, postwar political factions depended heavily on the distinction between those who had fought in the Resistance or with the Free French, and those who had supported Vichy and collaborated with the Germans.

In French Equatorial Africa and the Belgian Congo, there was administrative continuity during the war years. And while that meant high taxes and heavy demands on production, it did not lead to the political demoralization and breakdown of authority of French West Africa. The ironic result was that in Central Africa there was a less rapid development of African political parties.

For the Belgians, the political continuity was absolute. The Belgian government remained in place, and the Catholic party continued to govern as it had since the 1930s once postwar elections took place. The exception was a brief coalition of Catholics, liberals, socialists, and communists in the immediate aftermath of the war. For France, the Free French outside of France and the Resistance inside France began competing for the loyalties of the French as the end of the war came into sight. In re-establishing a French government, a new relationship would have to be thought out between the French nation and the French empire. In addition to the domestic pressures for a new government, the prospective formation of a United Nations organization as well as American and Soviet pressures for decolonization caused the French to seek a new arrangement. Also at stake were the loyalties of the inhabitants of French colonies.

The impact of the war on the outlook of French administrators is best indicated by the results of the Brazzaville conference of colonial governors convened in January of 1944 by Charles de Gaulle and Félix Eboué. Here the governors called for a new set of colonial rights. They began by stating that the colonies should remain with France, but they went on to recommend that the colonies have representation at the Constituent Assembly which would form the Fourth Republic, and that the constitution of the overseas territories be the same as that of France. They also recommended an end to forced labor, the extension of trade-union rights, the creation of a unified penal code for the colonies, an African development plan, and – to affirm their assimilationist vision – the abolition of polygyny in Africa.

The French Committee for National Liberation, a provisional government established in June 1943 in Algiers, began to implement some of these proposals. In August of 1944, for instance, it authorized trade unions in the colonies, thus formalizing the relationships opened since the CGT, the main French labor federation (in which Communists were quite active), had been sending delegations to sub-Saharan Africa since 1943. Joining the transport and civil service unions established immediately after this decree was the Syndicat Agricole Africain of Ivory Coast, the planters' association headed by Félix Houphouët-Boigny.

The abolition of subject status through amalgamation into the French nation was a vision of the future that many African leaders were happy to consider. But another means of abolishing colonialism presented itself. The Vietnamese, under the leadership of Ho Chi Minh and the Viet Minh movement, had no intention of remaining under French rule, and declared independence in 1945. The result was a long war until France admitted defeat in 1954. This vision had African echoes, based in part on Parisian contacts among political activists from Africa, Indochina, the Antilles, and North Africa in the 1920s and 1930s. In Madagascar the historically strong anticolonial movement grew greatly during the war years, and ended up in confrontation with the government during a major 1947 uprising. French repression of this uprising took some 80,000 lives. In a third vision, political leaders in Cameroon sought to use its status as a United Nations Trust Territory to achieve independence.

THE POSTWAR POLITICAL ORDER

The immediate postwar years, 1945–51, led in the French territories to a great political restructuring. Africans gained rights to electoral politics, trade-union organization, and steps toward citizenship, all within the French political community. The accession to these democratic rights was linked to the great postwar political changes in France and throughout the world. In a second stage of political change, the French African territories moved toward independence beginning in 1956.

The Belgian territories, in contrast, experienced no formal political change in the immediate postwar years. In political terms the Belgian colonies were isolated from Belgium and isolated from the rest of the world, and Belgium's political change after World War II was less drastic than that of France. As a result, the pressures for democratization in Ruanda–Urundi and the Belgian Congo were virtually suppressed until 1956. By then, however, the first hints of democracy were sufficient to open up an almost immediate demand for independence.

A French Constituent Assembly was elected in October of 1945; 64 of its 586 delegates were from the colonies, and 24 of these were elected by subjects. This assembly drew up a constitution by April of 1946 which established a French Union and made all colonial inhabitants citizens of the French Union. A separate condition allowed for ratification of the constitution by colonial voters, and thus would have implied their free consent to the union with France. This became known as the Lamine Guèye law, after the Senegalese deputy who proposed it. The constitution was rejected in May, however, by the citizens, and the colonials never got to vote on it. While debating the proposed constitution, the Constituent Assembly also passed a series of laws. One of these laws, proposed by Félix Houphouët-Boigny, abolished forced labor in the colonies. This law remained in effect even though the April 1946 constitution was rejected.

In the June election for the second Constituent Assembly, a more conservative body was elected. Where the Communists, Socialists, and Popular Republican Movement (MRP, a Catholic party) had each had equal power in the first assembly, the MRP grew at the expense of the others in the second. The consequence for the colonies was that the Socialists and the MRP agreed to weaken the provisions for the colonies. The distinctions between citizens and subjects, as well as varying levels of privilege among the subjects, were reflected in a complicated system of two electoral lists. The second constitution was adopted in October 1946. Most overseas voters opposed it, however, because they saw it as reaffirming colonial rather than assimilated status for overseas territories.

Under these deteriorating conditions, all the African deputies (there were 22) signed a September 1946 manifesto calling for a congress of African delegates and parties in Bamako, and inviting the metropolitan parties to attend. Marius Moutet, the Socialist Minister of Overseas Territories, gave initial support to the idea. As the date of the conference approached, however, new divisions emerged in French politics. Left, right, and center began to break apart on domestic and international issues. Only the Communist Party supported the colonial demand for full citizenship. Moutet and the Socialists soon turned against the idea of the meeting. As a result the African leaders closest to the Socialists – including Lamine Guèye and Léopold Senghor of Senegal – stayed away from the meeting. So did the metropolitan socialists and the MRP, so that only the Communist Party attended. With this was born the great division of postwar politics in French Africa.

In October of 1946 the Bamako congress, with delegations from most French African colonies present, created the African Democratic Assembly (Rassemblement démocratique africain or RDA). This was an interterritorial alliance of parties formed earlier in each of the colonies. Gabriel d'Arboussier of Senegal became Secretary General, and Félix Houphouët-Boigny became its leading figure in parliament. The RDA dominated the politics of French West Africa (and, to a lesser degree, French Equatorial Africa) for a decade.

During that decade, a dizzying series of elections and electoral changes cascaded past the African voters. Voters elected delegates to the National Assembly, to the Assembly of the French Union, to the Grand Councils in Dakar and Brazzaville, and to the territorial assemblies. From 1945 to 1958 they voted on four referenda, two constitutions, three National Assemblies, and three territorial assemblies. The territorial councillors elected members to the Assembly of the French Union twice, to the federal grand council three times, and to the French Senate three times. In some cities voters elected mayors and councils. The fact that the same leaders ran for offices at several levels made voting easier, but it made governing difficult. The Grand Council of French West Africa, for instance, often had difficulty gaining a quorum, since several of its members were in Paris at the National Assembly.

Voting was made more difficult because there were two electoral colleges; full French citizens made up the first college, while others might hope to gain admission to the second college. In 1946, the second college included veterans, civil servants, registered property owners, and holders of hunting or driving licenses. In 1947 the second college list was extended to include all persons literate in French or Arabic. In 1951 it added tax-paying heads of families, mothers of two veterans, and pensioners. In Cameroon, the second college included 40,000 voters in 1946 and 592,000 in 1953. While this extension of electoral rights was welcomed, it was a complex, unwieldy, and endlessly changing system.

By May of 1947 the RDA and the Communist Party opposed the French government, each for their own reasons. The MRP, which now dominated the government, made a move for African influence by pressuring the RDA, imprisoning its activists, banning its meeting, bribing wavering figures, and even falsifying elections, as in Ivory Coast, Upper Volta, and later in Guinea.

Socialist parties briefly sought to oppose the RDA throughout West and Central Africa. But the strongest Socialist Party, that in Senegal, split in 1948 when Senghor objected to Guèye's giving full support to French Socialist Party positions. Senghor and Mamadou Dia built the new Block Démocratique Sénégalais rapidly, and in 1951 Dia defeated Lamine Guèye to become Senegal's second deputy. To present the rationale for these actions, Senghor began propounding the ideas of African Socialism – socialism based neither on Marxism nor on European conditions, but on African realities. Senghor gradually assumed leadership of a parliamentary group of Overseas Independents (IOM) with support from the MRP in France, but this group never gained the organizational strength of the RDA.

In 1950 and 1951 the RDA, having survived the colonial administration's repression but now seeking an accommodation, pulled back from systematic opposition to the government. Houphouët removed d'Arboussier, who he saw as too close to the Communists, from the post of Secretary-General, and broke the formal parliamentary link to the Communists in October of 1950. In effect the RDA changed from an alliance with the Communists to one with the Socialists. But even as the RDA and the administration moved toward rapprochement, the administration falsified elections during 1951 in Niger, Sudan, Ivory Coast, and Guinea.

Administrative expansion paralleled the growth of electoral politics. The governments-general in Dakar and Brazzaville, spurred on by the new politics of development and social responsibility, sought to expand port facilities, schools, and hospitals. They were encouraged further by the demands of elected officials and their constituents, and they were funded in part by moneys raised through FIDES. (This money came partly from French funds for economic and social development, but mostly from additional taxes in Africa). To support scientific and technical studies, the Paris government set up ORSTOM, which sent French scholars and technicians to perform studies in the colonies.

Administrations in each of the colonies expanded similarly, including those in Lomé and Yaoundé. These two territories, along with Ruanda–Urundi, were now governed under the supervision of the United Nations Trusteeship Council. Missions from United Nations officials visited the Trust Territories every three years, beginning in 1948, and these visits provided inhabitants of the territories with opportunities to raise demands for better conditions. In Togo, these demands took the form of a pan-Ewe movement, in which members of the Ewe ethnic group in both British and French Togo sought unification of the two territories. In Cameroon, equivalent responses took the form of demands for independence.

Trade-union activity, legalized at the end of the war, became important both in electoral politics and administration of the French colonies. The administrative impact was that, in public employment, unions of African workers demanded wages, working conditions, and benefits equivalent to those of European workers. These demands of the railroad workers in French West Africa were partially met as a result of their 1947 strike. By 1950 African representatives in the National Assembly had gained passage of the Second Lamine Guèye law, which guaranteed equal salaries and benefits for equal work in government service, regardless of race. As a result, the salaries of African government workers shot up in the early 1950s, and government surpluses soon began to turn into deficits. This was followed by the adoption of a liberal labor code in 1952.

The political impact of trade-union growth was that political parties soon sought to benefit from the success of trade unions in mobilizing mass support. For instance, Ahmed Sékou Touré of Guinea came to prominence as a trade-union leader, and from this position he became leader of the Democratic Party of Guinea (PDG), an affiliate of the RDA. In education, politics, and economic life, Guinea had been a backwater. The postwar economy of Guinea grew very rapidly, both in agriculture (bananas) and mining (iron and bauxite). When the 1952 labor code led to a reduction in the work week from 48 hours to 40, the trade unions demanded a 20% raise in the minimum wage to prevent a loss of income. The result was a 66-day strike. Following the success of the strike, Touré began to use the union organization as the basis of the PDG, and spread its organization throughout the colony. In doing so, Sékou Touré relied not only on economic issues, but relied on the tradition of resistance to French rule under Samori Touré. With time, the trade unions in Guinea lost their independence and became an arm of the PDG, in part because of the intense struggle between the party and the colonial administration.

The political struggle of the late 1940s extended beyond Guinea and included all the territories where the RDA was active. It was most intense in Ivory Coast. There Houphouët-Boigny had built up his Democratic Party of Ivory Coast (PDCI) based on the organizational model of the French Communist Party, with local cells throughout the country, excellent communications, and an ability to mobilize thousands of militants rapidly. But while the tactics and the alliances of the PDCI owed much to the Communists, the objectives of the leadership were reform rather than revolution. Houphouët led a coalition of Ivorians ranging from large planters to agricultural laborers which contested the administration's policy of favoritism to a small group of wealthy white planters. The administration, in turn, saw the PDCI as disloyal and communistic and carried on a program of intimidation and isolation against PDCI leaders. Villages loyal to the PDCI were assessed higher taxes. Similar administrative campaigns against RDA-affiliated parties took place in other colonies, but generally the RDA parties were well enough organized to re-elect their delegates with each election.

In the course of this dispute, the northern portions of Ivory Coast were turned in 1947 into a reconstituted colony of Upper Volta. (Upper Volta had been divided among Niger, Sudan, and Ivory Coast in 1933.) Ouezzin Coulibaly had narrowly won election to the Constituent Assembly there in 1945, over a lieutenant of the Mogho Naba of Ouagadougou. He and Houphouët cooperated in the formation of the PDCI and the RDA. With the recreation of Upper Volta, the white planters now lost administrative control over their source of labor, but Houphouët was thereby deprived of the possibility of consolidating his electoral power over this area. Coulibaly continued to lead the RDA in Upper Volta, but had to maintain a delicate alliance of his own Juula with the Mossi leaders.

Then in 1951, with a new government in France and a new administration in Ivory Coast, the PDCI and the administration struck an accommodation. Houphouët-Boigny had made the first move a year earlier in breaking the RDA's parliamentary alliance with the Communists. The Ivory Coast administration ceased treating the PDCI as disloyal, and began supporting the development of both European- and African-owned enterprises. Ivory Coast became, more than ever, a privileged colony. Similar accommodations were made in most of the other territories, and within three years Houphouë-Boigny had become a minister in the French government.

In Ivory Coast, Houphouët's position as a canton chief made it possible for the RDA to form an alliance with the chiefs. In other colonies – Guinea, Sudan, and Cameroon, for instance – the RDA could win elections only after defeating the chiefs. In Guinea and Sudan the chiefs were defeated, but in Cameroon they were not. In Senegal, meanwhile, Senghor's BDS benefitted from close relations with the administration and was able to draw the chiefs into its network without confrontation.

Not all the RDA parties made accommodations, however. In Cameroon the Union of Cameroonian Peoples (UPC) remained committed to the ideal of independence. It carried on its electoral campaigns, but also sought representation at the United Nations in order to make its case. Out of frustration with their inability to change administrative policies, Ruben Um Nyobe and other UPC leaders turned in the end of 1956 to guerilla war.

POLITICAL INDEPENDENCE

The movement toward independence for francophone Africa began imperceptibly in the early 1950s, then accelerated rapidly from 1956. In the French territories, the existing political parties turned from a policy of assimilation toward the objective of independence. Independence was achieved, however, at the cost of balkanization; two large federations broke into their 12 constituent territories. In the Belgian territories, the belated first hints of democracy led immediately to a stampede toward independence, a stampede which threw social classes into bitter conflict.

The first United Nations inspection of Ruanda–Urundi in 1948 made no difference in the governance of the territory, though it led to some advances in education. The 1951 United Nations commission called on the Belgian administration to institute some reforms. A change in the Belgian government brought the first small changes; in 1952 the Liberal–Socialist government encouraged expanded education in Ruanda–Urundi and made the first steps toward holding elections. Local elections took place in 1953 and 1956. The administration, now becoming critical of autocracy, backed away from its previous support of the monarchy. It moved closer to the Hutu agriculturists, the largest social group in the colony, and away from the Tutsi pastoralists, who were few in number but socially dominant. Political parties formed rapidly, and the isolation of Rwanda and Burundi ended. Bloody conflicts followed on this sudden opening of electoral politics. The monarchies fell in both countries, and the Tutsi lost their dominant position in Rwanda and ended up as refugees in surrounding countries.

In the Belgian Congo, the late 1950s brought a resolution of the long-standing contradiction between the political isolation of the colony and its economic incorporation into the wider world. The administration finally scheduled local elections in 1957, in the major cities. The result was the immediate coalescence of a national political consciousness and of political parties. This flood tide of political conflict led in just over a decade to the formation of the present Republic of Zaire. The events were of such importance for Africa as a whole that they are discussed separately in the next section.

In the French colonies, the postwar extension of African representation (along with growing economies) had brought a substantial improvement in social services, which in turn gave popular legitimacy to the new political leaders. But as the legitimacy of political leaders came to depend on a steadily larger electoral constituency, a change in the orientation of political parties took place. The political parties formed in 1946 and 1947 were territorial or even inter-territorial in scope, and they were ideological in orientation. By 1952, however, new and reconstituted political parties had become ethnic and local in orientation. This narrowing of the geographic scope of parties had great importance for the nature of independence in the French colonies.

By 1956, it had become clear that the French territories were headed for some sort of self-government or sovereignty. Yet the framework for sovereignty remained undecided. Would the African states be governed as federations or as individual territories? Would they remain associated with France or become independent? As late as 1956 it seemed that sovereignty would go to African federations, and that they would remain tied to France. But by 1960 there had emerged, instead, nearly a score of independent countries.

The argument for independence came more from outside francophone sub-Saharan Africa than from within. The 1954 French surrender to the Viet Minh army at Dien Bien Phu led to the independence of French Indochina. In the same year the National Liberation Front (FLN) in Algeria began its war for independence. While the French government fought to retain Algeria until 1962, it responded to the Algerian crisis by granting independence to neighboring Morocco and Tunisia in 1956. Further, the 1957 independence of Ghana from Britain captured the imagination of patriots all over Africa.

The argument for federations was that the governments-general in Dakar and Brazzaville had been supreme for 50 years. Postwar centralization moved even more of the tax revenues and administrative power to these centers. The large size of the federations seemed to make them viable as political and economic units. And the Grand Council for each federation presented a legislative body through which Africans might gain control of the federal administrations. The 12 colonies which made up the federations were smaller, more ethnically homogeneous, and administratively weaker than the federations. African leaders in the Territorial Assemblies thus found that they had more power over the administrations in the various colonies than they had over the more entrenched governments-general.

The turning point came with the 1956 *loi cadre*, an enabling act adopted by the French National Assembly on the motion of Gaston Defferre, the Overseas Minister, and with the active support of Félix Houphouët-Boigny of Ivory Coast. This act followed the adoption of an act initially proposed to meet the needs of the United Nations Trust Territories of Togo and Cameroon, which were expected to move toward self-government. Then it was extended to the two federations. The act allowed for universal suffrage in a single electoral college and allowed the territorial assemblies to gain ministerial powers over the governments in each colony. The result was that the governments-general lost their political influence, and within three years they had dissolved. This was the "balkanization" of the French African colonies, as Léopold Senghor called it, which to this day is celebrated by some and regretted by others.

Why did the federations dissolve? One line of explanation emphasizes power politics, and another line emphasizes political structure. In the first case, politics within French West Africa had, by 1956, come down to a struggle between the RDA camp led by Houphouët-Boigny and the Overseas Independents (IOM) camp led by Léopold Senghor of Senegal. Senghor was close to the government-general in Dakar, and argued for the merits of a strong federal government. Houphouët argued that the federal structure served to benefit Senegal financially at the expense of Ivory Coast and other colonies. More practically, Houphouët had a strong political base in Ivory Coast, but this base, along with his other RDA alliances, was not strong enough to give him control of the Grand Council of French West Africa. The solution was to break up the federation by achieving greatly expanded powers for the territorial governments. Houphouët was well enough placed in Paris to get support for such legislation. French politicians Defferre and Guy Mollet may have supported the legislation in the expectation that, if the colonies became independent, 12 small nations would be more likely to stay close to France than two large ones.

But the federations may have been doomed for other reasons, since there was no secure base of African political power in Dakar or Brazzaville. In the French political system, power lay in Paris. From the time of Blaise Diagne, elected to the National Assembly from Senegal in 1914, Paris was where Africans had achieved significant reforms. The Dakar and Brazzaville governments-general were administratively powerful but politically impenetrable for Africans. The governors-general listened to the ministers in Paris rather than to subjects in the colonies. African political figures thus relied on local organizations to get elected, and sought legislation in Paris with which to bring reforms in Dakar and Brazzaville.

Meanwhile the war in Algeria brought both France and Algeria to a crisis. The army and the French settlers in Algeria threatened rebellion against the French government, which had become irresolute in its conduct of the war, and cries rang out for the return of Charles de Gaulle to power. De Gaulle, a conservative nationalist, had retired from politics in 1946 expressing contempt for the Fourth Republic, and apparently awaiting such a call. He returned to the public stage in 1958, and the Fourth Republic simply turned power over to him. He proposed a constitution for a Fifth Republic which weakened the National Assembly and made the president far more powerful than before. The new constitution was to be adopted by referendum.

In France, the 1958 referendum was on the adoption of the constitution and the selection of de Gaulle as president. In the colonies, however, the referendum was on whether to remain as republics within the redefined French Community, or to leave. In most of the colonies, the vote was overwhelmingly "yes" for ratification and remaining with France. But in three colonies – Niger, Cameroon, and Guinea   there were significant opposition movements, and in Guinea a resounding "no" vote led to immediate independence.

In Niger Djibo Bakary, the elected head of the territorial government, campaigned for independence in hope of reversing the effects of his recent loss of support by the French administration. But administrative opposition combined with his alienation of local allies to bring about his defeat. Niger voted just over 30% "no" and Bakary fell from power. In Cameroon the UPC, which was strong among the Bamileke people of the south, continued its long campaign for independence. But that campaign had taken the form of a *maquis* (guerilla warfare) since 1956, and the movement was near defeat in 1958. Cameroon voted heavily "yes."

In Guinea, however, Sékou Touré's Democratic Party of Guinea (PDG) had become a powerful and unified electoral organization. After sweeping the 1956 elections to the territorial assembly, the party moved to suppress the office of canton chief, the instrument of its previous oppression, and gained the administration's assent. Touré's response to the 1958 referendum evoked the colonial demands for federation and full citizenship in 1945. He offered to support the new constitution on the understanding that it guaranteed juridical equality and the right to self-determination for overseas territories. De Gaulle responded by avoiding the question of equality. He said that Guinea could have independence if it wanted, though it would have to accept the consequences of such a decision. Touré retorted that "we prefer poverty in liberty to riches in slavery." The voters of Guinea supported him and voted overwhelmingly "no." The French administrators, smarting from this rebuke, left immediately after the election, taking with them everything they could carry. The Guineans found government offices empty, and telephones ripped of the walls. France abstained when Guinea was admitted to the United Nations.

Within two years, however, all the other French colonies had gained independence, and with France's blessing. The logic of independent African nations had become inexorable, as all the other formulations failed. For instance, with the breakup of French West Africa and French Equatorial Africa, Senghor, Houphouët, and other leaders sought to form new federations. The Mali Federation, led by Senghor and Modibo Keita of Sudan, was to include Senegal, Sudan, Upper Volta, and Dahomey. Houphouët's Council of the Entente, formed in response, included Ivory Coast, Upper Volta, Dahomey, Niger. Neither of these groupings, however, had much practical importance. The Mali Federation shrank rapidly to Senegal and Sudan; after that alliance broke in 1960, the only remnant of the Mali Federation was that Sudan took on the name of Mali. The Council of the Entente continued to exist for over a decade, but only on paper.

Meanwhile, Senegal and Mali began negotiating for independence from France in 1960. As these negotiations began to bear fruit, Houphouët suddenly requested independence for Ivory Coast and the other states in the Council of the Entente. By the end of 1960, all of the French colonies in West and Central Africa had quietly acceded to independence.

CONFLICT IN THE CONGO

The political evolution of the French African territories was very rapid. But in Belgian Africa, by comparison, decolonization took place with blinding and catastrophic speed. The result was political collapse and civil war. The grave political crisis of the Congo (not to mention the revolutionary upheavals in Rwanda and Burundi) ranks with the civil wars of Nigeria (1967–71) and of Sudan (1966–72) as the conflicts which revealed most tragically the fragility of the independent African political order. More than African political fragility, however, the Congo crisis revealed the continuing power of outsiders – Belgian firms, the Belgian government, the United States government, the United Nations, and others – to divert African politics even after independence.

Only in 1957 did the Belgian administration allow elections for local government officials in the Congo. Elections began 12 years later than in the French colonies and they included no elections to territory-wide bodies. Only in December of 1959 was a Government Council established for the Congo as a whole. Political organizations thus formed at a local and regional level, rather than a national level, and ethnic politics thus had a relatively early start in the

Belgian colonies. Since almost all administrative positions of any responsibility were filled by Belgians, African demands for equalization of salaries achieved less prominence than in the French territories, as Africans were always in subordinate positions (whereas both French and African teachers, for example, served side by side but at different salaries until 1952).

Three leaders emerged with the vision of national politics, and one of them had the ability to convey it effectively. Joseph Kasavubu was the leader of the Bakongo Association (ABAKO) which grew to great strength in Leopoldville and among the Bakongo, but which never grew beyond those bounds. Moise Tshombe, of a wealthy Katanga commercial family, rose to prominence as leader of CONAKAT, the Confederation of Tribal Associations of Katanga. Patrice Lumumba gained a wider following. He was a postal clerk and a beer salesman while in his twenties, positions which were relatively humble but which gave him wide experience; more importantly, he became president of several urban associations in his home of Stanleyville. He was a brilliant orator, fluent in the main languages of the country. By 1960 he was the only political coalition to have support in every region of the country.

Lumumba came to prominence when he attended the All-Africa Peoples' Congress in Accra, Ghana, in 1958. Kwame Nkrumah, the founding president of Ghana and the leading figure in Africa's independence movement, called together representatives of political parties from all over Africa to discuss how to advance the independence movement. Lumumba, after his return from Ghana, toured and spoke with even more energy, calling for independence, and patterning the ideology of his Congolese National Movement (MNC) according to the model of Nkrumah's Convention People's Party (CPP).

Then in January 1959 riots shook Leopoldville. Thousands of people took to the streets, looting and attacking stores and administrative buildings. The Belgian government, profoundly shaken by this disloyalty, accelerated its movement to call together all the Congolese political leaders who could be identified and sat them down at a Round Table in Brussels late in 1959. In the course of two weeks' meetings, Belgium acceded to Congolese demands for immediate independence and an independence date of 30 June 1960.

From February through June, Belgian officials and Congolese political leaders struggled to set up a parliamentary regime and a government. The two strongest movements were Lumumba's MNC and the Kasavubu's ABAKO. Between them, these two groups held less than half the seats in parliament, and most of the rest were held by local figures. Ultimately, a government was formed with Kasavubu as president (and head of state) and with Lumumba as prime minister (and head of the government).

While political decolonization accelerated, there was no move toward administrative or economic decolonization. All top administrators and all military officers were Belgian; Belgians continued to dominate Congo's main firms; and Belgian and other expatriates dominated the clergy. The stage was set for an explosion.

The hostilities inherent in the situation were revealed at the independence ceremonies. King Baudoin gave a fumbling and paternalistic speech praising

Leopold II and Belgian colonial officials, and President Kasavubu read his brief and diplomatic remarks. Lumumba, however, took the microphone to give a fiery response:

> This was our fate for eighty years of a colonial regime; our wounds are too fresh and too painful still for us to drive them from our memory. We have known harrassing work, exacted in exchange for salaries which did not permit us to eat enough to drive away hunger, or to clothe ourselves, or to house ourselves decently, or to raise our children as creatures dear to us.
>
> We have known ironies, insults, blows that we endured morning, noon, and evening, because we are Negroes. Who will forget that to a black one said *"tu,"* certainly not as to a friend, but because the more honorable *"vous"* was reserved for whites alone? . . . .
>
> All that, my brothers, we have endured.
>
> But we, whom the vote of your elected representatives have given the right to direct our dear country, we who have suffered in our body and in our heart from colonial oppression, we tell you very loud, all that is henceforth ended.
>
> The Republic of the Congo has been proclaimed, and our country is now in the hands of its own children . . .
>
> We are going to put an end to suppression of free thought and see to it that all our citizens enjoy to the full the fundamental liberties foreseen in the Declaration of the Rights of Man . . .
>
> We are going to rule not by the peace of guns and bayonets but by a peace of the heart and will.

Lumumba spoke well, but too soon. Within days, the enlisted men in the army mutinied against their Belgian officers; the officers fled the country, and they were followed by large numbers of the Belgian civil servants. Lumumba grasped anywhere for African officers, and made Joseph Desirée Mobutu, a civil servant who had been a non-commissioned officer, into his army chief of staff. Meanwhile the army remained out of control, and evoked memories of the earlier mutiny of the *Force publique* in the 1890s.

On 11 July Moise Tshombe, of the mineral-rich Katanga province, declared the secession of Katanga and formation of an independent state. This was the only province in which Belgian officials had remained after June. These officials and the mining executives of Union Minière gave support to a movement whose African support stemmed from regional resentment of the centralizing tendencies of the government in Leopoldville. Shortly thereafter, the diamond-mining region of Kasai province declared its independence in alliance with Tshombe.

Lumumba turned first to the United States and then to the United Nations for support. But the United Nations was almost paralyzed. Then in early September, 1960, president Kasavubu dismissed Lumumba, which initiated a severe crisis, as no other leader could form a government. In this crisis, the American Central Intelligence Agency provided key information and support to Kasavubu and Mobutu, acting out of fear that Lumumba would become a Soviet ally. In ten days, army chief of staff Mobutu "neutralized" both figures and established his own regime. He soon arrested Lumumba; in November Lumumba escaped, and headed to Stanleyville where his strongest support lay.

He was intercepted by Mobutu's forces, and was turned over to Tshombe. In January of 1961 Lumumba was shot to death in Katanga.

At the beginning of 1961, the country lay in three fragments. Leopoldville (supported by the West) and Stanleyville (supported by socialist and anti-imperial states) each claimed to govern the whole country; regimes in Katanga and eastern Kasai (supported by mining interests) each claimed to have seceded. By August of 1961, however, a compromise regime had reunited Leopoldville, Stanleyville, and Kasai. Only then was it possible to obtain United Nations support for the suppression of the Katanga regime. The Katanga regime fell in January of 1963.

During the struggle for Katanga, a new force appeared on the scene: mercenary armies, based primarily on European soldiers of fortune. The most famous of these was Bob Denard, a former Belgian army officer, who fought for Tshombe's Katanga regimes until the end, and then offered his services to whoever would pay for another decade. In an astonishing switch, by the middle of 1964 Moise Tshombe had become prime minister of Congo and Bob Denard was fighting (again as a mercenary) to reaffirm the authority of the central government.

The events which brought about this change centered on a massive popular revolt led by peasants. It began in late 1963 among the peoples of the Kwilu region, but rebel bands met so little opposition from the national army that their movement spread rapidly to the east. At the same time, a larger peasant revolt broke out in the region adjoining Lake Tanganyika. The "simbas" (lions), as the eastern rebel soldiers were known, felt betrayed by independence, and expressed their anger towards the state, politicians, civil servants, teachers, and their Belgian and American external allies. As they captured towns, the simbas executed thousands of white-collar personnel. They took Stanleyville in August 1964, and proclaimed a revolutionary republic which would bring a "second independence."

The impotence of Leopoldville in the face of this movement paved the way for the return of Tshombe. Tshombe, in turn, was unable to arrange a peace with the insurgents, and turned again to a military strategy based on white mercenaries. As this army advanced, the rebels took several hundred Belgian and American hostages. In November 1964 the mercenaries and units of the national army reached Stanleyville; on the same day, a joint American-Belgian parachute operation (with French support) rescued the hostages, at the cost of about 100 hostages killed. This direct foreign intervention outraged many African and Third World countries, and new aid flowed to the rebels, though their cause was now lost.

In the capital, preparations for a new political order proceeded, with the drafting of a new constitution. Kasavubu and Tshombe emerged as the main political forces, but neither had power to achieve supremacy. In the face of this stalemate, the army installed General Mobutu as president. Parliament ratified the *coup* unanimously, and the First Republic came to an end in Congo.

Within two years Mobutu had skillfully consolidated a new regime which was unitary and bureaucratic. He abolished political parties, but brought political leaders into his regime as officials. In 1967 he brought forth a new, unitary constitution, giving the president great power, and established a single political party. His regime received general African recognition with the convening of the Organization of African Unity annual meeting in Kinshasa in 1967.

In later years Mobutu rehabilitated Lumumba and declared him to be a national hero. He launched a campaign of "authenticity" in which an authentic national culture was to be emphasized in every way. The name of the country was changed to Zaire (after an early Portuguese term for the river). Colonial names were removed from the cities, and the local African names were made official: Leopoldville became Kinshasa, Elisabethville became Lubumbashi, Stanleyville became Kisangani, and so forth. Finally, personal names had to be authentic; the president now became known as Mobutu Sese Soko.

DOMESTIC POLITICS

The main problems of African governments after independence fell into four areas. First was how to provide adequate *representation* for the country's political interests. Second was how to achieve effective *administration* of national affairs. Third was *development*; how to meet the public demand for improved economic and social life while facing deteriorating international economic conditions. Fourth was *social policy*; how to allocate power and resources among competing class, regional, and ethnic groups. Governmental success in one or more of these areas led toward establishment of a national consensus; significant failures led to demoralization, revolts, and even civil war.

Independent governments in Africa became, with few exceptions, more representative than their colonial predecessors. Virtually all the nations of francophone Africa gained independence with multi-party, parliamentary, democratic regimes. These parliamentary governments had been permitted to grow in the last few years of colonial rule. Indeed, without such structures, based on the European model, African nationals would not have been able to gain approval of their independence from the colonizer. Parliamentary democracy, however, did not last long in independent Africa; it collapsed under the weight of new governmental problems.

Where multiparty systems continued, they became embroiled in ethnic and regional conflict. In Dahomey, three regional parties traded power with each other and the army until, in 1969, they reached a truce by establishing a Council of Presidents. The three leaders were to rotate, changing places each year. As a result all were discredited, and a group of young military officers under Captain Mathieu Kérékou seized power in 1972. In many countries the parliamentary structure remained, but only a single party remained legal; this was the case for Senegal, Ivory Coast, Guinea, and Cameroon in the 1960s, and later in Zaire. In other cases parliament was abolished by military rulers, as in the cases of Togo, Mali, and Congo.

In all these cases the formal, electoral structures of representation weakened, after flourishing briefly in the decade surrounding independence. The voice of the people echoed only faintly when elections were uncontested or abolished, and more faintly still when governments put restrictions on the press. In a sense, domestic politics became reminiscent of the autocratic methods of the colonial era.

Elections, however, were not the only way in which constituents could make representations to government. Citizens of independent Africa, in contrast to subjects of colonial Africa, had a wider range of civil rights, and a state whose power rested to a greater extent on the consent of the governed. Constituents could use personal and family ties, rumors, or public demonstrations to make their wishes heard. The major problem with this sort of representational system was that, in cases where government lost the consent of the governed, there was no orderly means of transferring power; one was left with hoping that the right group of army officers would seize power. Thus the death of Sékou Touré in 1984 opened up popular discussion of Guinea's grim social and economic conditions, but the discussion was resolved only in a succession of military coups.

Meanwhile the civil administration of francophone African nations continued to grow and to assume new responsibilities in health, urban and economic affairs, as well as education and the registration of population. Almost without exception, these were centralized, national civil service organizations. The Senegalese became particularly proud of their tradition of stable administration, a heritage from France. The system of urban administration in Zaire, Rwanda, and Burundi was based on the Belgian model, though it was introduced only at the very end of the colonial era.

The centralization of administration in francophone Africa is revealed in aspects of the law. The national legal systems were based on the Napoleonic Code, and customary law lost virtually all formal standing with independence. Further, the working of the Napoleonic Code is such that old laws stay in place until explicitly replaced by the legislature, in contrast to the British system where the law may evolve through judicial review. Land law, however, changed in several countries; Guinea, Cameroon, Zaire, and other states nationalized all land. The Touré government in Guinea presented this act as transferring control of land from expatriate planters and mining firms to the people as a whole. Landholders in most areas of Africa felt differently. Since the beginning of the colonial era, they had fought efforts by the state to assert its ownership of the land.

The elaboration of a successful social policy remained the most fundamental and the most elusive task of government. Political leaders had to choose among the conflicting interests of social groups within each nation. First, the leaders had to take care of themselves and their families. Secondly, the state would not function unless political leaders met the needs of the bureaucratic bourgeoisie, the class which had taken the places earlier filled by colonial officials. The private bourgeoisie, threatened both by expatriate firms and by the public sector of the economy, needed state support to survive. The petty bourgeoisie was a much larger class with still less power. This class included the many shopkeepers, merchants, small manufacturers, repair shop owners, and transporters who populated the cities and towns, but who benefitted little from government regulation. Wage workers, the urban unemployed, and the rural populations each had specific interests. In addition, these class interests took the varying forms of regional and ethnic demands on government.

As an example of a common problem in social policy, wage workers and the unemployed of the cities demanded low prices for food, and the threat of their unrest encouraged governments to meet their demands. Much of the food eaten in the cities was imported, so that governments sought to subsidize its consumption, though they needed tax revenue to pay for the subsidies. As for food brought from the countryside, governments sought to keep its prices low. But in so doing they alienated the peasants who, while more distant from the centers of power, were far more numerous. Peasants remained the largest and the most disenfranchised class in African nations.

Three efforts at African socialism show the range of ideas and experience of the more principled francophone African leaders. Léopold Senghor in Senegal was one of those who coined the terms "African socialism." He meant by it a moderate socialism, like that of the French socialist party with which he was first affiliated, but he also meant a socialism drawing on the communal traditions of Africa. In practice this meant consulting closely with the French ambassador, but also with the *marabouts* of the Mourides and other orders. It meant maintaining an effective national administration, but it also meant dismissing Mamadou Dia, his vice president, when Dia pressed for a more militant policy.

For Modibo Keita, African socialism meant an attempt to unify African nations into a grand federation and, when that failed, an attempt to lay the basis for such a federation in his own domestic policy. After federation with Senegal failed in 1960, Mali sought to ally with Guinea and Ghana as a step toward unity and Mali broke from the franc currency zone as a sign of its independence from neocolonialism. But the inability to obtain outside loans meant that Mali financed its development through inflationary expenditures, and soon the Malian currency was worthless. Keita's political party was unable to maintain its broad, popular ties, especially as popular demands for improved services could no longer be met. The military overthrew him in 1965 and the country re-entered the franc zone in the 1970s.

Sékou Touré, who rose to power as a trade-union leader, and who led in the formation of an African trade-union organization (UGTAN), followed policies similar to those of Keita. The difference was that his organization was strong enough to deliver a vote for independence in 1958. The national feeling associated with this declaration of independence carried Touré for many years, but the lack of outside loans led Guinea also to financing through inflation, and the result further cut back the provision of services. Touré continued with the rhetoric of socialism, which he called "the non-capitalistic way," but his party organization withered and his support slipped away. Foreign enemies and domestic protestors became confused in his mind and the regime slipped steadily into oppression.

In conditions where the demands of citizens conflicted with each other and with the pressures of foreign firms and states, a strong man was sometimes able to achieve stability. Ahmadou Ahidjo of Cameroon, a Muslim and a northerner, was a strong man whose success reflected that of some earlier Latin American rulers. He assumed power at independence, and was able to repress the remains of the anti-colonial UPC rebellion. His authoritarian but dependable methods of rule achieved the federation of French Cameroon and southern British Cameroons in 1961, their amalgamation into a unitary Cameroon Republic in 1972, and a remarkable record of economic growth. In 1984 he suddenly resigned from the presidency, and handed power in an orderly fashion to Paul Biya, a Christian and a southerner. (Some months later, however, Ahidjo was implicated in an abortive move to overthrow Biya.) The best known African strong man was Mobutu of Zaire, who managed successfully to portray himself as the only alternative to anarchy. The economic results of his regime, however, were poor enough to undermine rather than advance a sense of national consensus.

Chad slipped from rule by an early strong man into civil war. The country gained its independence under the leadership of François Tombalbaye, who ruled the country through a bureaucracy and an army heavily based on his own Sara ethnic group for the south. Disaffection with this regime in many parts of the country caused Tombalbaye to invite French troops to support him in 1968; French troops remained in Chad thereafter without interruption. In 1975 his base of support had become so narrow that a group of Sara junior officers overthrew him and killed him.

Meanwhile, armed opposition in the Muslim north, especially in the desert areas, led to the formation of Frolinat, the National Liberation Front, in 1966. Two leading figures emerged in the next decade of fighting: Goukouni Oueddeye, the aristocratic leader of the northern troops, and Hissène Habré, who had achieved university education in France and served briefly as an administrator.

By 1978 this movement has displaced the southern-dominated government of President Félix Malloum, and the northern armies took over the capital of Ndjamena. Immediately, however, the northern movement fell into contending factions. Habré sought for a time to ally with Malloum. Goukouni was the leading figure in Ndjamena from 1978 to 1982. In 1980, however, he invited the Libyan government to send forces in to help him retain power. Habré fled the country, but soon re-established an army in Sudan.

With civil war threatened again, the OAU established its first peacekeeping force, drawing troops from Nigeria, Senegal, and Zaire, in 1982. Late in 1982, however, the Americans became significantly if covertly involved, as part of the Reagan administration's campaign against Libya. American support enabled Habré to build up a formidable army in Sudan, from which he entered Chad and took Ndjamena. This caused the collapse of the OAU peacekeeping force. Goukouni new fled the country and was soon back in Tibesti as leader of a rebel force, supported by Libya. Habré, meanwhile, played skilfully on political difference within the sough to dislodge Col. Kamougué as leader of the southern territories, and established firm military control over the region.

Habré was the strongest military leader in Chad and was adroit at political maneuvers. He had come from a position of a northern factional leader to the leader of all of Chad. He now had firm support from France, the United States, and Zaire. The Libyans presently moved back into Chad, and the civil war resumed. Domestic political conflict had become inextricably linked to international and Cold War politics. It was under these conditions of civil war that Chad had to endure the drought of the mid 1980s.

The governments of independent francophone Africa were more ambitious than their colonial predecessors. Their record on political and economic equity, while uneven, was far better than that of the colonial regimes; their record on economic growth was less impressive. With exceptions such as Ivory Coast, Senegal, Cameroon, and Gabon, the independent governments have been more unstable than were the colonial governments. In part, this is to be expected in any evolving political system. The twentieth-century governments of France and Belgium, for instance, were notoriously unstable even as they presided over stable colonial regimes. The historical factors contributing to unstable African national government may be divided into three categories: factors stemming from the colonial heritage, divisions among Africans which had existed prior to the colonial period, and the intervention of destabilizing outside forces in the period after independence. We have discussed at length the colonial impact on African government, and have discussed African social divisions more briefly. The third factor, neocolonial intervention, arose because African nations were poor and weak by comparison with major powers. France intervened directly and militarily in Gabon (1964), Chad (1968 and 1984), and in Zaire; Belgium and the United States did so in Zaire, notably from 1960 to 1964. More subtle interventions were those of aid counselors, ambassadors, and corporate managers. These interventions, though many were well-meaning and positive, tended to tip the domestic political balance unpredictably. Governments are overthrown when they are seen as misguided or unrepresentative. The domestic protests against the governments of independent Africa were not fundamentally different from those against colonial governments; the difference was that after 1960 the protestors had a real chance of bringing down the government.

INTERNATIONAL POLITICS

African nations gained admission to the United Nations, and for the first time in a century could participate in international diplomacy, now with a sounder basis then ever. Powerful countries sought their allegiance and promised them assistance: the Western bloc, led by the United States, the socialist block, led by the Soviet Union, and an emerging Third World or non-aligned bloc, in which India and China were prominent, though no single nation dominated.

International politics, like domestic politics, were initially dominated by the new nations' ties with the former colonial power. The division between pro-Western and anti-imperialist policies was made clear in the formation of two blocs of African nations in 1960: the Casablanca group, which included Ghana, Guinea, Mali, Morocco, and Egypt and the Monrovia group, which included Nigeria and most of the French speaking countries. The former French colonies formed an association known as the Union Africaine et Malagache (UAM), which served mainly as a channel for continuing economic ties to France. The absurdity of competing blocs become rapidly apparent, however, and in 1963 all the independent African nations met in Addis Ababa to form the Organization of African Unity. Now the differences between countries following radical and moderate policies were viewed as being within the range of polite discussion.

For the French colonies, diplomatic and cultural ties remained close, and were now carried out through the French Ministry of Cooperation. This ministry continued to arrange visas to African countries and among African countries. It dispensed aid, sent teachers and administrators to Africa and brought African students and civil servants to France for training. Such socialistic countries as Congo and Bénin sought to renegotiate the terms of their relationship to increase their own benefits, but they did not seek to end their links to the Ministry of Cooperation.

With the passage of time, the importance of former colonial powers diminished. This was particularly true for the Belgian colonies. Rwanda and Burundi each had thoroughgoing revolutions which set them in new directions. Zaire nationalized Union Minère and other expatriate firms, though Belgian interests still retained influence in the operation of the nationalized firms. In aid missions, the United States and Canada became important. In trade, the United States became a major trading partner for most of the francophone countries.

Aside from the economic expansion of American-based firms, the Cold War made itself felt in African politics. The Soviet Union sought to open up trade and diplomatic missions with African countries; the Americans sought to enhance their lead. Israel opened diplomatic missions and aid projects throughout francophone Africa. (With the 1967 Middle East War, in which Israel took substantial Arab territories, most African nations broke relations with Israel.) Similarly, Nationalist China opened diplomatic and aid missions in Africa, but these were replaced with communist (People's Republic of China) missions as China gained admission to the United Nations in 1972. With the course of time, francophone African nations moved gradually away from casting their UN votes with France (and then with the United States), and toward voting with the Afro–Asian bloc. Leaders in this direction were Congo, Guinea, Bénin, Mali, and the Malagasay Republic.

The main source of unity within the Organization of African Unity was the campaign against colonialism: against Portuguese rule in Angola, Mozambique, and Guiné-Bissau, and against white rule in Rhodesia and South Africa. In an effort to affirm African unity and to speed the end of colonialism in southern Africa, the Organization of African Unity called for a boycott of the 1976 Montreal Olympics. The reason was not the participation of South Africa, which had earlier been banned from Olympic competition, but the participation of New Zealand, which has associated itself with South Africa by allowing its national rugby team to play against the South African Springboks. Most African countries joined the boycott (accompanied by some West Indian countries), though Ivory Coast refused to go along. The boycott was a dramatic show of unity, as the Africans stood to gain many medals, and it served to advance the athletic isolation of South Africa. On the other hand, this action served as a precursor of the larger Olympic boycotts at Moscow in 1980 and Los Angeles in 1984.

Conflicts within the African continent came to balance the importance of Cold War and other extra-continental affairs. Most francophone countries sought simply to ignore the crisis of Zaire from 1960 to 1965, though the rise of a revolutionary regime in Brazzaville in 1963 led to direct support for the Lumumbist faction. Later on, the Brazzaville regime gave support to the MPLA party in Angola, and enabled it to launch assaults on the Portuguese in the northern enclave of Cabinda. With the civil war in Nigeria (1967–70), most francophone countries supported the OAU resolution which called for preservation of the territorial unity of Nigeria and support of the federal government. Cameroon, however, associated itself with efforts to fly aid to the Biafran rebels.

Boundary disputes have been less severe among francophone sub-Saharan countries than others in Africa, but several may be mentioned: a dispute between Niger and Bénin over islands in the Niger River, the claim of Morocco to control all of Mauritania, and the border dispute between Mali and Burkina Faso. The border dispute between Chad and Libya became linked to civil war within Chad.

The politics of guest workers provided a growing basis for international conflict as the number of migrants increased. Large numbers of West African workers moved to France, where they became important in the menial work force, and gradually moved into industrial production. At issue were visas, remittances of money to families in Africa, schooling, and social security. Of at least equal importance was the number of guest workers within Africa: workers from Burkina Faso in Ivory Coast and from Mali in Senegal. In times of depression, the foreign workers were expelled by governments seeking to maintain political support among their own nationals. The stream of expelled workers going back to their home countries, even more depressed, served only to reinforce the problems there. The first big expulsion of guest workers was that by Ivory Coast in 1961; most of those expelled were from Dahomey. They included well-placed civil servants as well as day laborers.

The politics of drought relief left African nations in desperation and confusion. Governments sought first to deny the effects of the drought of 1974, and then to resolve them without outside help. Only once matters had become severe were international humanitarian agencies allowed to contribute. These agencies, while far better funded than the national governments, were often lacking in the local background necessary to balance their good will. Their efforts provided short-term relief but no long-term benefits. In addition, the flow of large quantities of money and supplies provided an opening for graft.

The idea of regional economic integration returned from time to time. One form of this was admission of African nations to associate status in the European Economic Community. An earlier form had been the federations of French West Africa and French Equatorial Africa. The Central African Cystoms Union (UDEAC) became an effective successor to the latter Federation. But in West Africa after 1956, smaller groupings such as the Mali federation and the Council of the Entente sought, without effect, to achieve economic integration. Finally, in 1975 all the nations of West Africa joined to form ECOWAS, the Economic Community of West African States. This attempt to form an economic union across colonial lines had some initial successes, but was soon crippled by Nigeria's depression. The decline in oil prices reduced Nigerian income, and Nigeria expelled a million foreign workers, mostly Ghanaian, in 1981.

The politics of international debt suddenly assumed great importance in the early 1970s, and remained determinant thereafter. African nations, seeking investment funds to provide social services and permit economic growth, suddenly found that international banks were willing to loan large amounts on relatively easy terms. It was under these conditions, for example, that Mobutu in Zaire undertook a massive expansion of infrastructure in order to facilitate exploitation of the nation's mineral resources.

But the low interest rates and easy credit were not to last long. Prices began rising in the early 1970s, and then they rose far more rapidly with the petroleum boycott of the Muslim countries in OPEC (Organization of Petroleum Exporting Countries). As a result, interest rates skyrocketed, and the African nations learned about the variable interest rate clauses in their loan contracts. They now faced impossible debt burdens. Now the International Monetary Fund (IMF) stepped in to recommend means of repayment of loans, and to recommend austerity programs which would reduce national expenditures. Zaire was the most heavily burdened, but the magnitude of its debt was so great that it could threaten to default and thus induce the lenders to accept a much slower payment of the debt.

Thus, regardless of their domestic political and economic policies, the governments of francophone Africa found themselves united in support of the growing demand for a new international economic order. This idea, supported by the world's poorer countries, was that the wealthy countries benefitted from unfair prices and from preferential treatment by banks, and that international agreements should be made which would redress this balance. Despite years of discussion at the United Nations, however, little advance was made on this proposal.

On this issue as on others, the specifically francophone identity of the 17 nations began to be subsumed into a broader African identity. A suggestive example of this modification in identity comes from the year 1985. Abdou Diouf was the newly elected president of Senegal, having been chosen by Léopold Senghor as his successor. Diouf, in turn, was recognized in his own right by the African heads of state when they elected him president of the OAU for 1985. Soon after his election as OAU president, the repression of anti-apartheid demonstrations by the government of South Africa brought an international outcry. Diouf, a Muslim and a francophone head of state, but responsible now for African policy in anglophone South Africa, used his old francophone ties to make a strong and personal plea to François Mitterand, president of France, that France should take action against South Africa. The plea worked, and France, for the first time, spoke up strongly for sanctions against South Africa in the European Economic Community, with the result that moderate EEC sanctions were later instituted. The francophone unity and ties were still there, but they were now being directed toward participation in a wider African community.

NATIONHOOD AND DEMOCRACY

The nation is the unit of modern political affairs. The powerful nations of the world took on their modern identity as their economies industrialized, and as their educational systems expanded and instructed new generations in the history, the culture, and the destiny of the nation. So too did the nations of francophone Africa form themselves during the past generation. The 1960s were filled with the pageantry of nationhood in Africa. Flags fluttered, anthems were composed and sung, and schoolchildren learned the lives of national heroes. In a brief time they made remarkable strides toward gaining order and identity within their borders, and toward achieving recognition as full members of the community of nations.

On the other hand, the nations of francophone Africa failed to escape poverty and weakness. The achievements of national governments generally failed to match up to the hopes of their citizens. They fell into debt, and they remained exposed to the whims or the designs of great nations and powerful firms. The ability of government to do good or ill was shown to be limited and in some cases irrelevant. Many modern Africans have relied for survival on the informal economy and networks of personal relations rather than on public services.

Nor, Africans learned, does the creation of nations guarantee the enjoyment of democracy. Critics of African nations have argued that such regimes as Bokassa's Central African Empire and Burundi during the Hutu massacres were as arbitrary and capricious as the colonial regimes they replaced. Closer study, however, shows both the benefits and the limits of nationhood to democracy. African nationhood put an end to the systematic racial and national discrimination against Africans which had reigned since the nineteenth century. Nationhood required the state to base itself on the support of a significant portion (though not necessarily a majority) of the inhabitants. But nationhood did not guarantee democratic rights for individual African citizens, nor for such large grouping as the peasantry or the urban unemployed.

It may be asked, therefore, whether the national states of francophone Africa were viable. Could they survive the pressures of the years to come? Would another political structure better serve the needs of the hundred million people of francophone Africa? These questions may be considered by looking both at the past and at the future from the vantage point of 1985.

In past years, several alternative structures had presented themselves. One of these was to continue the colonial relationship, although virtually no Africans voluntarily accepted the condition of second-class citizen (much less that of subject) when full citizenship was available. Another alternative, long considered in the French colonies, was integration of the colonies into the French nation. The French Antilles took this path, but the African colonies did not. The reason, however, was not so much that Africans rejected full French citizenship as that the metropolitan French would not offer it. The opportunity for independence of federations was within the grasp of the inhabitants of French West Africa, French Equatorial Africa, and Ruanda-Urundi, but in each case the option was declined because the smaller units seemed more manageable and more historically justified.

Another potential unit of political action arose now and again for consideration: the African continent. The ideal of pan-Africanism emerged in the nineteenth century as a broad though vague version of African nationalism. The origins of pan-Africanism lie not in the inherent unity of African peoples, though a defense of pan-Africanism can be made on these grounds. Instead, pan-Africanism owes its existence to the heritage of colonialism and racism which Africans gained from their European rulers.

It was with a pan-African vision that Modibo Keita of Mali and Sékou Touré of Guinea joined Kwame Nkrumah of Ghana in announcing the unions of their three countries in 1962. In the nineteenth century, Germany and Italy had formed great nations out of many small states; perhaps the same would now happen for Africa. This union failed, as did several others. Such failures of pan-Africanism were balanced, however, by the formation and survival of the Organization of African Unity. This organization, for all its weakness, rapidly became the most effective regional body of nations on the globe, with the exception of the European Common Market. If it was ineffective as a gendarme or as an agency of African development, it remained effective as a forum of African opinion and an anchor for the further growth of pan-African consciousness.

The modern African nation, the political instrument for the emancipation of African colonies, faced competitors for the loyalty of its citizens. Within the nation they could look to families and ethnic groups. They could look to social class within the nation or across national boundaries. Or they could look beyond the nation to a pan-African basis of future political identity.

7

Culture and religion, 1940–1985

For two weeks in the spring of 1966, Dakar was the cultural capital of Africa. The First World Festival of African Arts and Culture brought writers, musicians, sculptors, artisans, and *griots* from every corner of Africa to the capital of Senegal on the tip of Cape Verde. President Léopold Senghor, the renowned poet of *négritude*, inaugurated the festivities. Performances, celebrations, lectures, and debates ensued in the conference halls, on the streets, in restaurants, and in the artisanal village of Soumbedioune, constructed at the seaside especially for the festival. African culture had regained its self-confidence, and it was the French-speaking Africans who led in proclaiming its renaissance.

Then the festival came to an end. The artists and writers returned home, and Dakar settled back into its workaday life. The modern achievements of African culture were certainly imposing when the creators were focused into a single location. But the difficulties, the deficiencies, and the crises in African culture re-emerged as the cultural leaders dispersed. Disputes among African artists, while creative in themselves, were also costly. Wole Soyinka, the Nigerian playwright, criticized the notion of *négritude* by noting that a tiger does not have to proclaim his "tigritude."

While colonial rule itself had ended, the spectre of Western cultural discrimination against Africa remained, just as the neocolonial influences of Western corporations and governments continued to constrain the growth of African economies. And, as with neocolonial economic life, some of Africa's cultural oppression was self-inflicted. For instance, after three score years of colonial rule, many Africans continued to respect European uniforms as symbols of authority more than those of their new national governments.

Africans now wanted to express the validity of their culture and their religious beliefs more explicitly than ever. In every area of culture and religion, a debate raged as to the nature of African culture. Was there an essentially African character to the culture of the continent, which was fundamentally different from that of other peoples? Or was African culture but a variant of a more universal human culture? According to the first view, the adoption of European forms and the use of European languages would necessarily undermine the integrity of African culture. In the second view, the adoption of Europeans forms by Africans might permit the formulation of an even more original African culture. Senghor himself was on both sides of this question.

His view of *négritude* was that there existed in blackness a special social quality, but he expressed this outlook in French language of such skill and precision that he was admitted to the French Academy.

In religion, the meanings of Christianity and Islam in Africa were debated in similar terms. Did Christianity make one less African than before? More African than before? Was Islam more African than Christianity? Echoes of the same discussion emerged in music, where Africans adopted new instruments and new forms. The new musical forms, as it happened, came more often from blacks in the Americas than from whites in Europe. Was this yet another means of assimilating Western culture, or was it a means of reinforcing African traditions? Finally, at the ethereal level of philosophy, Africans pondered the question of their existence. Was there such a thing as an African person, an African culture, or an African philosophy? Or were these artificial constructs created out of the minds of Europeans and the structures of colonialism?

The continuing transformations of culture and religion were felt all over the continent, but took some characteristic forms in francophone Africa. The relative backwardness of education in francophone Africa, as compared to anglophone and Arab Africa, was largely overcome in the years after independence. Use of the French language spread along with the expansion of education. Through the medium of French, new trends in popular culture spread across the continent, with Zaire emerging as a major center of innovation. From modest beginnings in early colonial years (when Dahomey was known as the Latin Quarter of West Africa) there emerged an elite francophone culture. In the generation after independence, most francophone African nations produced literary and scholarly writers of importance. One result of their work was the development of a cultural pan-Africanism among francophone writers, which may be contrasted with the contributions of anglophone Africa to political pan-Africanism. In religion, francophone sub-Saharan Africa includes the most heavily Muslim areas of sub-Saharan Africa, and the most heavily Catholic areas, as contrasted with the greater Protestant influence in anglophone Africa.

In this chapter we shall review several aspects of the culture and religion of francophone Africa in the years after 1940. We begin with the dilemma of African identity; Africans at every level of society have faced such a range of identities that their culture has become unique for this reason if for no other. We next turn to the extraordinary changes in African education, and then to the continuing transformation in African religious life. We explore several areas of popular culture, and conclude with an analysis of trends in francophone African literature and scholarship

THE PROBLEM OF AFRICAN IDENTITY

More than most other people in the contemporary world, Africans have found their identity ambiguous, and have found themselves called upon continually to redefine who they are. This problem of identity has made itself felt at all levels of existence: the family, the individual, ethnic group, nation, language, cultural tradition, and race. Which gods to worship? How to name one's children? Which lands to occupy? Which charters to use as the basis for government?

In francophone sub-Saharan Africa the changing focus of nationality illustrates some of the choices in identity. In the French colonies, many leading individuals had chosen the identity of French citizens. This assimilation into the French nation was even conceivable for the French colonies as a whole, following the model of Martinique, Guadeloupe and Guiana in the West Indies; such an option was openly discussed at the end of World War II, and was definitively excluded only with the *loi cadre* of 1956. An African national identity could logically have been focused on the two great federations, French West Africa and French Equatorial Africa, and this seemed most likely in the postwar years – but again, the *loi cadre* removed that option in 1956. The result was that the national identity of the inhabitants of French African colonies was focused on the eight colonies of West Africa, the four colonies of Central Africa, and the two trust territories of Togo and Cameroon.

Meanwhile, between the level of African nationality and that of French nationality, there emerged another plane of identity: the cultural unity shared by francophone Africans. This outlook was created by an elite who shared the background of African culture and the experience of French colonial rule. Although francophone Africa meant little as a political unit in the years after 1960, it grew in importance as a focus of broad cultural identity. In particular, the cultural and political leaders of the former Belgian colonies turned to assimilate themselves and their nations to the notion of francophone Africa.

For the Belgian colonies, the option of Belgian citizenship and assimilation to Belgium was never held out, either for individual Africans or for African territories. Ethnic identity, where it was not already strong, was imposed by the colonial state; the Belgian regime made sure that every inhabitant of the Congo was classified with a tribe. Meanwhile, the Belgian Congo as a whole emerged as an obvious national unit, though separatist tendencies arose within it, particularly in mineral-rich Shaba. There Europeans associated with the mines argued for separation from the centralizing influence of Leopoldville. Ruanda–Urundi, while formally administered as part of the Belgian Congo, never accepted the loss of its territorial identity. Nor did it accept amalgamation of the two kingdoms. Rwanda and Burundi remained two distinct kingdoms with separate colonial administrations, held together at the top by a Belgian government in Bujumbura. The attempts of Belgian and United Nations leaders to achieve a federation of Rwanda and Burundi at independence were rejected by the new national leaders.

For the newly established national units, determination of their territory was not sufficient to establish their identity. Several of the new nations took new names. In 1958 the colony of Ubangi-Shari became the Central African Republic. Prime minister Barthélemy Boganda argued that the colonial name (based on two rivers, both of which ran at the fringe of the country) needed to be replaced by a name more appropriate to the nation's future. (For several later and painful years, 1976–79, the country became the Central African Empire.) In 1960 the French Sudan became the Republic of Mali, as the new nation harked back to the great empire which dominated the western savanna from the thirteenth to the fifteenth centuries. But this was only after the failure of a larger enterprise: a federation of Senegal and Sudan. Other name changes were more subtle but none the less significant; the colony of Mauritania became the Islamic Republic of Mauritania.

Zaire assumed its new name in 1971, at the same time President Mobutu announced the "authenticity" campaign. What had been the Belgian Congo since 1908 and the Democratic Republic of the Congo since 1960 now became Zaire. Bénin assumed its present name in 1975. The military government declared it to be a people's republic, and declared that the name of Dahomey (taken from the old kingdom located in the southern part of the country) needed to be replaced by a name giving equal recognition to people throughout the nation. The new name, Bénin, was chosen not for any reference to the old kingdom of Benin, 300 kilometers to the east in Nigeria, but because the country borders on the great bay known as the Bight of Benin.

A final change of a nation's name reveals further aspects of the struggle for identity. In 1983 Captain Thomas Sankara, the new military leader of Upper Volta (a territory named by the French for the river flowing through it), decreed that the nation was hereafter to be known as Burkina Faso. This term represented a hope for the future rather than a turn toward the past. It was pieced together from the word "Burkina," a Mossi-language word, and the word "Faso" from the Mande language, and it means "the land of the incorruptible." Such a name is unique among modern nations; it not only reflects an intended spirit of reconciliation and national unity among various groups, but builds a moral code into the name of the nation.

This constant reconsideration and redefinition of identity has preoccupied francophone Africa in many more areas than in the naming of nations. Similar searches for identity are reflected in the choices of names of individuals (whether Christian, Muslim, or ancestral African). The same may be seen in choices of dress: whether to wear Western garb, whether to emphasize Muslim traditions of dress, or African dress – or how to mix the three, or how to develop African dress so that it fits the needs of modern society. In language, equivalent choices are whether to pursue the French language, whether to learn English as well, or whether to give primary emphasis to the development of African languages into literary languages. Similar choices arise in art, in literature, and in music.

EDUCATION

Education expanded at a spectacular rate in francophone Africa in the period after World War II, and especially in the years after independence. In 1940 less than 5% of the population of francophone Africa was literate in French (and similar proportions were literate in Arabic and in all other languages); by 1985 nearly 25% of the population of school age and above was literate in French.

State schools accounted for most of the growth in education, though mission schools expanded as well.

After World War II the French and Belgian administrations began responding to the wishes of African parents by supporting the construction of more schools and the hiring of more teachers. The reasons behind this expansion were not only the demand for education, but also the pressures of anti-colonial critics outside Africa, and the administrative desire to modernize the colonies in order to exploit them more effectively. But this initial expansion of schooling, associated as it was with the beginnings of formal African representative government, led to an explosion in the demand for education, and an explosion in the number of students in school. In French West Africa, expenditure on education rose from 3% of the total budget in 1935 to 4% in 1947, and to 13% of a much expanded budget in 1957; the percentage grew further after independence. Togo, Cameroon, Senegal, Congo, and Zaire came close to achieving universal primary education in the 1970s.

In French colonies, instruction was given only in the French language. As a result, those students who made it through secondary school became highly proficient in French; on the other hand, African languages were given no opportunity to develop as literary languages. The contrasts with adjoining British territories were sometimes dramatic. Hausa was written in Nigeria but not in Niger. Yoruba was written in Nigeria but not in Dahomey, Ewe was written in Gold Coast but not in Togo, Mandingo was written in Gambia but not in Senegal or Sudan. In Central Africa, Kikongo and Lingala were written in the Belgian Congo but not in French Congo.

In Belgian colonies, primary school instruction was mostly in African languages. The main languages which emerged were Kikongo in the lower Zaire valley, Lingala in the middle Zaire valley, Kiswahili along the eastern frontier, and Tshiluba in the southeast. In Burundi instruction was in Kirundi, and in Rwanda it was in Kinyarwanda. In one sense these languages emerged because they had already become regional linguae francae (or, in Rwanda and Burundi, the universal language) before the education system was established. In another sense, the division of Belgium into the two language traditions of French and Flemish prevented the imposition of a single European language on the African colonies, and local languages benefitted. French (and in some cases Flemish) became the language of secondary schools only. In fact, since secondary education in the Belgian colonies was primarily religious training, it was sometimes joked that the Congolese students could converse and write better in Latin than they could in French.

In Zaire, the achievement of independence brought an end to the Belgian prohibition on French-language instruction. As a result, literacy in French climbed even more rapidly than the growth of the school population; both parents and children saw French as the language which could bring social mobility. The same period saw the initiation of an opposite trend in former French territories. One by one, they began to implement primary education in local languages, to ensure broader literacy and as a means to protect the national heritage. Guinea was the first of these, but the effort was hurried and insufficiently funded, and had to be given up. The problems involved the delicate matters of deciding which languages (and which dialects of the chosen language) to use in education, and then the practical decisions of the orthography for the language and the preparation of adequate texts. Other countries proceeded more slowly, and by 1985 perhaps a majority of primary education was in African languages, with French introduced at the upper primary level.

In the French colonies, a commonly used text began with the words, "Our ancestors the Gauls were tall and fair." The phrase, often recited by African leaders in the era of decolonization, came to symbolize the cultural imperialism of the French, and the insensitivity to African culture which this entailed. Later on, however, French educators developed a set of readers based on the lives of fictional Senegalese boy and girl, Mamadou and Bineta. Mamadou and Bineta had the adventures of daily life, visited African cities, and even visited France, taking thousands of young African readers with them on imaginary tours.

Schools not only provided technical training and an avenue of social mobility, they also acted to socialize the students. Children were removed from their parents for a substantial portion of each week, and were inculcated with the values of the empire, the church, or the nation. In the Belgian Congo, for instance, the predominance of the Catholic Church in primary education was one of the main reasons why that country became overwhelmingly Catholic. In Leopoldville during the 1940s, the Catholic Church refused to allow confirmation or first communion for girls until they had completed three years of primary school. Since education at that time did more to prepare girls for marriage than for work, very few girls continued school beyond the third year. Eventually the state took a more direct interest in the socialization of the nation's youth, and in 1974 the primary schools of Zaire were placed under state control. By this time many more girls were completing school in order to qualify for work.

Even in the years after independence, education in francophone Africa was severely underfunded and carried on under difficult conditions. In the elementary schools, classes of 60 students were led by a single teacher whose materials were often limited to a single small blackboard; rote learning and stamina were the hallmarks of this education. In 1962 the average primary class size in Brazzaville was 62, and in the Congo countryside it was 66.

Education meant the hope for social mobility. It provided medical, technical, legal, and secretarial training. For many years, those with educations received far higher salaries than those without education. As a result, students and their parents came to expect that education should lead to an equivalent rise in income for all who gain a school certificate. But while the number of graduates rose steadily, the number of jobs did not, especially as economic conditions worsened in the 1970s. Francophone Africa suddenly found itself with many highly educated but unemployed men and women. These difficult conditions, however, served only to heighten popular demand for more and better education.

Secondary education remained restricted to Dakar and Leopoldville until after World War II, and many of the secondary students were European. Exceptions to this rule were to be found in the technical school at Bamako and in religious seminaries. In the postwar years, *lycées* and other secondary schools opened in the major cities of French and Belgian Africa. With independence, secondary enrollment grew rapidly: in Zaire, for instance, from 60,000 students in 1962 to 260,000 students in 1971.

The first universities of francophone Africa opened in 1954: the University of Dakar, operated by the state, and the Lovanium University in Kinshasa, a Catholic institution. In 1956 a state university opened in Lubumbashi, and others opened soon thereafter in Abidjan and Yaoundé. Within a few years of independence, most francophone African countries had universities. (In Zaire, the universities of Louvanium, Lubumbashi, and the Protestant Free University of Kisangani were amalgamated in 1971 into the National University of Zaire, UNAZA; UNAZA was later divided into three universities.) For the first decade after independence, the universities retained their affiliations with European universities, and French and Belgian professors were sent out to give the examinations of advanced students. With time, however, the universities established their independence.

Even at the oldest and strongest of these universities, classes were large, faculty members taught large numbers of classes, and the shortage of books meant that transcribing lectures was the main means by which students learned. The number of strong students which came through this gruelling and chaotic system is a tribute to the imagination and determination of the students.

The existence of universities led rapidly to their assumption of a role of social critic. (This, indeed, had been one of the reasons why universities were not built by the colonial powers.) Thus in 1968, when students in France led a set of demonstrations which were echoed throughout Europe and North America, students at the University of Dakar also led demonstrations in favor of expanded educational opportunity, as well as for an expansion of political rights in Senegal and against the power of French government and foreign firms over Senegal. In later years, governments closed universities in Bénin, Cameroon, Congo, and Zaire in order to bring student agitation to an end.

The great expansion of secular and Christian education in the postwar years put great pressure on Muslim education in francophone Africa. While Qur'anic schools expanded along with the Muslim community, and while higher religious studies expanded at a similar rate, the Muslim nations of francophone Africa found themselves governed by men trained in Western secular schools. To respond to this challenge, Muslim educators turned to institutions created during the colonial era, and created new institutions themselves. The School for Chiefs' Sons, established as a secondary school in the early colonial years in Senegal, was based on an Arabic-language curriculum. By the time of independence it had been expanded and amalgamated into the University of Dakar. The colonial regime gradually set up other Muslim secondary schools or *madrasas*. In the postwar years, private *madrasas* were established in Segou, Jenné, and Timbuktu; with independence, they began adding a broad secondary education to the basic curriculum in Arabic language and religious studies. The most advanced of students from these schools studied at the informal universities of these towns, with the most learned shaykhs. For formal university studies, the students sought to gain admission to al-Azhar University in Cairo.

RELIGION

The religious transformation of Africa continued and even accelerated in the years after 1940. Among the Catholics, the postwar movement toward increased power for Africans meant the admission of Africans to the church hierarchy. Africans became priests in large numbers only during the 1950s, when the first African bishops were appointed, including, for instance, bishop Kimbondo of Kisantu in 1956. But as Africans rose in the hierarchy, the hold of Rome over the African church was strengthened more than it was weakened.

The liberalization of the church associated with Vatican II, the council called by Pope John XXIII in 1964, coincided with a great expansion of Catholicism in Africa. Mass was now to be celebrated in vernacular languages rather than in Latin; this provided an advantage to African priests and especially to African parishioners. In 1972 Pope Paul VI chose to recognize the growing significance of the church in Africa by visiting Uganda, where he celebrated the canonization of the Ugandan martyrs – pages at the court of Kabaka Mwanga of Buganda who were executed in 1886 – who were soon to become saints. Pope John Paul II visited Zaire and Congo in 1980, on the centennial of the second evangelization of the Zaire valley. The teachings of the church in favor of unrestricted childbirth, in opposition to polygyny, and in favor of obedience to the state continued to be influential. European clergy continued to serve in African churches and missions in large numbers. Now, however, the rationale was that the universal church was sending its priests and religious wherever they were needed, rather than that civilized Europe was sending missionaries to convert heathen Africa. In this decolonization of the church, what had been known as missions now became churches, and those who had been apostolic vicars now became bishops.

The Catholic educational system in Africa, as elsewhere, developed students well trained in philosophy. From the early work in African philosophy carried out by a small number of priests, there now came to be a much larger number of religiously trained philosophers whose work went beyond the study of African thought in past times to propose the essentials of an African philosophy for the future. Valentin Mudimbe of Zaire and Paulin Houtondji of Bénin (a Protestant) are the best known of these philosophers.

In contrast to the deep involvement of the Catholic clergy (now dominantly African) in education, church leaders tended to stay away from political activism. (One exception stands out in the first years of independence. Father

Fulbert Youlou became the first president of Congo-Brazzaville, and ruled until he was overthrown in 1963.) In Africa there was little to correspond to the Latin American movement of "liberation theology," in which significant portions of the priesthood adopted a theological alliance of Christianity and Marxism, and a practical participation in social struggles to change or overthrow governments which neglected peasants or the urban masses. The Latin American church had, as a result, significant disputes with the Vatican; the African church, in contrast, remained on good terms with the Vatican.

In Protestant churches, the replacement of missions with churches, and of foreign missionaries with African ministers, proceeded even more rapidly. The Protestant churches responded flexibly to new social pressures as they expanded. The Kimbanguist church in western Zaire, legalized in 1959, grew to a membership of some four million in 1980. This church became a member of the World Council of Churches, and thus came to participate in broader church affairs through a federation, rather than through a hierarchy.

The smaller Protestant churches were no less revealing of changing social and religious patterns. One striking instance is the movement led by Marie Lalou of Ivory Coast. Born in 1915, Marie Lalou was brought up in the tradition of the prophet William Wade Harris. At a certain point, she found that she had received a message from God saying she should no longer have sexual contact with her husband. He remonstrated with her, then unexpectedly died. Her husband's brother then sought to take her as his wife, and she refused. The brother persisted, and he soon died as well. Her fearful community exiled her, but brought her back when she became successful in preaching and healing. She preached against witchcraft and against the forcible marriage of women. She gave her converts holy water, saying that only those who had no thought of malice toward another would survive after drinking it. Then in 1949 the colonial government summoned her to Abidjan for questioning. When she was released, it appeared to confirm the validity of her mission, and her church grew greatly in numbers until her death in 1951.

The missionary work of Muslims continued unabated through the middle years of the twentieth century. Yet as it expanded in Africa, Islam struggled to accommodate with modernism. This struggle had become explicit during the nineteenth century, when Muslim scholars in Syria, Palestine, and Egypt sought to argue that the technical backwardness of Muslims, as compared with European Christians, was an accident of history rather than an inherent deficiency in the religion and society of Islam. They argued that Islam was consistent with a scientific view of the world, perhaps more so than Christianity. Echoes of this debate rang throughout francophone Africa. Missionaries argued that Islam provided not only a true vision of the will of God, but a means to social advance on an individual and group basis.

At least until independence, however, the lack of state support for Muslim institutions in francophone sub-Saharan Africa meant that Qur'anic schools were not the equivalent of French-language schools. Pilgrimages, informal academies of saints, and Qur'anic schools spreading literacy in Arabic, held the Muslim community together and gave it contacts with the rest of the

Muslim world. Economic communities, notably the Mourides in Senegal, provided examples of successful Muslim response to challenges of the twentieth century. But African Muslims, chastened by colonial rulers early in the century, dared not talk of state power until independence was assured.

A Muslim renaissance in northern Africa during the 1950s opened new prospects for their co-religionists south of the Sahara. Gamal Abdel Nasser came to power in Egypt in 1952, an effective spokesman for Arab nationalism and for Arab socialism, and at the same time a proponent of pan-Africanism. The strength of Nasser's appeal was one of the reasons Britain granted independence to Sudan in 1955. The independence of Libya from Italian rule in 1951 was of special importance for Chad to its south, a region with which Libya had strong historic ties. The war for Algerian liberation began in 1954 and, supported strongly by Nasser's Egypt, continued until its victory in 1962. Meanwhile, Morocco and Tunisia gained independence in 1956.

With the independence of sub-Saharan Africa, six states had Muslim majorities (Senegal, Mauritania, Mali, Guinea, Niger, and Chad) and six more had large Muslim minorities (Burkina Faso, Ivory Caost, Togo, Bénin, Cameroon, and Central African Republic).

All of this political change, however, represented secular nationalism among African Muslims. A new trend emerged in the 1970s and grew in strength during the 1980s: militant Islam with a national coloring. This vision first gained strength among the Shi'ite Muslims of Iran who led a successful revolutionary movement against the American-backed Shah. Of the many groups and outlooks participating in that evolution, the day was carried by a fundamentalist approach which called, on the one hand, for a back-to-the-Qur'an approach in legal and social affairs, but pursued, on the other hand, the use of the most modern political and technological approaches. Ayatollah Khomeini spread his word to the Iranian public by means of tape cassettes.

This Islamic fundamentalism tended to bring a diminution in the status of women, and the attempt to govern on the basis of the shari'a (Muslim religious law) presented some problems in commercial affairs. Its uncompromising approach was both a strength and a weakness; it increased the enthusiasm of its followers, but it brought conflict with those who were not believers or enthusiasts. Muslims in sub-Saharan Africa were a bit slow to adopt this fundamentalist vision – as measured, for instance, by the veiling of women – but it still had its effect. Young people in most of the Muslim countries began to study their Qur'ans with more seriousness.

While Islam and Christianity have come to dominate the religious beliefs of modern Africans, the traditional religions have by no means lost their influence. In some areas the old religions have remained strong, not only by reaffirmation of the ancient beliefs, as in the case of the Dogon people of the hills of Mali, but also by adapting themselves to become relevant to the twentieth century.

Such is the case of the Bwiti cult of the Fang people of Gabon. It originated at the beginning of the twentieth century in reaction against earlier Fang religions, and later grew to prominence. Many Fang, after two generations of

Christian evangelization during which they always preferred the Old Testament to the New Testament, turned late in the colonial era to seek new sustenance from African beliefs. The ritual of the cult centers on all-night dances led by touring dance troupes, but its purpose is to bring the past and present into coexistence in a stable, imagined microcosm. Through dance and imagination, the celebrants of Bwiti seek to resolve the conflicts brought by money-mindedness, divorce, witchcraft, and generation gaps. The followers of Bwiti are urged to show love for others and to give mutual aid. Four injunctions were brought back from the grave by the founder of one branch of Bwiti:

> You shall not eat of men.
> You shall not keep the bones of men.
> You shall not go out in sorcery.
> You shall not steal others' belongings.

The first two injunctions refer to rejection of former Fang ancestor worship; the last two refer to the social conflicts which grew up under colonialism. Those who dance seek to achieve a state of moral cleanliness achieved with the aid of the ancestors, and hope to open up the potentialities of their personality. This religion is similar in some of its beliefs to variants of modern African Christianity and Islam. Yet it leads its believers not to the joining of a community of all mankind through universal religion, but to creation of an autonomous microcosm within Fang society.

The traditional religions of the Aja-Ewe peoples and Yoruba peoples of Togo and Benin, known by their generic terms for god, *vodoun* and *orisha*, demonstrated their continued strength and adaptability in another context. They remained widely celebrated by New World people of African descent in Brazil and the Caribbean, people who went from African life, through slavery, into the industrial life. In Togo and Benin as well, the gods took on new responsibilities. The Yoruba god Ogun, the god of iron and war, became the god of the highways.

Even where the old religions were formally replaced or absorbed by Christianity and Islam, their philosophy, their cosmology, and their institutions continued to be influential. This is seen on a trivial level by the retention of beliefs in magic and sorcery. At a more sophisticated level, the belief in fate among peoples of the Central Sudan made its weight felt in modern interpretations of society. In the novel *Princesse Mandapu*, author Makombo Bamboté of Central African Republic leads the reader to believe that when the princess dies in an accident, her death must still have a wider meaning that can be understood.

Aside from the developments in individual religious traditions, the diversity of African religious life was an important influence in itself. A few francophone African nations were dominated by a single religious belief (Muslim Mauritania, Senegal, Guinea and Niger) but in most cases contending religious traditions had to learn to coexist. In a world where Christians and Muslims have come into fundamental and antagonistic conflict, one may ask whether it has fallen to the African nations to work out the basis for a new religious tolerance.

Popular culture blossomed in francophone sub-Saharan Africa in the optimistic years leading up to independence and in the early years of independence. Even with the difficulties and disillusionments of the 1970s and 1980s, popular culture continued to develop.

One of the most successful forms of popular music has been the music of Zaire. This music had its origins in cabaret music which can be traced back to the 1940s and 1930s, and perhaps earlier. Night clubs grew up in the towns of the Belgian Congo. In the mining town of Elisabethville, they drew on the musical and dance traditions developed around the mines of southern Africa. In the administrative towns of Leopoldville and Boma, they drew on American jazz, Cuban rumba, and West African highlife. There and in commercial towns such as Kasongo, small groups of musicians played a mixture of European and African instruments, and composed songs drawn eclectically on music of the rural areas, but which romantically or humorously portrayed life in the towns. In the 1940s and 1950s some of these groups were recorded, and they began to have a regional reputation. As phonographs became available, listeners became acquainted with a wider range of music: dance music from the United States, calypso from the West Indies, and popular music of Brazil. In all of these New World traditions on which Zairian musicians drew, there had been significant contributions in earlier centuries by people of West Africa and Central Africa, so that the Zairians were in a sense drawing on a revised version of their own musical tradition.

By the 1950s the technology of portable amplification and recording had developed to the point where the music industry took off in Zaire. Instrumentation came to focus on electric guitars, percussion, and brass instruments. Franco emerged in the 1950s as Zaire's leading musician and songwriter, and he was followed by Rochereau. (With Zaire's "authenticity" campaign of the 1970s they became Luambo Makiadi and Tabu Ley.) With words in Lingala and French, and with a beat that owed much to the polkas which had been taken over by Mexican *mariachi* bands and then modified in Cuba and elsewhere in the West Indies, these musicians produced dozens of records which were played all over Africa, though particularly in francophone countries.

With the expansion in African ownership of phonographs, tape players, and radios, there developed a cosmopolitan African popular music. This music developed very much in contact with music of the African diaspora – black American musicians such as Louis Armstrong and later Jimi Hendrix were well known in Africa – but also developed and retained its own characteristics. While the high-life music of Ghana was the first step in the creation of this cosmopolitan African popular music, the musicians of Zaire soon overtook those of Ghana as those with the largest record sales.

Development of this visible, cosmopolitan popular culture did not, however, mean the end to local traditions of popular culture. Local traditions of song, dance, and storytelling did suffer, as more people moved to the cities, or as other traditions were brought in by people returning from the cities. But the development of national radio networks provided a means by which local culture could be reinforced as well as undermined. Radio in francophone Africa was state-run, whether in the colonial era or since, and state officials set limits on what could be broadcast. Nevertheless, beginning in the 1950s state radio systems began broadcasting in several languages, and began programs in which stories and music of various regions and ethnic groups were broadcast. Ivory Coast was one of the countries to organize regional broadcasts from the 1950s, as part of Houphouët-Boigny's policy of seeking to draw the nation together under the umbrella of his political party, the PDCI.

Dance underwent a transformation conditioned by the changing social and political structures of francophone Africa. The rural state and lineage structures which supported dance in precolonial years weakened with time, though social dances continued in the countryside. Dance in the urban areas was social dance, heavily influenced by the growing cosmopolitan culture. But the rise of new African states brought state support for dance on a new level; school children were called upon to perform dances, and some national dance troupes were formed. The most successful of the national dance troupes was the *Ballets africains de Guinée*. This troupe, organized and directed by Fodéba Keita, brought traditional dance of Guinea, full of great acrobatic leaps, to stages around the world in the 1960s and 1970s. In political terms, this dance troupe was a statement of the validity of African culture and an attempt to maintain contact with Western countries and African countries by the regime of Sékou Touré, which was in other ways isolated by the aftermath of its bitter separation from France in 1958. In cultural terms, it was a contribution to the elaboration of a cosmopolitan African culture, though one which lapsed because of the financial stringencies of Guinea, and which has not been followed up.

The plastic arts, especially wood sculpture, soared in their output and in their appeal. In the years after independence there developed an international market for African art, and also a cosmopolitan African market. The peoples who led in wood sculpture early in the century continued to lead: the Senufo of Ivory Caost, the Yoruba of Bénin and Nigeria, the Kuba of Zaire, the Fang of Gabon. But now, in addition to selling in their local areas, they were connected by networks of salesmen criss-crossing the continent, then flying to Paris, Marseille, and later New York. One example is the network selling butterfly portraits made in Central African Republic. In these portraits, multi-colored butterfly wings were fastened to black felt to form a portrait of, for instance, a woman carrying a basket on her head. A network of hawkers flew from Bangui to each of the airports of West and Central Africa and on to the cities of the North Atlantic, displaying the portraits for sale. Not all groups of African artisans sought to participate in this network. The artisans of Abomey in Bénin – brass sculptors, carvers, and weavers – resolutely held on to the sale of their own wares, which could only rarely be bought outside of Bénin.

The growth of a Western market for African art resulted in the purchase of much of these and other works. In the elite portion of this market, American and European shopkeepers made visits to African countries, purchasing loads of art work, and carried them home for sale. African countries soon found that, while the export of art work provided foreign exchange, the loss of so much art work was a threat to their national heritage. The result was new restrictions on exports, and then new patterns of bribery as exports continued. In the tourist art portion of the market, sculptures were sold both in small quantities by African merchants, and in large quantities through Western buyers.

While this large export art market was of great significance in determining the nature of African art production, of greater interest to us here is the African market for African art. The rural market for sculpture and other art forms had long existed, and people in one area continued to buy pieces made in other areas. In the cities, painters and decorators had begun to create and sell innovative works as early as the 1920s. By the time of independence, wage workers as well as influential bureaucrats bought sculptures, paintings, basketry, and cloth to decorate their homes. This cosmopolitan, urban African market for art established the values and set the tone for the artistic standard of modern Africa.

In contrast to expression in sculpture, for which the production and purchase allowed maximum freedom of choice and expression, the press in francophone Africa was severely restricted. In the whole history of francophone Africa, lively journalism was permitted only in a few times and places: Dahomey and Senegal in the 1930s, and French West Africa generally in the 1950s. Otherwise, the only free journalistic expression came from newspapers published in Europe or elsewhere, and in many cases possession of these newspapers was illegal in Africa. Senegal remained a country in which there were several newspapers, which carried on critical political commentary. Otherwise, the regimes of independent francophone Africa permitted only official newspapers, which were concise the lacking in features appealing to popular audiences.

For this reason, the most popular sources of written news in francophone Africa were news magazines published in France and North Africa. *Jeune Afrique* (Young Africa), created in Tunisia in 1960 and published thereafter in Paris, was consistently the leading such news magazine. It provided political commentary from a moderate socialist viewpoint, lots of photos, and coverage on all of Africa, though with emphasis on francophone Africa. The wide circulation of this and other news magazines did more than perhaps anything else to keep alive the ideal of pan-Africanism through the decades of the 1970s and 1980s in which Africans experienced disunity in so many areas.

Reporting on entertainers and on sports was also an important aspect of *Jeune Afrique*. Sports in particular became a passion of Africans involved in the cosmopolitan culture. First among the African sports was football (soccer) which African boys played on every lot available in city and countryside. National teams were pitted against each other in the African Cup; Cameroon and Mali were among the strongest teams. Sports were attached to another and more gruesome public issue: mortality on the highways. Sports figures, since they were always on the road, were more exposed than most to the dangers of travel on African highways. The combination of poorly maintained roads and poorly maintained automobiles meant a high potential for accidents. In 1967 *Jeune Afrique* and *Bingo* each had covers with photos of over a dozen leading sports figures who had died in automobile accidents.

Cinema first came to African cities in the interwar years, and the number of theaters became significant in the 1950s. French and American films were widely viewed and, as elsewhere, their heroes and their symbolism worked their way into popular culture. After independence, African film makers began to enter the market, first with documentaries and brief experimental films, and then with feature films. Ousmane Sembène, whose novel *God's Bits of Wood* provides a moving analysis of the social changes brought by the 1947 railroad strike in Senegal and Sudan, became better known as Africa's leading film maker. Between 1963 and 1976 he produced nine films in French, Wolof, and Diola languages. The films portray tragic situations ranging from contemporary neocolonialism (as in *Black Girl*) to historical tragedies (as in *Ceddo*). In *Emitai* he chronicles the 1942 revolt of a Diola village in Senegal precipitated by a decision of the women to hide their rice from French officials who had come to requisition it. Sembène films were sometimes banned, as they emphasized contradictions within African society as well as criticizing the impact of colonial rule. The films were made simply, but with a remarkable unity. Sembène once noted that the African film maker, working with such a low budget, necessarily had control over each step in production.

In 1969 a group of West African film makers held a small film festival in Ouagadougou, and then decided to repeat the experience. By the time of the third festival in 1971, 30 films from 17 countries were screened before audiences totaling 100,000, and Upper Volta had become the film capital of francophone Africa. The festival, known as FESPACO, became a regular biannual affair, and stimulated a growing film industry centered on Ouagadougou.

In each of the above areas, one may see the development of a lively and diverse popular culture. The diversity is part of the achievement, yet it seemed clear that the peoples of francophone Africa were working toward the creation of a more coherent and more well-defined national culture, as well as the development of a cosmopolitan African culture. The examples of dress and hair style may serve to reinforce this. A walk through the streets of Dakar revealed a remarkable array of styles of dress, mixtures of old Senegalese dress, modern European dress, and dress borrowed from black Americans. Who was to say which would triumph? In Zaire, President Mobutu decided to leave nothing to chance, and in his authenticity campaign decreed that no Zairois should wear Western clothes or straighten their hair in Western style.

LITERARY AND SCHOLARLY ENDEAVOR

In December 1947 appeared the first issue of *Présence Africaine*, the literary and critical journal which, from that time forth, was to reflect the cutting edge of francophone African thought. It appeared simultaneously in Paris and Dakar. Léopold Sédar Senghor of Senegal was its founder, and Alioune Diop, also Senegalese, was its editor-in-chief. Diop declared its purpose to be to "explain the originality of Africa and hasten its appearance in the world."

In literary terms, *Présence Africaine* launched the movement of *négritude*. Senghor and Aimé Césaire, the Martinican lawyer and writer, had done the groundwork for this movement with their Paris writings in the 1930s, and now they could proclaim to a wider and more receptive audience the beauty of blackness and the eternal strength of Mother Africa. In political terms, *Présence Africaine* was an organ for the critique of colonialism and for the rehabilitation and organization of Africans.

This combination of literary, scholarly, and political endeavor was embodied in the person of Senghor, who was elected in 1945 to the Constituent Assembly and then to the National Assembly, yet who pursued his literary efforts along with his political work. The appearance of *Présence Africaine* was a logical consequence of his situation. As a delegate, he lived most of the time in Paris. The same was true for Aimé Césaire, also a writer and a delegate, and for others of the contributors to the journal. At the same time, the appearance of *Présence Africaine* in Paris also enabled the journal to benefit from the support and the writings of leading French intellectuals and writers, such as André Gide, Jean-Paul Sartre, Albert Camus, and Georges Balandier.

In 1955 Alioune Diop founded the *Société Africaine de Culture*, an extension of the journal which organized conferences of black writers. The high point of his years of writing and organizing was the first Black World Festival of Arts, held in Dakar in 1966. This festival brought together writers and artists from all over Africa, and from New World countries from Brazil to Canada. (A second such festival, known as "Festac," was held in Lagos in 1977 and a third festival was held in Dakar in 1984.) *Présence Africaine* retained its bookstore near the Sorbonne in Paris, and opened a publishing house which published many important African literary works. With the success of this publishing house, other presses opened up, in Africa and Europe, specializing in African literature; in addition, African writers gained access to the more prominent French publishers.

The contents of *Présence Africaine* reveal the expanding scope of the francophone African intellectual community. In the early years, contributions were limited to those from West Africa, from the West Indies, and from France. With time, contributions from French Equatorial Africa began to appear. Contributions in English also began to appear, written primarily by black American authors. In the 1960s, contributions from Zaire began to appear. Thus, francophone sub-Saharan Africa expanded in the postwar years to include all the French and Belgian territories; at the same time, the francophone vision expanded to include English-speaking Africans and English-

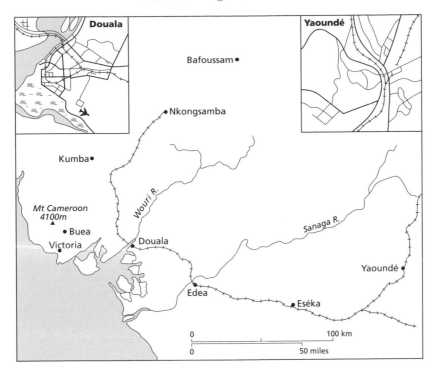

Map 12   Southern Cameroon, 1980

speaking Afro-Americans. Its mission was therefore a multiple one: French-speaking Africans, at the minimum, but people of African descent at the maximum.

The wide reception and critical acclaim for Senghor's poetry gave him the position of prominence in the literary movement, but many other distinguished writers entered the scene. Olympe Bhely-Quénum of Bénin wrote poetry and short stories of his home country. Camara Laye of Guinea wrote an autobiographical story of his youth, *Dark Child*, which portrayed village life as a gentle upbringing. The Guinean writer D. T. Niane translated the Mandingo epic, *Sundiata*, into French. This heroic story of the foundation of the great medieval empire of Mali, as presented in a concise and attractive French version, was adopted into the heritage of students throughout francophone Africa.

The best-known writer from Central Africa was Mongo Beti of Cameroon. His early novels, written in the 1950s, provide a playful yet insightful view of the conflicts in a decolonizing society. *Mission to Kala* does so in hilarious fashion from a young adult's point of view. With the frustration and defeat of the UPC movement for Cameroonian independence, Mongo Beti moved into exile in France and into bitter criticism of the Ahidjo regime. His *Remember Ruben* (after Ruben Um Nyobe) and *Perpetua* document the days of the *maquis* and its aftermath.

Of the many scholars who emerged in the francophone African tradition, two are particularly worthy of mention. Cheikh Anta Diop of Senegal devoted a lifetime of linguistic and archaeological research to demonstrating the links of ancient Egypt to African civilization. His work held out great hope to many in Africa who saw in it the rehabilitation of African culture, and who saw in his erudition the model for future African scholars. On the other hand, his analysis of the unity of Egyptian civilization with that of the Western Sudan remained deeply controversial for methodological reasons. Meanwhile, Cheikh Anta Diop also wrote in favor of the federation of all African states into a great union (he thought this was consistent with his analysis of ancient times) and these views too were widely approved by francophone African intellectuals.

The other key intellectual was not African by birth but West Indian. Frantz Fanon, born in Martinique, was trained in France as a psychiatrist and worked in Algeria during the war for Algerian independence. He eventually joined the Algerians as editor of the FLN newspaper. His writings began with the psychology of persons in the colonial situation, and turned gradually toward the political economy of decolonization. He traveled widely in Africa, and his analysis became central to francophone analysis of politics. His last book, *Wretched of the Earth*, was a strident call for peasant-led national liberation movements, and a deeply critical analysis of what he conceived to be the weakness and negative influence of the African bourgeoisie.

The distinctions in the views of Fanon and Cheikh Anta Diop were reflected in a debate over African philosophy which opened up at the end of the 1970s. Paulin Hountoundji and Valentin Mudimbe each argued that ancestral African philosophy and thought had no inherently unique qualities. They characterized as "ethnophilosophy" the search for essential African beliefs, and they argued instead that Africa had been "invented" as a result of the colonial experience. Their view, analogous to that of Fanon, was that Africa gained its uniqueness and its identity out of the struggles of the modern world. Pathé Diagne of Senegal responded by labelling their view as "Europhilosophy," and he reaffirmed the viewpoint of Cheikh Anta Diop, as explored through documents from ancient Egypt, that African thought has had systematic patterns over a long time. The debate continues in an effort to elucidate the nature of African identity.

FRANCOPHONE AFRICAN CULTURE

Through the development of a wide range of cultural forms, the people of francophone sub-Saharan Africa had by 1985 taken many steps toward achieving a new cultural synthesis. The emergent francophone African culture worked through the medium of the French language, it facilitated the development and the communication of numerous national traditions, it emphasized the commonality of all in a cosmopolitan francophone African culture, and it reinforced a broader pan-African identity which extended to all of Africa and to the African diaspora in the New World and, increasingly, in Europe.

There remained, however, great gaps and tensions within this emergent culture. The greatest gap was between elite culture and local popular cultures, corresponding to the immense social distance between rural isolation and deprivation and the jet-setting of the wealthy and powerful. The formation of national cultures or of a supra-national francophone African culture was hindered by the fact that, even in 1985, only a minority of the inhabitants of francophone Africa were French speakers, and hindered further by the fact that the French language still bore the stamp of the colonial heritage. Radio and television in many African countries included significant programming taken directly from France.

Yet this unevenness – these cultural tensions – need not be seen as evidence of cultural incompleteness. The ambiguity of identity, the mixture of languages, the economic systems beyond the control of the national state – all these elements of francophone African culture reflected the realities of life in the mid twentieth century perhaps more realistically than did the national cultures of the well-established North Atlantic nations, whose world views were held within national constraints more appropriate to the nineteenth century than to the global nature of twentieth-century society. Thus francophone African culture, itself still evolving in directions as yet undetermined, became a culture of such strength that its appeal spread beyond the borders of the African continent, and began to offer contributions to a more universal view of humanity.

8

Democracy and dependence, 1985–1995

The seven previous chapters of this volume address African encounters with colonialism up to 1985. They narrate the creation of a modern African culture from the interplay of African cultural heritage and European colonial tradition. In turning now to the years after 1985, we find colonialism fading from its prior position as the dominant factor in African experience. To interpret recent years we must add a level of complexity, and address not only the creation but also the evolution of modern Africa. In its evolution, modern African culture draws on the contemporary influences of its own nascent traditions and on the global forces emanating from every continent, while continuing to draw on the historical influences of its African and colonial roots.

This interplay of factors yielded complex sources of change. By 1985, for instance, the leaders of African nations had exercised formal responsibility for nearly a generation, so that their own patterns and proclivities became factors in determining the African future, though the colonial heritage remained visible everywhere. New ethnic conflict burst forth in Burundi and Rwanda, while old rivalries separated ethnic groups in Senegal and Mauritania. The economic stagnation of the 1980s reflected the failures of African governments, both socialist and liberal in political persuasion, but also the failures of international organizations and great-power allies to bring relief to African economies. Even among global influences, it is useful to distinguish between the continuing heritage of colonialisms and newer global factors. The former included the special relationships between France, Belgium and African nations, and also the remnants of racism; the latter included the Cold War and its demise, global economic restructuring, democratization movements, and global cultural trends. To repeat, the dual heritage of colonialism and the African past had now to share the spotlight with evolving African traditions and with new global developments.

In the political turmoil of the early 1990s, francophone Africans widely adopted a terminology which divided public affairs into the arenas of the state (or "the power") and "civil society." Governments faced narrowing bases of popular support, declining fiscal resources and increasing pressures from international organizations. Governing elites lost their recognition as the rightful leadership of the nation, and came to be seen as distinct interest groups seeking only to retain power. As African governments developed their own patterns, so too did civil society. Circumstances varied from nation to nation – from a relative stability in Ivory Coast to wild fluctuations in the insurrections of Chad – but certain overall patterns emerged throughout the region. The new patterns of civil society included the dominance of urban areas in national affairs, the growth in numbers and social significance of young people, the forceful demands for more public services as these services contracted because of economic stagnation, and the rising assertiveness of skilled and self-conscious professionals.

This chapter, in surveying the period from 1985 to 1995, focuses on government. The government of African nations became an increasingly complex and contentious issue. In francophone Africa, as elsewhere on the continent, many people became impatient with their leaders and with each other during the 1980s. One novelist, Amadou Ousmane, expressed this impatience in his title, "15 ans ça suffit!" – "Fifteen years is enough!" – in a tale criticizing the corrupt and ineffective government of an imaginary country in the West African sahel.

The institutions and rules of African politics remained in flux: the search for legitimacy and legality as well as order led to numerous experiments. These experiments, however, failed to bring to an end either domestic coercion or foreign interference. Those impatient for political reform in Africa could look in various directions for solutions. Dissatisfied soldiers could mount military coups; urban and rural civilians could hold public demonstrations; insurgent groups could organize military insurrections. Newspapers, conferences and elections might also be useful tools for political reform, but governments tended to restrict such means of free expression. Governments in power occasionally took proactive measures, cultivating constituencies within the country, but generally utilized defensive and negative means to retain power: they manipulated the constitution, appealed to constituencies outside the country, and used coercive force. Still, those in power had occasionally to learn when to give it up.

This chapter emphasizes a narrative of political contestation. To lay the groundwork for this story of political debate, we explore only certain aspects of socio-economic and cultural affairs. In particular, we will focus on the social transformations, changes in cultural identity, and economic difficulties for all of Africa, and the specific form of those changes in francophone African countries. For instance, the general decline of African public institutions – schools, health facilities, highways – served to weaken African social fabrics during the 1980s. As it became more and more clear that independence had not solved Africa's economic problems, the pressures on governments became more and more severe. Some developments seemed positive: cities grew dramatically; microelectronic technology advanced in key sectors of the economy; domestic agriculture bounced back even as agricultural exports suffered; and the incidence of malaria declined significantly. An accounting of such ameliorations seemed insufficient, however, to people who were conscious of the arbitrary powers of police, the limits on health facilities, and the blockages in education. For those who had gained education, employment became rare and salaries even rarer. Skills and ambitions had grown greatly since independence, but opportunities ceased to expand.

In cultural affairs, the continuing search for an identity led to thoughtful critiques and to contending statements of national, francophone and pan-African identity. This volume has used the term "francophone sub-Saharan Africa" to refer to the region under study from 1880. It was only in the 1980s, however, that people in the French-speaking African countries began commonly to describe themselves and their countries as "francophone." Use of the term had been cultivated from the 1960s in French diplomatic and cultural circles, and with the aid of such leaders as Leopold Senghor of Senegal, Habib Bourguiba of Tunisia, and francophone political figures in Quebec. African leaders began to adopt the term, thinking partly of links to France and to a global community through the French language, but thinking also of pan-African politics, and of allying francophone nations to build strength in dealing with the more populous and wealthier anglophone African countries. In the 1980s, as Africans outside of government adopted the term "francophone" to refer to themselves and their nations, they used it to refer to links among themselves rather than with France. The francophone movement thus became both an exercise in neocolonialism and a framework for democratic and pan-African aspiration. In both these guises, it was to provide a springboard for efforts at political reform.

The pressures building up within francophone Africa for political reform grew steadily more substantial, until they burst forth with great transformative power at the turn of the 1990s. Political change in francophone Africa provided an important chapter in the global wave of democratization movements, and the francophone African countries contributed a particular form for those movements – a series of national conferences. These conferences stemmed from local and international roots, they brought new governments to several countries, and they introduced a new vocabulary of politics to all of francophone Africa. The democratization movements brought declarations of new rights, especially for freedom of expression and multiparty politics.

By 1993, in Africa as on other continents, the democratization movements had encountered numerous frustrations. In Togo and Zaire, the national conferences lost their momentum, and dictatorial presidents reaffirmed their powers. And in the highland nations of Rwanda and Burundi, movements for multi-party government collided with military power and with militias breathing the fire of ethnic exclusivism. The hopes for national reconciliation met frustration, and the results turned to assassination, murder and genocide.

Poverty and stagnation, while shared widely throughout Africa and the world, did not suffice to determine the character of people's lives. In the nations of francophone Africa these common problems fit into a particular institutional and cultural framework. French-language education systems, government bureaucracies patterned on French models, the continued tutelage of France herself, and the common cosmopolitan culture of francophone Africa all served to keep the political developments of francophone African countries in close interaction with each other. Thus, on the one hand, frustrated ambitions of an increasingly well educated and well informed citizenry ran headlong into confrontation with penurious authority as salaries simply ceased to be paid to schoolteachers, government officials, and even soldiers. On the other hand, at the end of the 1980s, independent newspapers burst irrepressibly onto the streets of francophone African cities, from which they had been absent except for a brief time just before and after independence.

ECONOMIC STAGNATION, SOCIAL TRANSFORMATION

In the early 1970s, the world economy came to the end of an extraordinary period of growth stretching over nearly three decades. Asian economies continued to grow thereafter, but African countries came, one by one, to the end of an era of rising incomes, improved health conditions, and expanded literacy and educational opportunity. That juncture was marked by sharp rises in oil prices, which served as a harbinger for a period of price inflation and of high interest rates.

The promises of postwar governments – in Africa and elsewhere, whether dictatorial or democratic – focused on economic development. Economic growth in Africa came to a virtual halt in the 1970s, but economic transformation continued. Urbanization, the crisis and decline of state-run enterprise, and continued technical change were three major examples of the changes that accelerated after 1985, though in an atmosphere of overall stagnation. That this was a general decline of African economies, not just a series of responses to ineffective leadership, became clear as even the Ivory Coast economic miracle came to an end.

African economies were marginalized in the world economy, then put into receivership. As national economic planning ministries progressively lost even the illusion of control, international structures assumed a growing role in African economic policy. The World Bank and the International Monetary Fund, with offices and economists based in Washington, D.C., combined to impose "structural adjustment" programs on debtor nations, requiring the dismantling and privatization of public enterprises. Programs of public investment, which had previously been touted as wise investment in infrastructure, were now labelled by travelling experts as causes of social disaster. The attack on public investment came partly because of corruption in government service and public enterprise, and also because the interest rates on current and previous debt became so high that payments went entirely to debt service and not to retiring the principal. Structural adjustment programs focused mainly on cutting back government expenditure through layoffs of public servants, salary cuts for those still employed, and privatization of government-owned enterprises. In the short run, the main benefits of these economic reforms were to increase the flow of funds to the holders of African debts, and their main problems were in increasing African economic hardship.

The longer-run benefits of these programs were slow to emerge, with the result that the World Bank and the IMF became exceedingly unpopular among African publics. An outstanding example of this sentiment came with the protests of Zaire against Belgium and the IMF in 1987-88. President Mobutu, acting more as opportunist than as nationalist, saw hope of rebuilding his sagging popularity by refusing to pay the obligations required of Zaire in its loan agreements. The results, because of Zaire's mineral wealth, included a new series of delays of payments. Still, this conflict revealed the changing relations among African nations, the IMF and World Bank, and transnational firms.

The monetary changes of francophone Africa further demonstrated the pattern of transformation without development. The monetary system of Zaire struggled with disaster from the early 1980s. The national bank continued to finance its debt by inflationary measures, and the currency moved steadily toward worthlessness: from carrying bags of currency in the late 1980s, citizens moved in the early 1990s to preferring the currency of its neighbors, especially the CFA countries.

In Congo and the other countries of the CFA bloc, mere membership in a stable currency union was insufficient to protect them against monetary crisis. Insufficient liquid funds were circulated by the central banks, and commercial banks simply closed their doors. Benin in 1990, for instance, had no regularly functioning banks, though it had an active cadre of informal money-changers. Rumors of devaluation of the CFA franc circulated for years, but no action took place until the death of Felix Houphouet-Boigny in December of 1993. Within a month the board of directors of the central bank (still dominated by France) announced a devaluation of the CFA franc by 50 percent, which lowered the cost of African goods on world markets, but increased the cost of imported goods in CFA countries.

Agricultural exports lost ground steadily in world markets, and peasants fled the countryside in search of better chances. Domestic agricultural markets showed signs of improvement, as some of the remaining farmers fed the burgeoning cities. But the lack of real opportunities in the cities led to the development of new urban crises. Governments lacked resources more than ever. Public services such as road repair came to a halt, and the growing heaps of garbage – reinforced by the appearance of plastic packaging – lay unattended except by scavengers.

Even in these difficult times, not all economic change was negative. The "informal economy" – the activities of small scale entrepreneurs, opportunists, thieves, and others operating beyond the law and standard business procedure – became more and more essential to the achievement of any economic transaction. Even schooling came to be conducted by informal teachers. The cities of francophone Africa grew into major metropoli in precisely this period. Somehow streets, waste disposal, fuel, electricity, water, transportation and schools appeared for the millions inhabiting these bustling cities.

From the 1980s the cities became truly the hubs of African life, though not necessarily centers of optimism. Kinshasa and Abidjan, at five and four million inhabitants the metropoli of francophone Central and West Africa, respectively, were now accompanied by other cities of more than a million in population: Dakar, Lubumbashi, Yaoundé, Douala, and Mbuji-Mayi. To these were added nearly a score of urban areas with populations of over half a million by 1995: Bamako, Bangui, Brazzaville, Bujumbura, Conakry, Cotonou, Kigali, Kisangani, Lomé, Ndjamena, Niamey, Ouagadougou, Pointe Noire, and even Nouakchott in the Mauritanian desert.

With the colonial frontiers lifted, new economic connections arose between neighbors. Thus, Benin returned to modest economic growth by acting as an entrepot for trade with Nigeria. Nigerian plastics and petroleum products went to Benin and the west; imported goods from Europe, America and Asia came into Cotonou, and passed imperceptibly across the border to Nigeria. Since most such trade was illegal, this represented the informal economy at the international level. And the key determinant of economic growth in Benin was not whether its government followed the structural adjustment policy of the World Bank, but whether the border with Nigeria was open.

Families in cities and countryside underwent great pressures in these times. In Mauritania, the drought of the 1980s drove people to the city so that Nouakchott, created as a tiny administrative center with its back to the sea, grew to over 600,000 by 1990, a third of the population of the country. Children became partially or fully cut off from their families through the death or divorce of parents, through migration, or through neglect and alienation in large families. They gathered near movie theaters, supermarkets, or transport centers. Groups of such children, from perhaps six years of age on up, lived partly by theft, partly by working in small trades, and largely by sharing meager resources among themselves. Some maintained contact with parents, others did not.

In the confusion of the city, street children could become indistinguishable from those who had families. The children in Quranic schools, after reciting their lessons by rote in Arabic, were expected by custom to beg in the streets for the cost of their meals. The children sent to state schools, who sat in classes with most of a hundred students, reciting by rote in French, might easily slip off their uniforms in alienation, so that the three groups of children could become confounded. Street children, even living impoverished in Nouakchott, managed to find drugs for momentary relief from the pain of their existence. Prostitution, not uncommonly, provided the funds for their downward cycle. After years of such existence, some of these children expired in one disaster or another, while others managed to take up more normal lives.

The informal solidarity of street children was but one example of the ways in whch urban and rural groups sustained organizations for defending their collective interests. Trade unions in urban areas were among the most prominent of these, and organized street children played a central role in the 1991 insurrection in Mali. But the problems of inequality between and within families remained severe. The agronomist René Dumont, widely respected for his early critique of the economic difficulties of independent Africa in the 1960s, went on a West African speaking tour in 1989 to plead for the release of African peasant women from conditions of subjugation.

At another end of the social scale, professionals – men and women – became increasingly prominent. The professionals included academics, government servants, religious leaders, doctors and lawyers, teachers, and university students headed toward these occupations. They were francophone, cosmopolitan, and imbued with ideals of progress for their class and their nation. Frustrated with the limitations on their personal and national advance, they called for political change and moved to seek out common cause with urban workers, with urbanites at the edge of employment, and with the rural population. Ecological issues – the destruction of forests by foreign loggers or the burying of toxic waste in African soil – sometimes provided linkages among these distinct social strata. A complex map of groupings, with links and contradictions among the divisions by status, region, and ethnicity, lent itself to rapid alternations between expressions of national unanimity and sharp divisions across one divide or another.

People from any social grouping could become refugees. Migrants had been prominent in francophone Africa for generations, as men went away to work or to serve in the military, and as children went away to school. But the political strife of the years after independence created refugees on a scale perhaps exceeding that of the years of colonial conquest or the preceding era of slave trade. Repeated coups in Chad brought retaliation and dispersal for the losing populations. Rwanda and Burundi underwent accelerating refugee crises. Drought brought flight from dessicated areas of Mauritania and other sahelian countries. Flight from political oppression sent many people out of Guinea during the Touré regime, and some of these sought to return during the succeeding regime.

Disease also struck with little regard for social status. In the mid-1980s, a sudden and rapid spread of acquired immune deficiency syndrome (AIDS) came to be recognized, notably in Kinshasa. The first response of Zairian officials to the discovery of AIDS was denial, but it was followed later by a coordinated Zairian and international attempt to monitor and limit the disease. In response to the vexed question of whether the disease had originated in Central Africa, health officials satisfied themselves ultimately by asking traditional healers whether they recognized the symptoms of AIDS. The issue was difficult, since many of the symptoms of AIDS are also the result of malnutrition and exposure. The healers responded that the symptoms were new, thus contradicting the thesis that AIDS had long existed in Central Africa on a small scale. What remained unresolved was the question of the ultimate origin of the AIDS virus, and the means by which it had spread so rapidly through the population of Central Africa. Meanwhile, the infection spread rapidly through the adult population of Kinshasa and most other Central African cities, and spread from there to the countryside. The horror of the widespread illness and death was only beginning.

THE FRANCOPHONE MOVEMENT

The initial impetus for the francophone movement came from France. And while the movement has come to develop a major cultural significance, one may ask whether, at base, it is not more political than cultural. In the 1960s

French leaders sought to preserve a position of influence for France and for French culture in a world where Europe was losing its earlier centrality. France had lost her empire and, even by a generous estimate, no more than 6 percent of the world's population spoke French. Part of the vision of the francophone movement was to preserve, or perhaps to increase, that proportion. In the words of one French spokesman for "francophonie," Xavier Deniau, the term had meanings on linguistic, geographic, spiritual and mystical levels. One might add that francophonie came to be buttressed by various national and international institutions.

In the 1960s and 1970s, French leaders thought of "francophonie" as comparable to the Commonwealth, the organization of nations formerly colonized by Britain. The Ministry of Cooperation, founded in 1961, handled relations with former colonies, especially in Africa. The organizations of former colonies, such as the UAM (Union Africaine et Malagache, founded in 1961) and the OCAM (Organisation Commune Africaine et Malagache, replacing it in 1964), served not only to bind former colonies to France, but to oppose radical, socialist and pan-African visions of African politics, which were personified by such anglophone leaders as Kwame Nkrumah of Ghana and Julius Nyerere of Tanzania. Supporters of francophonie emphasized that it was more informal and flexible, and less state-centered, than the Commonwealth. Thus, African and other francophone ministers of education met annually with the French minister of education, and this helped to lead to the formation of the ACCT (Agence de Coopération Culturelle et Technique) in 1972. All of these structures, in practice, were influenced greatly by the French Ministry of Cooperation. In 1973 the presidents of francophone African states met with President Pompidou of France in what was to become a regular annual meeting.

Another side of the francophone movement was more easily seen as a voluntary association of states and peoples having shared historical experiences reflected in use of the French language. And if the Académie française remained the authoritative body on matters of the French language, it was Leopold Senghor of Senegal and Habib Bourguiba of Tunisia who campaigned most publicly for formal recognition of the special place of the French language and French culture in modern civilization. Senghor, after stepping down as president of Senegal in 1980, was appointed to the Académie française in 1983, and became one of its best known and most respected members.

With the beginnings of popular acceptance of the notion of francophonie, a new set of institutional initiatives arose. In the 1980s a series of international conferences convened delegations from many states defining themselves as francophone. Paris was the site of the first conference of heads of state of "countries having the French language in common," in February of 1986. The second francophone summit took place in Quebec, in September of 1987, and the third met in Dakar in May of 1989. If France appeared as the leader in one sense, in another sense the French had to compete with the Canadians, Belgians and even the Swiss as wealthy donor countries offering the benefits of expertise and contributions to the poorer nations. At the

Quebec conference, Canada cancelled its debts from seven francophone African countries.

The francophone movement had its impact in cultural as well as political affairs. The radio services of France and Canada beamed increased programming to Africa, and African radio and television stations broadcast programs provided to them without charge by France, Belgium, Canada and Switzerland. And a francophone university consortium founded in 1972, AUPELF (Association des Universités Partiellement ou Entièrement de Langue Française), gained momentum during the 1980s.

The francophone movement could not have grown to the dimensions it reached without the support of significant sections of the populations of many countries, willing to associate themselves with a multinational and multiracial cultural community identified by language. In Africa, the articulation of a francophone identity represented in part a move of resistance against being swallowed up into the English-speaking world; in another sense it served as the statement of a broad and cosmopolitan linkage among Africans.

This emerging francophone African identity drew in part on the colonial tradition. But the number of French-speakers in postcolonial Africa was vastly greater than in colonial times. The same was true for the former Belgian territories. That is, the addition of Zaire, Burundi and Rwanda to the francophone group reflects not only the substitution of France for Belgium as the dominant European power in the region (though it is that), but also asserts a cultural identity shared with other nations of Central and West Africa. While this tradition was shared primarily at the elite level, it reached beyond politics to education, literature, film and music.

When the third conference of francophone heads of state met in Dakar in May 1989, it was the bicentennial of the French Revolution as well as the high point of the Chinese student demonstrations at Tienanmen. The holding of several academic conferences on the bicentennial – in Dakar, in Haiti, and in Benin, for instance – served to highlight the issues of democracy and human rights that reflected the universal appeal of the French revolutionary tradition. Thus did the francophone movement become linked to the movement for democratization. The fourth conference of francophone heads of state, scheduled for Kinshasa in 1991, was cancelled on the insistence of Belgian and Canadian governments critical of the corruption and oppression that characterized Mobutu's regime; the conference was rescheduled for Paris in November of 1991. The 1993 conference met in Mauritius; in this era the African heads of state met with the French president in even-numbered years, and the wider francophone organization met in odd-numbered years.

The case of Zaire reveals both the power of francophone identity and its limits in Africa. At the end of the colonial era only a tiny minority of Zairians (then Congolese) spoke French, and virtually all of them were male. The rapid postcolonial spread of literacy, education, and urbanization brought an expansion of French language usage. According to one set of estimates, 1.5 percent of the country's population spoke French in 1955, and 4 percent in 1975; one might guess 8–10 percent in 1995. The proportion of female speakers of French rose but did not equal that of males. The expansion of French language in Zaire was closely tied to the expansion of an urban, petty-bourgeois segment of society.

The apostles of francophonie in the 1980s labelled Zaire as the second-largest francophone country, and Kinshasa as the second-largest francophone city. Yet Zaire seemed unlikely to escape a complex multilingualism. Lingala was the language of music, of presidential addresses, of daily life in government and in Kinshasa. But if Lingala was the spoken language of Kinshasa, it made little progress as a written language. French was the written language of the city – as seen in street signs, posters, newspapers and in government documents. French dominated plays and television as well as the press; French was the language of the national anthem and even for the doctrine of authenticity. Zairian researchers found French to be used in vertical relationships among people of uneven rank; people of equal rank, no matter how high, tended to speak Zairian languages among themselves.

Given these limits, French might have lost its place to another of the leading languages of Zaire – Lingala, Tshiluba, or Swahili – except that each of these languages also suffered from limitations on its growth. Similarly, in Central African Republic, the creole language of Sango, emerging from the urban crucible of Bangui, became virtually the new national language, but was slow to become a literary language. The contrast with anglophone Africa is inescapable: there, strong literatures and educational systems developed in languages such as Swahili, Hausa, Yoruba, Shona and Xhosa.

As the number of French-speakers in Africa expanded with time, both African and European specialists came to complain about the quality of the French they spoke. Some complained about the quality of instruction. Some complained about the shrinking place accorded to French literary classics in the curriculum; some argued that the writing and teaching of African literature in French was the main hope for the quality of French expression in Africa. Others argued that the francophone Africans were taking revenge on the language they spoke, deforming it deliberately in protest against neocolonialism.

The underlying issues were whether French was to remain a foreign language in Africa, or whether it would become an African language; whether it would be a first or a second language to its African speakers. Would "French" in Africa follow the Parisian standard? Would it become a set of regional dialects? Or would "French" grow through creolized mixes with other languages? Substantial documentation on these issues appeared in 1984 with publication, by AUPELF, of an inventory of the lexicon of French as spoken in Africa, showing the development of much new vocabulary and new forms of terminology in African French. The developing regional variations were considerable: standard French remained relatively strong in Senegal and Benin; a characterisic local dialect appeared to be emerging in Ivory Coast, and in Zaire a Lingala–French creole known as "Indoubill" emerged in Kinshasa.

Under these conditions, African thinkers undertook the critique of francophonie as well as its celebration. One Zairian critic of francophonie, writing

in the 1980s, wondered why Africans had continued so long after independence to pattern "our manner of living comfortably as a carbon copy" (*"en
copie conforme"*) of their former colonial masters. Guy Ossito Midiohouan, of
Benin, launched a more extensive critique with the complaint that he was often
called a "professor of French" rather than a "professor of literature." By that
he meant that students assumed he would be teaching the superiority of
French culture rather than teaching modern literature, especially by African
authors, in the French language.

Midiohouan expressed hope for the long-run development of African languages as literary languages, and for that reason he argued that "the proper
usage of francophonie" in Africa should be to utilize standard French as a
foreign language for communication among Africans of different languages.
The problem with the development of creoles or of regional French dialects,
for him, was that they would restrict the literary development of African
languages. He argued that, in contrast, French leaders hoped for the African
creolization of French in order to assure the widest possible survival of the
French language in some form. Thus Midiohouan (the critic of francophonie)
advocated standard French while the leaders of AUPELF (supporters of
francophonie) were content with creolization. Midiohouan's vigorous critique
of the construction of francophonie included a single point of praise – the 1972
decision at a conference of francophone African education ministers to include, in the teaching of literature, works in French by African authors.
Midiohouan wished to preserve the French language but not French culture in
Africa. When Leopold Senghor was elevated late in life to the Academie
française, Midiohouan criticized his role in propagating "francophonie," and
stigmatized him as a collaborator with France in opposition to African unity.

THE NATIONAL CONFERENCES

The shape of the world changed from 1985 to 1995, and the shape of francophone Africa changed with it. A wave of democratization movements, peaking
from 1989 to 1992, brought to an end the world's polarization into Cold War
camps dominated by the United States and the Soviet Union. The democratization movements were more ideologically complex than a victory of capitalism
and liberalism over socialism, and were more socially specific than an uprising
of the disenfranchised masses. While these movements varied widely in their
character and their outcome, they shared a fundamental similarity in reflecting
widespread demand for reform by members of a specific social fraction:
educated, urban, professional employees, many of them centered in public
service; along with artists, students, and intellectuals. The stories of 1989-92
are, first of all, their stories.

The progressive alienation of African populations from their governments
became a commonplace of the 1980s: governments were unrepresentative,
unelected, and unpopular. Related to this growing split between government
and the governed was a steady transformation of military forces into instruments of domestic repression. In theory, armies were to protect the security of

the nation against outsiders, while police forces were to provide for domestic security. This distinction had never been implemented fully in colonial Africa, where most people lacked the rights of citizens, and where army and police served a foreign ruler. After independence, all Africans gained the formal rights of citizens. Their new and small armies, meanwhile, occasionally took up work in administration, and turned to domestic repression when their policies failed along with the policies of civilian governments.

Thus were African nations primed for upheaval, even before the demonstrations at Tiananmen and the dismantling of the Berlin Wall in 1989 came to magnify the political pressures within Africa. It required only a spark to ignite a political brushfire and a breeze to send the conflagration in one direction or another. Events in Benin provided the African spark, and for a time the breeze from Benin prevailed. With the Persian Gulf War and the breakup of the Soviet Union in 1991 the political winds shifted, and by 1994 the disastrous conflicts in Liberia, Rwanda and Burundi came to govern the political tone of francophone Africa.

The changes were rapid. In 1985, only a few bright spots had illuminated the political landscape of francophone Africa. Senegal had a relatively open political system, Burkina Faso under Thomas Sankara had entered with enthusiasm into a campaign for enlightened self-sufficiency, and Cameroun appeared to be prospering. Yet each of these countries would falter, and it was the unheralded Benin that reversed the downward spiral of an Afro-Marxist regime, creating an innovative, democratic opening.

First to falter was Burkina Faso. President Sankara, for all his energy, charm and ebullience, could not escape the contradictions of his nation's society, nor the narrowness of his military base in politics. Sankara allied himself with the interests of the peasantry and of women, and found himself in increasing conflict with urbanites, especially with trade unionists, and with men. The result was his assassination in an October 1987 coup d'état, which brought to power his close associate, Blaise Campaoré. The loss of Sankara's heroic figure brought expressions of grief from all over Africa. In Burkina Faso itself, the reaction was muted: all the contradictory forces remained in play, but they acted with caution.

In Guinea, a long decline finally reached bottom. The regime of Ahmed Sékou Touré, which began with proclamations of social revolution and pan-Africanism, suffered from real and imagined persecution by foreign and domestic enemies, and retreated into dictatorship and misery. Touré died in 1984, a military regime under Col. Lansina Conté replaced him, and the many refugees from Guinea began cautiously considering whether to return home.

The complex international responses to the demise of Touré provided reminders of the importance of great-power conflicts in African affairs. The International Monetary Fund and the European Community placed strong pressures on Guinea and other countries to comply with proposed trade, migration and finance policies.

Senegal's prestige in maintaining formal, multiparty democracy emerged tarnished from the 1988 legislative elections, in which the Diouf government ensured its victory with transparent acts of electoral fraud. Student protests of election results led to an "année blanche": the government annulled students' work for the year. In the next year Abdoulaye Wade, leader of the opposition, agreed to participate in a government of national union with Diouf, only to be drawn into complicity in the disastrous conflict of Senegal and Mauritania. Meanwhile the earlier federation of Senegal and Gambia was completely abandoned.

In April 1989, as Chinese students demonstrated for democracy at Tiananmen, and on the eve of an international conference on Senegal and the bicentennial of the French Revolution, an incident of theft in Dakar set off a wave of mutual killings opposing Senegalese and Mauritanians, and opposing black and moorish Mauritanians. Abdou Diouf responded by expelling all Mauritanian nationals from Senegal in May, and periodic battles continued within Mauritania and on the frontier between the two countries for the next year.

Meanwhile, a set of Algerian events came to be influential for sub-Saharan countries, in part because French diplomats concluded that they reflected a sensible policy of gradual but controlled opening to greater democracy. The single-party regime of the National Liberation Front (FLN) had responded to student protests at the end of 1987 with a massive crackdown which in turn brought widespread popular condemnation of the government. In attempt to accommodate its critics, the government decreed that multiple parties could exist beginning in October 1988. The revised constitution of February 1989 permitted a freer press, and the number of newspapers in circulation expanded rapidly. It was this controlled opening that appealed to French policy-makers.

In Benin the bank crisis and the shortage of revenue meant that public servants were paid infrequently during 1989. Public-school teachers were officially on strike for much of the year, while central government officials struck more informally, simply not showing up for work. In September the university teachers' trade union took the strong step of withdrawing from the national trade union federation (affiliated with the governing party and the government), on the grounds that it was not defending its members' interests. When no retaliatory moves came, other trade unions moved rapidly to disaffiliate, and soon a general strike was proposed for early December. Rumors flew orally and in the newspapers now sold on Cotonou streets, and demonstrators gathered and marched daily in large towns and small. University students and the Communist Pary of Dahomey, with its base among Cotonou's youth, each contributed significantly to the protest.

A few days before the strike deadline, the governing party met and decreed that three months of back salaries would be paid to government employees, that Marxism-Leninism was no longer the official national ideology, that the use of the term "comrade" was no longer required in public salutations, and that a "national conference" should be held. The strike was postponed, and beginning Christmas Eve the treasury opened for three days to pay back salaries for two (not three) months, with funds apparently provided by the government of France.

Plans for the national conference went ahead, led by Robert Dossou, dean of the university law school and a close confidant of President Kérékou. Dossou argued that the conference was an extension of conferences held by the governing party in earlier years. He consulted with the French (who preferred to support Kérékou, and relied on the Algerian example for inspiration), with the Americans (who were closer to the political opposition), and with opposition leaders of several factions. In January, after several attempts, a rough consensus had been achieved on the groupings to be represented and the number of representatives for each grouping. The actual selection of delegates depended on the procedures followed by the various regional, occupational, and confessional groupings.

From February 19 through 28, 1990, roughly two hundred delegates met at the Hotel PLM-Aledjo in Cotonou. The proceedings of the meeting were broadcast from gavel to gavel by the national radio service, and significant highlights were broadcast each day on television. Within these nine days, the delegates elected a leadership, declared themselves sovereign, passed legislation, and convinced the sitting president to agree to their selection of a prime minister and of a High Council which would oversee the preparation of a constitution and hold new elections. The rhetoric and imagery of the conference invoked, at once, traditions of the French revolution, pan-Africanism, and multiparty politics.

The transition was carried off with such elegance and efficiency that it became a script, followed in remarkable detail by imitators of the Benin conference in five or six other francophone African countries, and in less detail elsewhere. Official and unofficial videotapes of the proceedings circulated all over the continent, conveying the message of peaceful popular upheaval – a "civilian coup d'état" as it was briefly called in Benin. Among the key elements of the script was election of the Catholic bishop as president of the conference: Isidore de Souza, in the prime of life and from an old Ouidah family, provided an effective mix of firm leadership and supple adjustment to sudden pressures. The assertion by the conference of its sovereignty brought it into open conflict with Kérékou. In perhaps the most dramatic moment of the conference, Kérékou appeared and spoke to defend his leadership, yet effectively conceded sovereignty to the conference. While numerous commissions addressed the specific issues before the nation, the appointment of the High Council and the prime minister held center stage. Mgr de Souza was selected to preside over the high council and, in a contested election, Nicéphore Soglo, a World Bank economist and arguably the American candidate, won selection as prime minister over Albert Tévoedjré, who was closer to France.

The sense of national renewal gave weight to the philosophy and terminology which dominated the conference. A slim but compelling list of links to French traditions was evident: the formal similarity of the conference to the Estates General of 1789, the appeals to the ideology of citizenship and universal rights. But also present were the ideas of liberation theology, and a vision of civil society based more on the thought of the Italian revolutionary Antonio Gramsci than on that of Plato. The notion of the "forces vives" (active forces) of the country and of codifying the rights of each fraction of the population against tyranny were responses to the conditions of the 1980s. Still to go, after adjournment of the national conference, were establishment of an interim government, writing and adopting a constitution and, after a year, electing a new legislature and a president. As Benin settled down to quiet implementation of these dramatic reforms, the model of the national conference spread from country to country.

The democratization movements of francophone Africa were grounded in the domestic political tradition of each nation, and fueled by worldwide currents of political contestation and change, including the pan-Africanism linking Africa and the Americas. The popular uprisings of the 1980s against unpopular governments in Iran, Philippines and Haiti laid groundwork for these movements. Continuing war in Angola showed that great-power intervention was still to be feared; elections and independence for Namibia in 1989 showed that democratic change could sometimes prevail even against heavily armed states. The Soviet withdrawal from Afghanistan in 1989, and the sudden collapse of unpopular governments in eastern Europe later that year, contributed to the same positive atmosphere. Civil war in Liberia, however, showed that the establishment of stable national communities was by no means inevitable.

The present analysis is intended to demonstrate, in addition, that the strong common roots and the shared traditions of francophone African nations brought close interactions and commonalities to the experience of their democratization movements. The national movements became more than a collection of distinct cases of political change, and took shape as components of a continental movement – growing, evolving, and finally receding. The demands for convening conferences of the "forces vives de la nation" and for establishing a pluralistic political order became the most prominent elements in this wave of contestation. The heritage of the Estates General of 1789 and the critique of absolutism provided the common ideal underlying these demands.

In each case there were years of pressure building up to the convening of the national conference; in each case the demand for a national conference was mixed with a complicated game of elections and a complicated dance with military power at home and with tentacles of the great powers abroad. Perhaps more importantly, each nation passed a series of turning points that would mark the national experience ever after.

The spread of an active popular press, and the decline of government control of radio and television, characterized this era. Weekly and daily newspapers appeared by 1987 in Senegal, by 1989 in Benin, Cameroon and Ivory Coast, by 1990 in Zaire and Mali, and thereafter in Congo, Niger, Gabon and elsewhere.

Public demonstrations had been endemic if largely unreported for francophone African countries in 1989. Occasionally events reached the news, as in Niger in early February of 1990, when in Niamey a demonstration by university students seeking better conditions brought a murderous retaliation by the army and police of Niger, killing children of high government officials among others, thus setting in motion widespread protest against the regime of Ali Saibou. Upon the conclusion of Benin's national conference such demonstrations accelerated, notably in Gabon, Ivory Coast, Cameroon and Zaire. The problems of economic deprivation, unpaid salaries, corruption and unrepresentative government seemed general, and the Benin model became widely attractive.

In terms that came increasingly into popular use, "civil society" expressed dissatisfaction with "the power" of government. Students sought better conditions, teachers and other public servants sought to have salaries paid, rural populations complained about prices, urban populations complained about the lack of work. These movements were national in scope, though their activists made accusations that the Power had, in its corruption, shown favoritism to certain ethnic groups.

Governments in francophone African countries, facing this amplification of already severe public pressure, tended at first to respond either with full-scale repression or with clumsy concessions. In Cameroon, Central African Republic, Togo and Ivory Coast, governments held out against concessions. In Zaire, President Mobutu conceded the right to form opposition political parties in April, but in May the national police repressed a protest by university students in Lubumbashi, at the cost of eleven lives, and caused a national scandal.

The most adroit offering of concessions came in Gabon, where president Omar Bongo responded to urban demonstrations with relatively minimal repression, and quickly convened a national conference under his own leadership. The conference, from March 23 through April 20, proposed modest reforms. Still, with the return of riots in June 1990, Bongo benefited from the arrival of French troops, nominally to protect French property but just as much to protect him. The succeeding legislative elections brought a minority of opposition figures to the legislature, and the country settled down into relative quiescence with a government that was slightly more open than before.

In a slower but more sure-footed response to the script for the national conference, the aged Félix Houphouët-Boigny of Ivory Coast developed an approach which might be called a counter-script. By the end of 1990 he had declared for multiparty government, had convened a congress of the governing party, and had conducted elections for the presidency, the legislature, and local governments from which he and his party emerged victorious. While the script for the Benin-based national conference spread across the continent in the form of videotapes of the proceedings, the Ivory Coast-based counter-script of elections without conference circulated in quiet meetings among officials, including ambassadors from France.

Ivory Coast began the year 1990 in nearly desperate straits, with its vaunted economy suffering greatly, with students and public servants on strike for better conditions, and with religious authorities criticizing the human rights violations of the regime; the aged president seemed to have lost his grip. In May, as segments of the military, uneasy and underpaid, began brandishing their armored vehicles, Houphouët-Boigny was able to meet with them and calm them. New political parties began to form, but some of them were "phantom parties," working in concert with the government.

In June of 1990, at the seventeenth conference of French and African heads of state, French president François Mitterrand spoke out for democracy, saying that "development supposes a minimum of democracy; democracy supposes a minimum of development." It was a statement for which Houphouët-Boigny was prepared: France sought to support democratic reform, but did not propose to abandon long-time allies even when, as with Gnassingbé Eyadema of Togo, they ruled largely by force.

By the end of 1990 Houphouët-Boigny, in a series of well-timed maneuvers, had regained control of the situation. A carefully planned October 1990 congress of the governing party, the PDCI, brought announcement that a prime minister, Alassane Ouattara, would be appointed. A sudden presidential election was called for October 28. The opposition, despairing of its demand for a national conference, agreed to participate and united behind one candidate, Laurent Gbagbo, who gained 18 percent of the vote against Houphouët. Within another month legislative elections were held and the PDCI, renewed from its presidential victory, prevailed. In yet another month, municipal elections again brought the PDCI back to dominance, though opposition candidates prevailed in some cases. This strategy could not solve the economic problems of the country, but it succeeded in isolating and dividing opposition groups, often identifying them with ethnic labels.

By 1991 the basic strategies of "civil society" and "the power" were fully developed. For another two years these two strategies remained locked in contention until all the countries of francophone Africa had either changed their government and its structure or reconfirmed the existing government in place. The outcomes were roughly half and half. The countries holding national conferences included Gabon, Niger, Mali, Congo, Togo, Zaire, Madagascar, and Chad. The countries in which the second script would dominate included Cameroon, Central African Republic, Burkina Faso, Guinea, Senegal, Mauritania, Burundi, and Rwanda. Of all of them, the countries which gained new leadership or new institutions were Benin, Niger, Mali, Congo, Madagascar, Chad, Central African Republic, Rwanda and, briefly, Burundi.

This dance of the two strategies – national conferences and a new political order, as demanded by Civil Society, or controlled elections and reaffirmation of the existing political order, as demanded by the Power – continued until 1993, when the last of the national conferences adjourned in Chad. The outcome depended on the strength and organization of the two sides, but also on successive innovations in tactics and rhetoric, and on the emergence of new factors both in the affairs of individual nations as well as in the changing influence of global affairs.

Two additional factors entered this equation of political struggle. First was great-power intervention, especially from France, but also from the United States, and from the United Nations and the World Bank. The government of France systematically provided support to the Power, and only came to support the option of a national conference or opposition candidates for president when it appeared that the government would otherwise lose power completely to the aroused citizenry.

Second was the military option, both domestic and external. The domestic attempts at military coups, though all failed, nevertheless affected the political climates of Ivory Coast, Benin, Congo, Mali, Togo, and especially Burundi where a second coup, while it too failed, killed the head of state and derailed the country from democratic reconciliation, sending it toward a renewal of genocide. Then in both Rwanda and Chad at the end of 1990 – under the shadows of darkening clouds of war as the United States and its United Nations allies prepared to reconquer Kuwait and invade Iraq – rebel groups entered the country and drove toward the capital. Idriss Deby in Chad, aided by Sudan, was rewarded with instant success, as Hissène Habré fled before the end of December. The less experienced soldiers of the Rwandan Patriotic Front, aided by Uganda, met initial reversal but continued their struggle.

As the successful completion of Benin's national conference in February 1990 brought one defining moment, so did the massive re-election of Houphouët-Boigny in October 1990 bring another such moment, in which the demand for a national conference was effectively blunted in Ivory Coast. In an immediate application of Houphouët-Boigny's approach, Blaise Campaoré of Burkina Faso, after rejecting calls for a national conference, convened the "assises nationales" in December of 1990 – in effect, a congress of the governing party rather than an open national forum. With this device, he was able to defuse opposition, and then to schedule and win national elections a year later.

If Houphouët-Boigny's development of an electoral strategy regained a modicum of consensus for Ivory Coast, Paul Biya's application of a similar strategy in Cameroun brought the country to a political and economic impasse. When Yondo Black had gone so far as to declare the foundation of a party in April of 1990, Biya had Black arrested. An atmosphere of confrontation and impasse developed steadily, though it was relieved for a time in June and July as the Indominable Lions, Cameroon's entry in the 1990 World Cup of football (soccer), came within an eyelash of making the final four, and played as well as the teams from Germany, England, Argentina and Italy that did make the finals.

Matters seemed to have calmed a bit by December, and Biya promulgated a law on democratic pluralism. No sooner did he make the announcement, however, than Celestin Monga published in *Le Messager* an open letter critical of Biya, and at the beginning of January Monga and publisher Pius Njawe were arrested. For all of 1991 Biya firmly refused any move toward a national conference, though Douala and other major cities remained largely on strike. The inability of opposition leaders to unify meant that the parties were diffused in the March 1992 legislative elections, and that Biya was able to eke out a victory over John Fru Ndi in the October 1992 presidential election.

The protests of Civil Society, if blunted in some countries, gained influence in others, notably in Mali and Congo at the beginning of 1991. The events in Congo most closely followed the pattern of Benin, not least because Congo too was governed by a Marxist regime of military origin, but which would make concessions rather than repress popular demonstrations. In the People's Republic of Congo, President Denis Sassou Nguesso had been ably backing away from an aroused populace: he assented to formal declaration of a multiparty state, abandonment of Marxism-Leninism and, finally, convening of a national conference. The Congo national conference convened on 25 February and adjourned on 10 June 1991. It lasted over a hundred days rather than ten days, yet otherwise it followed most closely the Benin model. The conference confronted the president and won recognition of its sovereignty; it selected the Catholic Bishop (Mgr Ernest Nkimbo) as its president, its actions were spurred on by strikes and threats of strikes, and it imposed on the president a High Council and a prime minister who had served as a World Bank economist (André Milongo). The apologies offered by Sassou Nguesso for the excesses of his regime matched and went beyond those of Kérékou in Benin.

Meanwhile, in Benin the drama of political renewal through the national conference moved through its next set of stages. The legislative and presidential elections were scheduled for March 1991, and it was certain that Prime Minister Nicéphore Soglo, Albert Tévoedjré and others would run for the presidency. Then in February the incumbent president, Mathieu Kérékou, announced his candidacy. Kérékou gained 26 percent of the vote, mostly from his home region in the north, behind Soglo with 36 percent. In the aftermath of the first round, rumors of a military coup circulated in the capital, but the second round of elections was held in April, and Soglo won with 67 percent of the vote as compared with 32 percent for Kérékou. After his defeat, Kérékou settled down quietly to life in Cotonou, and became an active communicant in the Catholic church and a close confidant of Mgr Isidore de Souza, who had presided over the national conference. Thus was an orderly and relatively peaceful transition in power completed in Benin.

As the national conference slowly unfolded in Congo, political confrontation came to a head with an insurrectionary result in Mali. There, President Moussa Traoré, who had come to office by military coup in 1984, was among the first to announce "multipartisme" in October 1989. But from there no further change was permitted. The failure to grant raises or even to pay salaries for public servants, especially teachers, brought growing unrest and a move, as earlier in Benin, for the public-employee unions to break from government control. Two broad political coalitions formed to contest the government – CNID, formed of old political parties and led by Mountaga Tall, a young lawyer, and ADEMA, led by historian Alpha Oumar Konaré.

Two sets of public demonstrations brought down the government of Mali, and children played a central role in each of them. In January of 1991 trade unions went on strike, led by unpaid teachers. When the teachers ended their strike under government pressure, students in primary and secondary schools went into the streets on their behalf in Bamako and other cities, and were joined (or sometimes led) by children who were not in school. These youthful mobs destroyed property of supporters of the Traoré regime in three days of riots. Then on April 22, as Traoré still rejected demands for a national conference and instead organized a party conference, demonstrators challenged the assembled party leaders at the Bamako football stadium. Troops fired on women and children in the front ranks of the demonstrators, and the resulting deaths provoked an outcry and an immediate insurrection. Moussa Traoré and his wife Mariam were arrested on April 25 by a faction of the military siding with the rebels. For a time Mali was governed by a coordinating committee led by Amadou Tumamy Touré, interim head of the army, and by Alpha Oumar Konaré of ADEMA and Demba Diallo of the Mali association for human rights.

In the case of Mali the national conference met after the old government fell. The conference, held from July 29 to August 12, 1991, nevertheless followed the pattern of other successful conferences, assuming sovereignty, setting up an interim government, planning for a new constitution, and scheduling national elections. The elections, held in January 1992, confirmed Alpha Oumar Konaré as president.

Three other national conferences opened in the summer of 1991, in addition to that of Mali. In Niger, president Saibou had managed to postpone a conference scheduled for March. Even then, there was a last-minute debate over the number of women delegates at the conference. Women claimed more seats, and had to face accusations that they were acting on behalf of the government to delay the proceedings. In Togo and Zaire as well, the supporters of national conferences managed to overcome the months of delay by the Power. (In Central African Republic and Mauritania, the governments held out against aroused publics and avoided scheduling conferences, though the president ultimately lost power in the first.) The delay in Togo included riots in Lome followed by a crackdown in which the military was discovered to have thrown nineteen bodies into the lagoon. Public outrage gave impetus to a national conference following the Benin script, which convened in July and, after months of deliberations, appointed Joseph Koffigoh prime minister as it concluded its work in November 1991.

The national conference of Zaire, opening in August 1991, included an innovation in structure. The inhabitants of Kinshasa had watched the Congo national conference on television for four months, as Brazzaville is just across the river – as a result, they knew the script very well. At the same time, the conference in Zaire was different. In previous national conferences, determination of the number and distribution of delegates, plus their method of selection, had been by informal bargaining among the parties. In the resulting discussions, the term "civil society" came into use to refer to the general population of the nation. In Zaire, the term "civil society" became formalized and institutionalized: the delegates to the conference were divided into the Power, the opposition political parties, and Civil Society (meaning church groups in particular, but also ethnic and professional associations), each with about a third of the seats. The Zaire conference was not adjourned until December 1992, and in the interim it was suspended for months by the action of President Mobutu. The political parties declined to join civil society in opposing the government, thus revealing the complicity of some of them in government power; Mobutu, meanwhile, remained isolated on his yacht in the Zaire, sowing discord among his opponents with nearly his usual success.

In Madagascar the opposition developed two new tactics. First, in an expansion of a trend visible in other countries, religious groups joined together to form an ecumenical association which issued strong criticism of the government. Second, when President Didier Ratsiraka refused any concessions, the opposition brought huge demonstrations into the streets of Antananrivo, Tamatave and other cities from June through August of 1991. Rather than call for a national conference, the opposition called simply for the resignation of Ratsiraka, and appointed a shadow government from the streets. When the shadow ministers sought symbolically to occupy their ministries, troops arrested several of them, resulting in a further escalation of the confrontation. The decision of the demonstrators to go to Ratsiraka's presidential palace 20 kilometers outside of the capital (one can hardly avoid mentioning the comparison to Versailles) resulted eventually in a massacre of some demonstrators by the presidential guard. The resulting outcry forced Ratsiraka to give way, and to allow for the convening of a national conference at the end of 1991.

Where Mobutu worked to derail Zaire's national conference through political maneuvers, Gnassingbé Eyadema took a more direct approach in Togo. For instance, in October of 1992 his military took forty hostages among members of the High Commission appointed by the national conference in late 1991; the result was that prime minister Joseph Koffigoh, appointed by the national conference, became dependent on Eyadema who, in turn, continued to benefit from French support. The response, by March of 1993, was a midnight attack on Eyadema's residence by young officers, but with its failure the re-establishment of Eyadema's control of the government became complete, though occasional public outcry continued. In April of 1994, Eyadema was able to appoint a new prime minister, Edem Kodjo, who would work with him closely yet maintain his reputation as a pan-African diplomat.

The last of the national conferences met in Ndjamena, Chad, from January to April of 1993. In one sense it resembled that of Mali, in that the old regime had fallen before the national conference. The difference was that Idriss Deby had conquered power by invasion from Sudan, driving Hissène Habré into exile in Senegal, while Moussa Traoré was overthrown by a domestic insurrection. In Chad, Deby ruled for two years from his seizure of power in December 1990 before convening a national conference. Still, it brought some broadening to that fragile and divided nation's political structure. The French government and the French garrison in Chad shifted their allegiance from Habré to Deby.

Authoritarian and unpopular government in francophone Africa did not end sharply with the wave of national conferences. Yet the years 1989-91 brought a quantum leap in the availability of an independent popular press, and in the level of popular political participation. On the other hand, the constraints on effective national political communities remained in place – economic stagnation, the disproportionate power of the military and police, the weight of international organizations and great powers in the politics of each nation, and the heritage of popular distrust for all governing figures that expressed, quite logically, the previous century's experience.

DISILLUSIONMENT AND DISASTER

The popular movements for political change were sure to lose momentum on the shoals of one difficulty or another. As it happened, the crisis brought by the Iraqi occupation of Kuwait in September 1990 and the resultant Persian Gulf War of January 1991 changed sharply the character of global politics. From a period in which unarmed popular masses forced changes on their rulers, the focus of events turned to military confrontations among groups of nations, directed by the great powers. After two years of claims for the rights of individuals within nations, the debate shifted to the rights of nations to interfere with other nations. United Nations Secretary-General Boutros-Ghali suggested, for the case of Iraq, that the UN's principle of the sovereignty of nations should be applied selectively, in cases where the national leadership appeared to the UN to be violating human rights.

In the aftermath of that conflict, the USSR collapsed in August 1991 to yield a web of competing states, and with it collapsed the bipolar framework that had dominated the world since 1945. New and old conflicts, fueled by the Cold War, nevertheless continued – in Yugoslavia, Cambodia, and Afghanistan; and, within Africa, in Sudan, Chad, Angola, Somalia, and Liberia.

The short-term impact of the international political climate can bring either positive or negative changes to life in individual nations. Under certain circumstances, the international climate can help smooth tensions, by creating pressures to allow the dialogue, debate and compromise which might work out inequities. Under other circumstances, the international climate can reinforce inequalities, undermine consensus, and provoke violence within affected nations. From 1990 to 1992, after the peak in the success of democratization movements, the international climate changed sharply from the former to the latter. The precarious democratization movement of Zaire would falter in 1992; and in Rwanda and Burundi the results would be far worse.

The impact of domestic political ideology, though it changes more gradually than the international political climate, remains powerful. In this case it was the ideology of tribalism, institutionalized by the identity cards of the Belgian colonial regime. Perhaps the most basic distinction in political ideology is the balance of individual and group rights. In dealing with conflicting interests of individuals and groups, this is the choice of whether to pursue compromise through law and procedure, or to define groups with sharp boundaries and impose absolute predominance of one group over another. The ideology of group identity, raising distinctions between Hutu and Tutsi to an absolute level, came to poison the history of the East African highlands. For the cases of Rwanda and Burundi, the short-term decline of democratization movements combined with the long-term impact of tribalistic ideology to bring accelerating disaster from 1993 to 1995.

In Burundi, a Tutsi-led military oligarchy briefly lost power in 1993, but regained power thereafter. Then in a wave of killings in late 1993, anti-government Hutu militias carried out mass murders and Tutsi troops retaliated. In Rwanda, a Hutu-led regime gave support to the Hutu militias which conducted massacres focusing on Tutsi in 1994, after which a Tutsi-led rebel movement gained control of the country. Refugees from both countries poured into Zaire and also Tanzania, where their conflicts continued in refugee camps, compounded by problems of disease and hunger. The total number of deaths by massacre is unknown but seems to have been several hundred thousand, with many thousands more lost to famine and epidemic in the aftermath.

The most devastating events in these two countries were the October 1993 coup which killed President Melchior Ndadaye of Burundi, the genocidal killings in Burundi during October and November of 1993, the shooting down at Kigali in April 1994 of the airplane carrying the presidents of Rwanda and Burundi, and the three months of genocidal killings in Rwanda from April through June of 1994, brought to an end by the conquest of power by the Rwandan Patriotic Front and the arrival of a substantial force sent by the United Nations. The narrative of the build-up to these events gives emphasis to tragedy, for it reveals that these horrific results were by no means inevitable.

Irony compounded tragedy in that the differences between Hutu and Tutsi had become largely arbitrary. Rwandans shared a single national language and culture, and so did the Burundians. They could trace ancestry to different strata in the precolonial kingdoms. More determinant was that the Belgian regime had insisted that each person carry an identity card with a unique label – Tutsi or Hutu – and independent governments continued the practice. The "ethnic" distinctions between Hutu and Tutsi were largely arbitrary, determined as much by social and administrative accidents as by coherent ancestry, but they became murderous. To quote Jean-Pierre Chrétien, on Burundi (1988):

> Fear is no longer in the decor of the drama, it has become the principal actor. What is it to be Hutu or Tutsi? It is neither to be Bantu or Hamite, serf or lord! It is to remember who killed someone close to you fifteen years ago or to ask yourself who will kill your child in ten years, each time with a different answer.

Rwanda and Burundi, both governed by military regimes in 1991, were nevertheless undergoing the same pressures for democratization as other African governments. The government of Rwanda, dominantly Hutu, and that of Burundi, dominantly Tutsi, had to worry about the same problems of corruption, shortages of public facilities, and inadequate employment opportunities as other governments. The ethnic divisions got out of hand only when these problems too became exaggerated.

In Rwanda – the northernmost of the two countries, nestled against the border of Uganda – the continental wave of democratization movements launched two developments in mid-1990. In July President Juvénal Habyarimana, just back from the conference of francophone African heads of state with President Mitterrand of France in La Baule, announced that he would initiate a process of democratization, by which he meant a multiparty system of government. Second, in October, a group of young Rwandan Tutsi exiles in Uganda, organized as the Rwandan Patriotic Front and including Paul Kagame, launched their first military incursion into the homeland many of them hardly knew.

The two processes developed for two years. A new constitution was promulgated in 1991, and a coalition government, led by opposition political parties, took office in 1992. Meanwhile the RPF was able to gain a foothold in a small area of northern Rwanda. These developments set the stage for negotiations between government and rebels, and the possible admission of the RPF into the coalition government. An agreement at Arusha, Tanzania, in July 1992 set forth the procedure for bringing the RPF into the government; the United Nations organization was to assist by deploying a peace-keeping force.

Meanwhile, a third process had been developing in Rwanda. The Interahamwe militia, composed of militant young Hutu, armed itself under a leadership preaching ethnic exclusivism and extermination of Tutsis; the Hutu Power faction, led by Jean Kambanda, represented the political arm of the same approach. Radio-Télévision Libre Mille Collines ("thousand hills") broadcast this same brand of exclusivism. Rwandan military leader Col. Bagasora showed himself to be linked to each of these groups.

Efforts to implement the Arusha agreement were long but half-hearted. It took over a year to get UN Security Council agreement to deploy the peace-keeping force. Even then the administration, the army, the political parties in the coalition, and the RPF each delayed, at one time or another, in pressing ahead to implement the Arusha agreement. Rwanda's first female prime minister, Agathe Uwilingiyimana, came into office in July of 1993, and pressed harder than her predecessors for a national compromise. President Habyarimana relied increasingly on ties to extreme Hutu groups, yet had also to conduct discussions with the RPF. Suspicions rose sharply with the unsuccessful October 1993 military coup in Burundi to the south, and the killings which followed it. Further delays in the settlement continued until April 1994, when the destruction of a plane carrying Rwandan President Habyarimana and Burindian President Ntaryamina set off a wave of assassination and genocide in Rwanda.

In Burundi, where a Tutsi minority maintained its power through control of all national institutions, particularly the military, the pressures of demands for democratization had nonetheless become potent. A combination of international and domestic pressures brought national elections in June of 1993, and these brought Melchior Ndadaye to the presidency and formation of a dominantly Hutu government. In an atmosphere of relief and celebration, Burundi seemed launched on the road to reconciliation. The army remained entirely Tutsi, but Ndadaye's supporters easily quelled a minor rebellion by troops in July.

When another military coup was mounted in October 1993, President Ndadaye underestimated it and declined to run to safety. He fell into the hands of the conspirators, who executed him brutally, along with his family. The coup then collapsed, but the sense of optimism disappeared from Burundi. A new government formed, under Cyprien Ntaryamira, but it proceded with caution and sought accommodation to the wishes of the Tutsi military oligarchy. Meanwhile the Parmehutu militants (a group similar to the Interahamwe of Rwanda) sought an opportunity to make war against the military rulers. Their tactic was often to launch massacres of Tutsi in urban and rural areas, and then to flee the country to escape the military.

Both countries entered 1994 in situations that were tense but not yet hopeless. In Rwanda, negotiations continued on implementing the Arusha accords, but two or perhaps three sides also prepared for war – the military led by Bagasora, the RPF, and perhaps the moderates surrounding Prime Minister Uwilingiyimana who dominated the government. Then on April 6, presidents Habyarimana and Ntaryamina flew from the Rwandan capital of Kigali to Tanzania to meet with President Mwinyi of Tanzania on implementing the Arusha accords. Just as their plane was landing on its return to Kigali, it was destroyed by a surface-to-air missile, and all aboard were killed. The site from which the missile was launched is known, but the author of the assassination is not. Each of the parties is accused and suspected, including France and Belgium.

Genocide began within a day, and war within two. In Kigali, the Rwandan military killed prime minister Uwilingiyimana, and then the heads of the constitutional court, the national assembly, and other ministers. Radio Mille Collines claimed that the RPF had shot down the president, and in so doing set the tone for retaliation. The Hutu militias joined the army in a week of general killing in Kigali, in which the Tutsi population was largely exterminated. The main exceptions were young women whose fate was rape and imprisonment as concubines of their captors. Descriptions of the killings indicated that men were killed with guns, while women and children were dispatched with machetes. Churches in this Catholic country were a major site of massacres, as attackers executed victims who had huddled there in hope of sanctuary.

On April 8 the RPF declared war and began a rapid advance, occupying much of the country within weeks; the massacres mostly ended in areas under RPF control. Beginning on April 9, French and Belgian missions in Rwanda removed almost all foreigners from the country. As the great powers stepped back, the killing of remaining Tutsi moved to the countryside and continued for three months, limited only by the advance of the RPF. France took the lead in the great-power discussions at the United Nations, but argued for minimal action, at least in part because it had been allied with the Rwandan government and military. The United States, more dominant than ever in the Security Council after the Gulf War and the collapse of the Soviet Union, also preferred minimal action.

In July of 1994 the United Nations moved to take stronger action, and set up Operation Turquoise. By this time the RPF controlled the majority of Rwanda, and fearful Hutu populations, including the militias who led in the killings, streamed to the Zairian border in the west, and also to Tanzania in the east. The UN landing did stop the killing, but it also interdicted the advance of the RPF. UN and other international groupings set up camps serving mainly Hutu refugees near Goma, in Zaire, where an epidemic of cholera soon broke out because of contaminated water. This wave of refugees added to earlier waves of Rwandan refugees in Zaire to produce an explosive mixture that would later affect all of Zaire.

Overall, the great powers offered a cautious and dilatory response to this crisis. In contrast to the 1990 crisis in Kuwait (where the United States and the United Nations committed extensive resources to reversing the Iraqi occupation) or to the 1992 crisis in Somalia (where the US and other powers intervened in civil war), international peace-keeping and relief missions for Rwanda and for refugees in Zaire and Tanzania were modest and late. Finally, in 1995, an international court was established, affiliated with the World Court, to investigate charges of genocide in Rwanda, Burundi, and what had been Yugoslavia.

COSMOPOLITAN CULTURE

Culture of the 1990s in francophone Africa reflected both the heights of optimism and the depths of despair warranted by the contradictory events of the time. African countries, while hardly growing in wealth during the 1980s, nonetheless participated in cultural changes and technical developments of their own invention and of the wider world. Thus, as one of many innovations within the second economy, there developed in francophone countries the metaphor of the "maquis," or outlaw. The term referred first to restaurants that avoided paying taxes and license fees, and then expanded to refer to any cultural activity having an anti-establishment flavor. The arrival of cheap presses and photocopiers supported the massive expansion of the popular press at the end of the 1980s. (As of 1991, Guinea was one of the rare francophone African countries not to have a sizeable independent press.) The spread of inexpensive cassette-tape players put recorded music into the hands of many more young people, so that the traditions of live music and ancestral dances began to be undermined even in isolated villages.

Musicians had the largest audiences among African art forms, followed perhaps by visual artists. Writers and film-makers continued to have relatively tiny audiences, yet they were important in codifying the outlook of that cosmopolitan class which was to have such a crucial role in the political conflicts of the 1990s. This class drew as well on magazines (*Jeune Afrique* and *Afrique Asie*, for instance), on television, and on the radio (both the national radio stations and, equally important, Radio France International, Africa No. 1, and other international services). For less privileged strata, football provided a common passion. When the Cameroon national team came within an eyelash of making it to the final four in the World Cup tournament of 1990 in Italy, a national and pan-African pride soared in many African breasts.

The music of Kinshasa, with its melodic lead guitars and its lyrics in Lingala peppered with French, maintained its dominance on the continent. But as Franco died of AIDS and Rochereau moved into retirement at the end of the

1980s, space opened for the next musical generation. Mbilia Bel, who had sung for years with Rochereau, now became the star of Kinshasa, along with her male singer Rigo Star. Others of the new generation moved further afield: for Kanda Bongo Man and Koffi Olomide, the attraction of intercontinental markets was stronger, and they moved to Paris. Koffi Olomide took two West African names (one Twi and one Yoruba) and began using synthesizers to imitate the kora and balafon. Thus music became more cosmopolitan, but threatened to move away from its base.

The universities of francophone Africa had become well established by the end of the 1980s, though they suffered perpetual crisis. Faculty members, though often able and well trained, faced immense classes, and lacked resources for research and teaching. Students sought scholarships which arrived only occasionally, and their demonstrations commonly brought the closing of universities and the declaration of an "année blanche," in which all courses were annulled.

One dimension of African scholarly life remained able to thrive, because of the existence of CODESRIA. The Council for Development of Economic and Social Research in Africa, based in Dakar and supported by UNESCO, brought scholars from anglophone and francophone countries together, to set and implement a scholarly agenda. UNESCO funding for CODESRIA ended, however, when the United States withdrew its membership and support for UNESCO, alleging that UNESCO gave too much support to Third World agendas. CODESRIA was later able to gain support from the American-based Ford Foundation.

Literature flowered in this difficult era, perhaps because of the very complexity and difficulty of the times. Gone were the earlier stories of young men growing up, or even of righteous struggle against corruption; village scenes, earlier obligatory, were now commonly absent. In prose of complex but attractive French, the authors of this era used metaphor and irony to present a worldly and yet deeply rooted critique of modern Africa. In *Fatoba, l'archipel mutant*, Cheick Oumar Kanté of Guinea used the metaphor of an island nation connected to the mainland by a great bridge to portray the reconstruction of the lives of inhabitants and visitors by domestic and global factors. In *Kin-la joie, Kin-la folie*, Achille Ngoye wrote in a more literal but equally engaging fashion to describe the folly of daily life and of the national existence in Zaire. Véronique Tadjo, a literature professor at the University of Abidjan, wrote with terse, fragmented and yet powerful prose to convey the conflicts in the lives of urban women, in *A Vol d'Oiseau*. In a more optimistic yet still critical vein, Nouréini Tidjani-Serpos conveyed the background to the democratization movement of Benin in a novel centered on a successful auto mechanic, *Bamikilé*.

With such a range of cultural arenas, various groupings came to prominence in each of them. Women such as Mbilia Bel of Zaire and Angelique Kidjo of Benin gained growing visibility in music. Women also gained stature as novelists, but had little place in popular magazines – the only women to appear in *Jeune Afrique* were European and American film stars. The dominance of

West Africa in film and of Central Africa in music remained unchanged, while novelists flourished whether in West or Central Africa, and among them authors both of Muslim and of Christian faith.

The cultural production of francophone Africa underwent immense transformation during the twentieth century, in part because the media changed dramatically (from oral to written prose, from live to recorded music), in part because of new languages (French, Lingala, Swahili and Sango were hardly used in 1900), and especially because the lives of the people had changed so much. The development of this lively, cosmopolitan and new African culture, in the course of a century during which African culture had experienced rejection from both within and without, serves as a positive sign for the future of the continent.

In the difficult circumstances of the late twentieth century, many Africans turned to their spiritual life and to religious leaders for counsel and leadership. Leadership of religious organizations was now African in most cases so that, while foreign missionaries continued to stream to Africa, they now worked in the service of African Christianity and Islam. Religion in francophone Africa thus became more cosmopolitan, without giving up its local specificity. Particularly among Christians, a strong African leadership had been allowed to develop only during the previous generation, and church leaders did indeed seek to offer commentary not only on matters of faith, but on public morality and on the conduct of the state. Ecumenical associations become influential in Madagascar, Mali and other countries, and Catholic bishops served as presidents of the majority of the national conferences held in francophone Africa. (In Mali and Niger, dominantly Muslim countries, history professors served a presidents of the national conferences.) Africa maintained its multiplicity of religions and its variety of tendencies within each religion. Neither Christianity nor Islam was monolithic, and no religion was controlled fully from top down, not even Catholicism.

Islam in francophone Africa was colored by the long history of the religion in West Africa, by its interaction with other African religious traditions, and by currents passing throughout the Muslim world. The relative tolerance of varying religious viewpoints and of secular states in African Islam, for instance, owes much to the heritage of African religion. But Muslims faced a choice between what the Kenyan scholar Ali Mazrui has called Islamic expansion and Islamic revivalism. The dominant trend was that of Islamic expansion, in which established sufi orders such as the Tijaniyya and Qadiriyya continued to gain converts in both urban and rural areas, at the expense of local African religions, so that Islam became the dominant religion in francophone Africa.

Islamic revivalism emerged in francophone Africa in accord with its growth in other parts of the Muslim world. The growth of a fundamentalist youth movement in Senegal was one such example. A somewhat different example emerged in Mali, where an immigrant group of Muslim leaders came to be known as Wahhabis, in a reflection of the strict group of that name in nineteenth-century Arabia. The newly arrived Wahhabis followed a different law system, yet gained influence by providing schools and health services which could not be provided either by the state or by other religious organizations. The government of Moussa Traoré responded to revivalism by attempting to adopt an Islamizing posture; after the insurrection overthrew Traoré, the new government became dominated by a secular approach. As Islamic identity expanded, religious disunity sometimes became as visible as the unity: at the 1993 national conference in Chad, spokesmen for Sunni and Shiite tendencies contended for leadership with each other and with leaders of the Tijaniyya and Wahhabi religious orders.

African Muslims became steadily more connected to Muslims elsewhere. Charter flights took thousands of pilgrims each year from African capitals to Mecca for the hajj. Such nations as Saudi Arabia, Egypt, Libya and Iran offered grants for universities and social services, as well as investments in banks and construction. If these did not bring about rapid African change, they did give the Muslim countries of francophone Africa a set of cultural and economic ties distinct from the neocolonial ties to France and her Atlantic allies.

Yet the other Muslim countries seemed to show little interest in African culture. In 1991, Senegal hosted the sixth international meeting of the Organization of the Islamic Conference. This organization, formed 1969, grew to include many nations after the attempted arson of the Jerusalem mosque by a member of a Jewish fundamentalist movement. The government of Senegal carried out construction of substantial conference facilities in Dakar, and hosted delegations from 44 countries. Still, heads of state declined to come from several major Arab countries – Saudi Arabia, Morocco, Syria, Algeria, Egypt, and Libya.

The influence of Christianity continued to grow, but in a less public fashion. Missionary work no longer dominated African Christianity as it had, for it was now a matter of servicing the needs of an established congregation. The most outstanding of those needs were for social services and a functioning political community. Thus it was that African prelates, foreign missionaries, and African congregations turned as much to saving lives as to saving souls.

A number of the Catholic bishops became national political figures. Bishops presided over the national conferences of Benin, Togo, Congo, and Zaire; and bishops were central in the ecumenical associations of Madagascar and Mali. These church leaders enunciated an ideology of social activism somewhat like the liberation theology of Latin America, yet managed to maintain close ties with the socially conservative Pope John Paul II. Protestant Christians, while numerous in Central Africa and parts of francophone West Africa, were less active than Catholics in national politics. The largest Protestant denomination, the Kimbanguist church of Zaire and Congo, focused its energies on religious devotion and on family and social service, though it did have seats in the national conference of Zaire. Only in Madagascar were Protestants a leading force, as they set the tone for the Ecumenical Association which led the opposition to President Ratsiraka.

The old religions of Africa might seem to the casual observer to have lost the initiative, surviving in the 1990s mainly as local modifications to Islam and Christianity. Occasionally they made the headlines, as when President Nicéphore Soglo of Benin sought the support of traditional religious leaders in his 1996 campaign for re-election. But a comparison with the Americas suggests that Africa's ancient religious heritage might experience a renaissance. In the cities of Brazil, the United States, and the Caribbean, the African-based cults known as Candomblé, Vodun, and Santería grew in the late twentieth century through a ritual and a theology that appeared to speak in an effective fashion to the needs of an urban population in the industrial age.

In religion as in other areas of cultural expression, African cities and rural areas became crossroads of global exchange because of the variety of traditions and outlooks contending for space. Between Christians and Muslims, and with other groups as well, Africa would become an important terrain for working out new accommodations among religious traditions, and between religious and secular approaches.

BEYOND IMPUNITY

In Africa and all over the world during the 1990s, people discussed with intensity the concept of democracy. In the same breath, people in francophone Africa also spoke of the problem of *impunity*. Impunity refers to a situation in which powerful people may act as they wish without fear of reprisal or need for justification. Arbitrary arrest and taxation were holdovers from colonial Africa, when governments could act with impunity, justifying themselves by the right of the civilized to structure life for the uncivilized. Postcolonial corruption and nepotism represented extensions of the colonial culture of impunity into independent Afica. The unlimited power of army and police in national affairs reinforced the culture of impunity. The toleration of genocidal slaughter was perhaps the height of impunity, but the recurring tendency of international organizations to dictate policy to African nations in their debt was another sort of impunity.

The strength of African popular impulses for democracy at the beginning of the 1990s expressed more than a call for new political parties and more elections. It was a call for the end of impunity, the formation of consensus, and the establishment of responsible government. To end impunity meant the establishment of some common rules which all would respect; to form consensus meant accepting democracy as a practice of give and take among conflicting parties confronting serious social issues. A responsible government would follow these practices, and step down when it lost public support.

This call for the end to impunity was a cautious claim, rather than a utopian dream. It probably seemed obvious, to anyone growing up and learning of the world from an African vantage point, that life would be unfair. But it seemed that there should be limits to the unfairness of life, and those limits should be enforced by common agreement. This was the proposition on which masses of people – wealthy and poor, urban and rural – expressed themselves repeatedly in their calls for national conferences and national consensus.

Meanwhile, the inhabitants of francophone Africa sought to apply imagination and humor to surmounting the unfairness and the difficulties of life. The hopes for rapid economic growth of the immediate post-independence era were gone – the term "development," so commonly used by Africans and by international experts in the late colonial and early postcolonial years, had left the vocabulary of the mid-1990s. For a time it was popular to speak of the "maquis," drawing on a French slang term for outlaws. The term came into use in reference to restaurants (in Abidjan and then elsewhere) which avoided paying taxes, and then came to refer to any institution which might seem anti-establishment. But the maquis restaurants became commercialized rapidly, and in any case the notion of escaping taxes seemed contrary to the ideals of civic responsibility which dominated during the era of democratization movements, so the term lost its popularity.

More lasting was the term "débrouiller," meaning to "muddle through." The French term from which it comes refers to fog, so the activity can be seen as "clearing the fog." Men, women and children of francophone Africa, tired of living in precarious circumstances yet proud of their skills in survival, spoke of their towns as places in which life centered on struggling to get by. They lived in "la cité de la débrouille."

9

Epilogue

On a dry day in the wet Cameroonian climate, the morning sun peers over the hills on the east side of Yaoundé. The central bank building looms above the city, gleaming in the early light yet casting its shadow into the commercial center. In the streets below, piles of paper and plastic lie strewn outside the doors of the night clubs – the bottles and cans have already been collected by pre-dawn scavengers. In the old residential quarter of Mvog-Ada, roosters call the day into existence. In the newer quarter of Essos, the day begins with the motorized sound of generators, compensating for undependable central power. On streets throughout the city, meanwhile, vendors light their charcoal, set up plank benches for customers, and prepare to serve breakfasts of instant coffee (laced with canned and sugared milk), freshly baked bread, and scrambled eggs.

In the northern quarter of Tsinga, a comfortably established family begins its day at the breakfast table. The cook sets out a breakfast like that of the sidewalk cafes, but with the addition of papaya slices. The children are sent off to school: public school for the girl, a Catholic prep school for the boy. The man of the house takes the car to inspect the construction sites he directs; his wife, running late, hails a taxi rather than wait for a bus, and climbs into the seat crowded with two passengers already heading for the center of town. By avoiding the wait she not only saves time, but escapes having to endure the smell of the burning and festering trash in the nearby field. (In Tsinga, recent and destitute immigrants from the rural north of Cameroon live interspersed with established urbanites, and the refuse heap reflects the contributions of both groups.)

The taxi works its way along the crowded Boulevard du Général de Gaulle. As it approaches the city center it enters the Place de l'Indépendance, where men sit at desks with manual typewriters, ready to type letters or documents. The driver waits patiently through the congestion in the commercial district along rue de Nachtigal, passing the central market, the cinema, and the Japanese- and Korean-owned stores selling electronic goods and textiles. The taxi stops to drop off and pick up other riders, and finally deposits the woman at City Hall, where she works as a receptionist. With its round and vertical architecture, the city hall is one of the structures which has made Yaoundé the most architecturally striking of Africa's cities.

Dawn and dusk show the beauty of the city, nestled among hills punctuated by streams, its major buildings illuminated electrically and its neighborhoods illuminated by kerosene lamps. But the brightness and heat of mid-day force one's attention on the holes in the streets, and the sights and smells of uncollected trash of every sort. The streams flowing into the Mfoundi River serve as a prime dumping spot for refuse, as well as a place for washing clothes.

The doubling of Yaoundé's population every ten years had led, at the end of the 1980s, to the crisis in refuse disposal. Its specific causes were multiple: the combination of new arrivals from the countryside, not accustomed to urban needs for careful disposal, the expansion of new forms of paper and plastic packaging, and a growing demoralization of the political community, each worsened the crisis. From 1979 the French firm of Hysacam held the contract for refuse collection in Yaoundé, but it gradually became clear that Hysacam could not do the job and the municipality could not pay the fees, so the contract was annulled in 1991. In the aftermath, a mix of city collectors, private refuse firms, community groups, and individual scavengers attempted without great success to process the city's trash.

In suburban Tsinga, as in the city center, a growing number of lives came to center around the refuse heaps. An urban pig-farmer was able to spend half his day collecting food for his animals from refuse heaps, and the other half of the day caring for the pigs. A father of five, he was able to send his children to Qur'anic school with his income from collecting aluminum, bottles, iron and machinery; he carried his finds by taxi to the firms that would purchase them for recycling. Women scavenging in the refuse heaps included those who sought household items (such as plastic and aluminum containers or used clothing), and those who collected items for sale, such as cement sacks and other paper. Some actually prospered: a collector of scrap metal bought two trucks and engaged numerous employees, delivering his findings to the military and major firms.

If the city appeared in decay at its center, it was still in construction at its periphery. The head of the family in Tsinga quarter, though a secondary-school graduate with some university training, had found his only secure income as a construction contractor. In the days of his youth he had worked with his father in constructing the family house, mixing imported cement with local sand to make the cement blocks which are the essential element of modern African home construction. Working his way through school as an occasional construction laborer, he learned both the techniques of design and construction, and the skills of gaining title to land and negotiating with municipal officials to gain electrical connections. On this as on other days, he drove from plot to plot, making arrangements at each. The plots all had partially constructed homes, as the families waited until they had money to make the cement blocks and to hire the workers to complete construction. This man's occupation was marginal yet sucessful – Yaoundé had many people in substandard housing, yet few who were homeless. Known as a contractor, he held no license, but was able to maintain his income with an active campaign of contacts with families in need of help in constructing homes, and with experienced workers in need of a paying job.

A morning's tour through Yaoundé provides many instances of continuity and change. Change in modern Afica has a new level of recognition: everything seems to have changed in town, and much has changed in the countryside. Yaoundé began as a clean and elegant little capital city. The heaps of trash, the evening fires causing as much pollution as they eliminate – these are new in one sense, but in another sense they are the inevitable extension of building a city without civic consciousness. The people of Yaoundé complain about an unrepresentative government, yet they have not found a way to support an orderly handling of their city's affairs.

The reason for the historian's emphasis on change is in order to analyze the causes of change. In the view presented here, the forces of change stem not only from foreign pressures, but also from the conflicts among Africans, their wills for improvement, and their imaginative responses to the problems they faced. Change has occurred not only among the social elite, but in all levels of society. The direction of change has been not simply toward replication of European society, but rather toward specifically African patterns of modernity. Further, we have emphasized that change was fundamental not only in areas of technology, but also in the social structures and culture of Africans. It has been the purpose of this book to demonstrate the depth of the changes and the transformations of these societies – as well as to demonstrate that the transformations took place within the bounds and patterns set by the pre-existing societies.

The basic problems faced by African societies have changed during the past century. For most of the nineteenth century, Africa had much cultural and political autonomy. Even in the nineteenth-century years before French and Belgian colonization, the lands which became francophone Africa underwent major social transformations. At that time most of the continent was linked to the world economy by a mercantile capitalist order, which made Africans into slaves both overseas and at home; it developed growing conflicts among classes and ethnic groups in Africa. In the middle years of the nineteenth century, Africans developed new mercantile links to the world economy through the export of agricultural produce. Overall, the issue of slavery came more and more to dominate Africa's relations with the rest of the world, and to dominate the economic system and social conflicts of African territories themselves. At the same time, the expansion of new economic opportunities within Africa and the expansion of the European-dominated world economy led inexorably to the political clash. The result of that clash was the colonial occupation of Africa.

In the colonial era, the issue of slavery receded rapidly into invisibility in public discourse. The colonizers focused on the political and economic subjugation of the continent. African links to the world economy were now guided as much by the workings of administrative policy as by the activity of merchants. Meanwhile, the colonial ideology of the racial and cultural inferiority of Africans brought a profound humiliation to the colonized. Africans were put in the position of striving for recognition of their culture, and for recognition of their rights to self-government. They had at once to reassert the value of their ancestral civilization and to demonstrate the ability to assimilate francophone civilization. Colonization at once exploited the many divisions among Africans and minimized those divisions by lumping all Africans into a single racial category. As a result, Africans expressed remarkable unity in their national movements during the crucial decades of the 1950s and 1960s. This unity, however, was political rather than social.

The international recognition of African nations successfully contradicted the colonial denial of African political rights and cultural equality. The precolonial heritage of slavery was thus set far into the background, and the colonial heritage of racial discrimination was denounced by all (though perpetuated by some). Now, in the late twentieth century, the African economies were linked to the world economy through corporate ties and through international finance. African polities were linked to the world political system through a welter of bilateral and multilateral ties, and in a continuing atmosphere of Cold War. Now the conflicts within African nations rose to the surface, as conflicting class and ethnic groups strove to gain control over the nation's resources.

These problems of the late twentieth century – development of national institutions and national culture, and the attempt to define and assert positions of equality in the world economic order – are thus fundamentally different from the problems which earlier generations faced during the colonial era and the precolonial era. To repeat, the key difference is not only that technology has improved, nor that religious beliefs have changed, nor even that family structures have changed. The crucial difference in Africa today is that the types of problem facing Africans in the late twentieth century are different from the problems of earlier periods. Francophone Africans of today face new kinds of freedom and of oppression, new kinds of equality and of inequality, new kinds of wealth and of poverty, new kinds of health and of sickness, new levels of independence and of dependency.

This concluding chapter turns now to a review of the francophone African urban landscape in the mid-1990s. The contrast between this modern landscape and that of the 1880s will help to show how far each of the trends discussed in previous chapters has progressed. In the concluding section, we undertake an analysis of conflicting visions of African destiny, as enunciated by various leading individuals and groups in contemporary francophone Africa. By comparing the modern visions to those of a century ago, we may gain an appreciation of what has remained the same and what has changed during this busy century.

THE FRANCOPHONE AFRICAN LANDSCAPE

Kinshasa celebrated its centennial in 1981. A century earlier, Stanley had founded his station of Leopoldville at Malebo Pool near the two villages of Nshasa and Ntampo. Nshasa remained the population center of the area. Its name, soon modified by Lingala-speakers to Kinshasa, remained the common name of the growing city even while the Belgian maps labelled it Leopoldville. At its centennial, Kinshasa included 2.5 million inhabitants, and thus exceeded the combined population of Abidjan and Dakar, the next largest francophone African cities. Kinshasa's 1981 population was an astonishing five times its size at independence two decades earlier, and the city continued to grow by 150,000 inhabitants each year: 100,000 through births and 50,000 through immigration from the countryside. By 1995 the metropolitan area had reached a population exceeding five million.

The city's splendid center was maintained and further embellished in the early years of independence. Exclusive boutiques, patronized by men and women in stylish dress, dotted the wide and tree-lined streets. The elegant buildings constructed in the colonial era came to share space with towering new structures. This was "Kin-la-belle," where well-to-do Kinois and Kinoises prided themselves on leading the good life.

Though it built rapidly upward, the Central African metropolis spread outward even more rapidly. Government-sponsored housing developments covered great areas at the edge of town, but privately built homes (some with permits and many without) outnumbered them. Rainfall declined as the extent of the city grew. In the area surrounding the city, wood was cleared out almost entirely in response to the need for firewood. The gallery forest of Lukaya lost from 20 to 200,000 tons of wood per year.

Transportation became a growing problem as the city grew. Roughly 80 percent of the vehicles in all Zaire were centered in and around the capital. The problem in transportation was not so much the shortage of vehicles, but the shortage of good roads; road work had not kept up with the growth of the city, either in construction of major highways, or in maintenance of local streets. The state took over the city transportation system in the years 1971–73 as part of the Zairianization campaign. Then a system of private taxis grew up to supplement it.

Despite the importance of the state in Zaire's economy, most working Kinois held jobs in the private sector. Unemployment in Kinshasa hit 25 percent in 1981 and rose thereafter. But for those who held jobs, roughly two-thirds worked for large and small private enterprise, and one-third worked either in the public sector or in mixed enterprises owned jointly by the state and private firms. Among the main areas of work were transportation (including rail, river, and air transport), work in food processing, metallurgy, textiles, and construction. Artisanal production, shopkeeping and marketing accounted for a large amount of employment.

The economic and social tentacles of the city reached far into the countryside. The food for this huge and growing population came primarily from the lower Zaire region, but an increasing proportion was brought in by rail and air from distant areas of the country. Manioc provided the basis of the Kinois diet; other important foodstuffs were bread, bananas, rice, fish, beans, and meat. A new threat to the food supply arose after 1980; bacterial blight cut down yields of manioc throughout Central Africa, and it took years before new and resistant varieties were developed and introduced.

Health conditions remained remarkably good in the city. Death rates declined to half the rate of rural Zaire, and to levels comparable to some European countries. In 1981 a survey found one doctor for each 4,000 inhabitants, six times the ratio for the population of Zaire overall; and three hospital beds per thousand population. But the endles sproblems of rapid expansion eventually began to bring new health problems. Illegal construction of houses, lack of such infrastructure as sewerage, running water, and electricity – these problems eventually caused the incidence of malaria to rise. Air pollution began to grow in importance. Then, in the mid-1980s, recognition of the sudden and rapid spread of acquired immune deficiency syndrome (AIDS) through much of the city's population brought a major new public health problem.

Kinois of the 1990s lived in family settings. This was a sharp contrast to the colonial era population, which was heavily male, and in which there were few children. Some aspects of the colonial heritage, however, hung on. Every adult was required to have an identity card, and movement from one section of the country to another required administrative approval and a travel permit. Similarly, those employed were still required to have a work permit, as had been the case under the Belgians. In colonial days, this had served mainly to restrict the movement of people, and to prevent the growth of cities. In the years after independence, it no longer prevented the movement of people nor the formation of normal family units in the cities. Instead, as the Zairois passed through the bureaucracy, they made payments – in firewood, manioc, cigarettes, or money – to officials as the price of achieving their desires.

The city, while more friendly to the family than in earlier years, did not become friendly to marriage. As early as the mid-1960s, the rate of divorce had become so high in Kinshasa that couples often declined to register their marriages, in order to avoid the possible costs of registering their divorce later on.

But if marriage suffered in the city, both childbirth and schooling had now come to prosper. Rates of fertility rose to over 50 children per 1,000 females per year, which meant a population growth rate of over 4 percent per year at low urban rates of mortality. Virtually all children went to primary school, and a growing proportion went to secondary school. Further, girls now attended primary school in almost the same proportion as boys. In colonial years, only one-third of the city girls went through primary schools, as there was virtually no work for them which required an education.

Almost all children in Kinshasa attended elementary school, and the proportion entering and completing secondary school grew steadily until economic crisis halted the growth. By 1981 the number of primary and secondary teachers had risen to 13,000. Schools were crowded, and teachers complained regularly of the conditions. Periodically, they struck for better conditions and closed the schools.

Another 15,000 city officials handled other aspects of city government. Municipal government only gradually took form. The city had no real municipal government until 1929, and then its government was set up as capital of the whole Belgian Congo. In 1941 Leopoldville was divided into the European

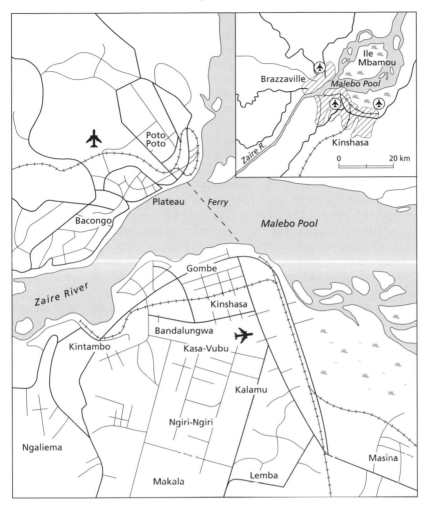

Map 13   Kinshasa and Brazzaville, 1995

zone and the "*cité indigène*" or native quarter. Only at the very end of the colonial period, in 1957, did the Belgian administration introduce the normal Belgian system of municipal government, that of communes; the city was divided into fifteen independent communes, with a council of representatives for each. This system of government survived until 1971, when it was replaced by a single centralized government, rather on the French model. By the mid-1980s, demands for the election of city officials began to be heard widely, but the Mobutu government held firmly to control of the city administration, arguing that it could ensure the highest quality of administration by making appointments based on merit.

Brazzaville, a twenty minute trip by ferry across the Zaire River from Kinshasa, remained in a sharply different world. Though the two cities were united by the Zaire valley, by the history of regional commerce, and by the cultural unities of their peoples, the century-long existence of the border had set up major differences between them. Brazzaville had never approached the size or population of Kinshasa. Though both cities drew immigrants from the Kikongo-speaking environs, Kinshasa became more and more a Lingala-speaking city, while Brazzaville remained a Kikongo-speaking city. Each was the nexus of a great commercial and administrative network, but the links between the two were minor and mostly illegal.

Just as Kinshasa developed with the European center of Leopoldville and the two great African quarters of Kinshasa and Kintambo, so did Brazzaville develop with a European center linked to the two great African quarters of Bacongo and Poto-Poto. Bacongo and Poto-Poto were laid out in roughly 1910, as Brazzaville first began to grow under the influence of the government general and the concessionary companies. The city then expanded in great jolts: the years of railroad construction (1921–1934), the early war years (1940–41), the post-war years (1947–49), and again in the late 1950s and 1970s.

The years after independence brought great expansion in the scale of the city, and yet also brought considerable improvements in the quality of life. As in Kinshasa, many women moved to the city, so that the sex ratio become nearly equal, and the number of children in the city rose sharply. New quarters opened up, though with conflicts over the ownership of land, as it was being sold both by the city and by private landholders, who had conflicting claims. Efforts were made to pave new roads, and to extend electrical and kerosene lighting, and water drawn from public fountains. Most houses had metal roofs rather than thatch. Kitchens were generally separated from the rest of the house, because of the danger of fire from the wood fires for cooking. One fortunate area of town, where most houses had water and electricity, became known as "Camp Chic" and "Tahiti."

Neighborhood organizations focused increasingly on church groups. Catholics, who comprised roughly half the city's population, were formed into groups based on their parish church, parish schools (that is, until these were nationalized) and into social and cultural groups for both men and women. Protestant churches included the two overseas mission groups, but also included three more recently formed groups. These were the Salvation Army, the Kimbanguist Church (formed in Zaire, but influential in Congo as well, especially among Bakongo people) and the Matswa movement. The latter movement, based on the personality of André Matswa, became a religious movement after World War II.

The women of Brazzaville, even though they were bringing up many children of their own, had money incomes as well. They managed this by acting as hosts to young immigrants from the countryside, who cared for their children while they worked. As long as the city was small enough to permit the cultivation of crops nearby, some women had managed sizeable farms; as land became scarce, small vegetable gardens became the rule. Other women sold produce in the market. Chief among these were the manioc sellers – manioc was the main staple of the inhabitants of Brazzaville, as of other Central African cities. They sold manioc as meal, as flour, and in loaves; they also sold palm oil and palm wine. On a smaller scale, many women set up stands at their own houses and sold their wares to passers-by. Still other women became seamstresses, and began to challenge the tailors for their control of the market for clothing. Finally, a small but growing number of women had salaried employment, mainly as teachers and paramedics, but with the passage of time as clerical employees too.

Dakar, like Brazzaville, grew at a moderate pace after independence, rather than at the extraordinary rates of Kinshasa, Abidjan, Conakry, or Bangui. Dakar was now the capital of Senegal only, rather than governing all of French West Africa. New construction there was in tourist hotels rather than in government buildings. Exceptions were in the expansion of the university and in the expansion of the central bank, which retained its influence over all of francophone West Africa.

The central bank building provides a wonderfully ambiguous symbol of Dakar's position in the world. The building itself is of very original construction, seventeen stories high with an oval floor plan, and decorated with brown stone replicas of traditional sculptures including those represented on the CFA coins and bills. It was designed by the Senegalese firm of Goudiaby and N'Gom, who won an international competition for the contract. The tower sits prominently on the waterfront at the beginning of the corniche, overlooking the harbor. Yet this symbol of the independence and individuality of West African culture housed a central bank whose governors were beholden almost entirely to France, in that the CFA franc remained tied to the French franc at the rate of 50 to 1 (exactly the rate at which it was set in 1949), so that the CFA franc changed in value if and only if the French franc changed. (CFA referred to "Colonies francaises d'Afrique" when the term was coined in 1946; the acronym was preserved by changing the reference to "Commmunauté financière africaine.") In return for dependency, this arrangement brought monetary stability to the former French colonies, in contrast to the great fluctuations in exchange rates experienced by Zaire, Rwanda, Burundi, and Guinea, each of whose currencies was governed by its own central bank. Yet the dependency was reaffirmed in 1994 as the central bank devalued the CFA franc by 50 percent.

The Place de l'Indépendance dominated central Dakar. This great square, laid out in 1895, was surrounded with banks, airline agencies, and restaurants; hotels formed the next concentric circle beyond the square. The location of these offices revealed the service base of the economy of Dakar; at slightly more distance to the north were the administrative offices of the state, and to the south were the transportation centers of the port and the railroad. At strategic points around the square were the hawkers of curios, the would-be tourist guides, and the beggars. All of these marginal people congregated in the areas where there was the most hope of finding people open to their particular claims. The beggars included middle-aged persons with leprosy, though these were smaller in number than they had been in earlier years, and children who were victims of polio. The polio victims were an ironic reflection of improving health conditions. Had they been raised on the untreated water of old, they would have been exposed to the polio virus as infants, and would have recovered unscathed. But since they were raised on an improved but imperfect urban water system, they were infected with polio at ages beyond five, and thus were crippled.

The Dakarois walked rapidly along the narrow sidewalks, to and from work, or queued up for the buses which ran with remarkable regularity to destinations throughout the city and suburbs. The piety of this heavily Muslim sociey was everywhere in evidence, perhaps more so than is warranted. For hidden along the side streets were numerous speakeasies. There it was possible to have a quiet sip of beer or gin, and to avoid flouting in public the prohibitions against consumption of alcohol.

Dakar remained a tourist spot for Europeans and for Africans as well. Artisans sold their wares at Soumbedioune, at the Mauritanian market, and on the streets. A favorite tourist jaunt was to take the motor launch to the island of Gorée, and to walk its quiet streets. The buildings once occupied by the William Ponty school were now a girls' finishing school. Population of the island had declined, and by the 1980s the houses had been taken over as vacation homes by European and American businessmen, but also by such luminaries as Leopold Senghor, Félix Houphouët-Boigny, and Mobutu Sese Seko. Most visitors to the island toured the old French fort and the "Maison des esclaves" or Slave House, including the quarters in which slaves were held before being shipped to the Americas. The curator of the museum, Joseph NDiaye, gave emotion-charged descriptions of the sale and loading of the slaves, and told his credulous audiences that ten million slaves passed through this very fort. In fact this figure was exaggerated, for ten million is close to the total of slaves leaving all the ports of western Africa, and Gorée was a minor port in the slave trade. The symbol of the island, however, retained its power. During the 1990s, public opinion and the action of African governments brought to UNESCO the proposal to build, on Gorée, a major monument to commemorate the victims of the Atlantic slave trade.

Beyond the plateau, the corniche, the harbor, and the public buildings of Dakar lay the Medina, the popular quarters. Dominated by the great mosque, the Medina extended for three densely populated kilometers north and east of the Plateau. Houses there were built mostly in concrete, though some in scarce thatch; water and electricity reached certain nodal points in each neighborhood, but little further.

The new urban focus of West Africa in the 1980s was Abidjan; more than twice the size of Dakar, it nearly matched the Nigerian metropolis of Lagos in size and intensity, and exceeded it in brilliance. Abidjan's growth and prosperity stemmed from its importance as a port and commercial center, and later as an industrial center. It did not become capital of Ivory Coast until 1928, and in the 1980s it was slowly relieved of its function of national capital as the center of government was gradually transferred to Yamoussoukro, the home of

President Houphouët-Boigny near the geographic center of the country. With the death of Houphouët-Boigny in 1993, governmental functions moved rapidly back to Abidjan.

Abidjan is perched on the Ile de Petit-Bassam and on a series of peninsulas protruding into the Ebrié Lagoon. North of the island, across the Houphouët-Boigny Bridge and the de Gaulle Bridge, lies the Plateau. It was originally laid out as the European quarter, and in the years after independence it came to support a host of skyscraping buildings, large and small shops, hotels, banks, corporate and government offices, and luxury residences. On the island and directly facing the Plateau lies Treichville, which began as the African residential quarter but rapidly became the industrial section of town. The port, railroad yards, food-processing plants, construction and manufacturing enterprises were centered here and across another bridge at Petit Bassam on the coastal sand spit, alongside the short canal leading to the Atlantic. The workers, about equally split into those of Ivory Coast nationality and expatriates from Burkina Faso, Ghana, Mali, and elsewhere, steadily extended their settlements eastward to Koumassi and then to New Koumassi. Meanwhile an exclusive residential quarter developed north of the lagoon in Cocody. Despite the striking contrasts between wealth and poverty in the city, and despite the sharp rise in unemployment which came with the virtual halt of Ivory Coast's economic growth in the mid-1980s, the city continued to exude the impression of bustle and expansion which had been its hallmark since World War II. Supplies of food to the city, however, were restricted by the spread of maize streak virus through the countryside, which cut back production of the region's main food crop.

The petty producers of Abidjan showed remarkable ingenuity in finding ways to create employment and eke out incomes. Alongside the soap factory in Treichville, Malian women manufactured their own low-priced soap by processing refuse from the factory. On the Plateau, young boys found work washing cars and guarding them against theft. Girls who carried water for sale found that at times they could do better by washing the mud-covered feet of pedestrians. Walking bankers visited each of their many clients daily, collecting small savings deposits from those who had no other place to put their money. Tailors carried sewing machines on their heads while in search of clients; young men with schooling but without jobs acted as scribes, and some specialized in falsification of documents.

CONFLICTING VISIONS OF AFRICAN DESTINY

Each generation must eventually yield its position to the succeeding generation. This transition, while it often passes imperceptibly, sometimes appears in sharp definition. Such was the case for the passage of influence during the 1990s from the first generation of post-independence leaders in francophone Africa to a second generation. In national political affairs, a combination of retirements, deaths and political upheavals brought new individuals and new philosophies to power. In cultural affairs, the passage of time and changes in

taste brought new individuals and new, more cosmopolitan styles to prominence. In economic affairs, twenty years of economic hardship at home, in the
face of global concentration of economic power, brought both innovations
and accommodations to face the difficulties.

Those who emerged to contend with the first generation of leaders, throughout francophone sub-Saharan Africa, came from urban and professional
strata. They included male and female professionals in education, administration and religion, university students, and leaders in popular culture – who
spoke out against what they saw as the stagnation and corruption in national
life. Their rhetoric gave emphasis to a vision of *human rights* as the basis for the
social order. Most easily recognized among these were expatriate academics
whose writings set forth this vision. Prominent among them were Achille
Mbembe of Cameroun, who moved to the United States, and Ernest Wamba
dia-Wamba of Zaire, who gained release from prison after an international
campaign and moved to Tanzania.

While these cosmopolitan figures, coming from situations of relative privilege, were most visible in raising criticisms of the Power, the rural populations
and the urban poor also played a part in the generational change. The
members of this majority, though they had little direct access to the levers of
political power or the microphones of public discourse, nevertheless had the
experience of dramatic changes in their lives and a desire to gain some of the
improvements they had been promised. By the 1990s the majority of African
populations had grown up after independence. The members of this second
generation were less satisfied than their parents with the explanation that it
was necessary to sacrifice for the benefit of the nation in order to overcome the
effects of colonialism.

Some areas of life had indeed improved rather than worsening in the
generation since independence. Mortality conditions had improved, levels of
education and literacy were rising, and African ties to neighboring countries
and to other continents were growing. But African economies were not growing, especially by contrast with those in Asia. And the narrow, nationalistic
reality behind the populist rhetoric of the entrenched political leaders made
clear that the benefits of national life were to go to a select few. For the rural
and urban populations that had felt more disappointment than fulfillment in
post-colonial years, the response was not so much an articulate expression of a
vision as a forceful complaint: "*ça suffit! – that's enough!*"

Felix Houphouët-Boigny stood out as the most influential and effective of
the first generation of post-independence leaders, and he maintained his hold
to the end. His vision of *state capitalism*, set in place in the 1950s, maintained
significant strength even with the sharp economic decline at the end of the
1980s. Even during the last two years before his death at about ninety in 1993,
he choreographed a convincing response to the democratization movement in
Ivory Coast which challenged his regime. An opposition to Houphouët-
Boigny had arisen in the course of the democratization movements, and
succeeded in gaining a permanent place in the national discourse, yet remained
far from gaining power.

The most prominent opposition leader, Laurent Gbagbo – a college professor in his forties – exemplified the second generation of post-independence activists. Gbagbo was skilled as a writer, speaker, and organizer, and could rely on significant popular dissatisfaction with the regime as a source of support. Yet he was unable to gain a central place in Ivory Coast politics, and his failure exemplified the difficulties of the second generation in overturning the patterns left by the first.

Houphouët-Boigny, in his response to the opposition, relied heavily on old alliances – with the overseas banks and corporations which invested heavily in Ivory Coast, with the government of France, and with the Catholic Church. These outside ties, as well as his adept use of his political party and elections, helped to turn back the opposition. To reaffirm his influence over the Catholic Church, for instance, Houphouët-Boigny won agreement by Pope John Paul II to consecrate his huge and controversial cathedral at Yamoussoukro. His long-standing ties to François Mitterrand brought continuing French support for his regime.

Throughout francophone Africa, as in Ivory Coast, international influences played a role in the growing distance and conflict between the Power and Civil Society, and in the generational shift of the 1990s. These international influences, while perhaps as powerful as ever, were now different from and more complex than the straightforward colonial dominance of Africans for the century beginning the 1880s. In 1880 the international forces had consisted of a few imperial powers, the Catholic church, some Protestant denominations, and European merchant firms. By 1995 the great powers were not only those of Europe, but also the United States, Japan, Russia and China. (In another change, the nations of Asia and Latin America were now sometimes able to make common cause with those of Africa.) Overseas corporations, while more powerful than ever, were now based in a wider range of countries. Organized religion now meant Islam as well as Christianity. And, in perhaps the greatest change, several types of international organization had taken shape: the World Bank and International Monetary Fund as representatives of international business, the United Nations and its numerous organs as service organizations, and numerous health, environmental and other organizations. From this range of international influences came a range of contending visions of African destiny.

From outside the continent, Africans felt the impact of several visions of *global tutelage*, through which powerful institutions sought to establish policies and constraints. The World Bank and IMF carried out a policy of *structural adjustment* – urging relentless belt-tightening, layoffs and privatization on African governments. France preached *francophonie*, which may be seen as an updated form of *assimilation*. French President François Mitterrand remained as influential in African affairs of the 1990s as he had been in the immediate post-war years, and his retirement from the presidency in 1993 and death in 1995 still left France's assimilationist policy toward Africa in effect. Belgium steadily lost influence over its former colonies, though commerce and migration caused ties between individual Belgians and Africans to grow at the personal level. At a greater distance, governments of the United States empha-sized a vision of the strengths of *Western Civilization*, urging Africans to tie their future to it.

If the outside world offered Africans tutelage in economic and political affairs, this was far less the case for religious and cultural affairs. Among Christians, Africans participated in the global discussions of *ecumenism*, the effort to share traditions and even organizational structures among various Christian sects. In Islam, Africans participated as members of an increasingly connected, global Muslim community. This very unity brought to each Afri-can country the debates within Islam – whether, for instance, to emphasize the strict-interpretationist views of *fundamentalism* or the less literal views of *Islamic modernism*. In other areas of culture, Africans received mixed messages from the world beyond the continent. On the one hand, dramatic increases in the overseas popularity of African music, literature, dance and styles of dress suggested that Africans should look to themselves and their heritage for cultural strength. On the other hand, the impact of Western elite culture and of Western popular culture, now conveyed by powerful electronic media, put pressure on Africans to look outward for cultural inspiration.

The career of musical enthusiast Georges Collinet reflected the mixture of continent and overseas in determining new visions of African life. Collinet, who was born in Cameroon and educated in the French language, came to work from the 1970s for the Voice of America. This US governmental radio service, broadcasting to Africa, linked Cold War political analysis with nurtur-ing African links to the US. Collinet's own work on VOA was to play African music. In so doing he traveled and developed ties with musicians all over Africa; he turned to urging them to continue working creatively in Africa rather than migrate to the money in Paris. In the late 1980s he created a US radio show, "Afropop," which did much to popularize African music in the US. The program then became "Afropop Worldwide," reflecting the interest of Collinet and his audience in hearing music from all the African disapora. The result was to expand the scope of African music, and also to bring overlaps in the musical traditions of French, English, and several other languages.

This example, linking corporate and governmental influences within Africa and abroad, also reminds us of the growing ties of cultural and even political identity within what came to be called the African diaspora. In Africa, mem-bers of the new African generation saw themselves partly in alliance with and partly in opposition to these numerous international influences, but focused primarily on advancing their position at home. In response to visions of francophonie or Western Civilization, Africans could seek out a UN-based *cosmopolitanism* or a developing though informal *pan-Africanism*.

African society of the 1990s, meanwhile, was stratified in far different ways from the 1880s. While peasant farmers remained the largest social class in Africa, these farmers were now tied to global communication networks, and family members migrated back and forth to urban areas. The cities included large new classes of wage workers, and even larger classes of people who earned their living through petty enterprises both legal and extra-legal. Near the peak of African social orders stood the professional class, itself highly stratified and ranging from schoolteachers to powerful heads of ministries. The complexity of this social order encouraged people to think in cosmopolitan terms.

A continental version of the new generation of African *cosmopolitanism* was that of the Zairian singer Mbilia Bel. She began her career singing with Rochereau, then built an equally large audience on her own. She remained in Kinshasa, however, in contrast to such other Zairian stars as Koffi Olomide and Kanda Bongo Man who moved their base to Paris. Mbilia Bel developed a male co-star, Rigo Star, and kept her music current by such devices as titling a 1990 song "Tenanmen." Released within months of the demonstrations in Beijing, this Lingala-language love song made no specific reference to China, yet hinted at the relevance of global affairs. Mbilia Bel's cosmopolitanism, if discreet, was in contrast to Mobutu's official doctrine of *authenticity*. A slightly different vision of African culture was that of the literary scholar Guy Ossito Midiohouan, who expressed dreams of African cultural autonomy, hoping that literatures would be able to grow up in African languages as music had in Lingala.

A new factor on the African scene was the vision of *gender equity*. The importance of women in African life had rarely been denied, but claims for social equality were new. In one striking example, women of Niger held out for greater representation at the beginning of the 1991 National Conference. They encountered accusations that their demands were impeding the conference. The accusations became all the more forceful as the roof collapsed in the auditorium where the delegates had convened. But the conference moved to the basketball stadium, in a step that clearly evoked the movement of the French Third Estate to the tennis court in 1789, and women did gain some additional seats. Thus did women in this largely Muslim country challenge their relative absence in positions of political leadership. In so doing, they also challenged the scarcity of women in African public media – for instance, their almost total absence from the pages of *Jeune Afrique*. In 1993, economist Mahamane Ousmane campaigned for president of Niger with a strong emphasis on women's issues and women's votes. He owed his margin of victory to their support, and then faced the need to provide these constituents with the improvements he had promised.

Many Africans sought to navigate a route between World Bank structural adjustment and the regulations of African socialism with *deregulation*. Popular dissatisfaction with African regimes rumbled in seismic tones beneath the continent's surface, then broke into the open as waves of protest, making claims for *human rights*.

The new generation swept to power in half the countries of francophone sub-Saharan Africa, but in the remaining countries the old rulers and their proxies maintained political control well into the 1990s. Houphouët-Boigny was able to pass power on to a younger proxy, Henri Konan Bédié. In this he matched some cases of the 1980s, in which Abdou Diouf maintained leadership in Senegal after Leopold Senghor passed the baton to him, and Paul Biya held on to dominance in Cameroon in the wake of Amadou Ahidjo. In Gabon, Omar Bongo held to power as the successor to Leon M'Ba, though his conversion to Islam was a distinctive step.

The changes in leadership were nevertheless more significant than the continuities. Mobutu Sese Seko, the second most prominent of the surviving first-generation leaders, lost his grasp during the nineties, and was ultimately driven from power, leaving his country in a shambles. His opponents posed a *cosmopolitanism* against his *authenticity*. These and other visions of political community were played out not in national isolation, but in global interconnection. Economists, generally with World Bank ties, became heads of state in such countries as Benin, Congo and Niger, but once in place found that they needed to give primacy to local agendas rather than to impose structural adjustment.

In Mali, the country with perhaps the sharpest break from its past, a historian came to national leadership. Alpha Oumar Konaré rose to influence as the spokesman for a broad alliance of pro-democracy forces based primarily on urban professionals. His ability to enunciate a policy of openness and conciliation helped to guide the country through a difficult period of alliance among elements of the military and various political factions. The approach may be called *constitutional accommodation*, in that it relies at once on the formal governance of a written constitution and on informal negotiations among interest groups. By the mid-1990s, Mali had become a country with returning economic activity and lively political contestation. Even the conflict between central government and the Tuareg peoples (whose homeland overlapped the desert areas of Mali, Niger, and Algeria) seemed closer to peaceable resolution.

For others who shared the vision of constitutional accommodation, the outcome was not always positive. Agathe Uwilingiyimana was notable not only as the first woman to become prime minister of Rwanda (in 1993), but for having staked out a ground for conciliation in a political situation fraught with polarization. As leader of the moderate, dominantly Hutu coalition of political parties seeking accommodation with the invading RPF and with the increasingly Hutu-extremist President Juvénal Habyarimana, she worked to implement the Arusha accords. The killing of Habyarimana as his plane was shot down set loose the armed forces, which surrounded her house and, after a few hours, shot her and her family to death. The Rwandan genocide thus began with the killing of a Hutu national leader by Hutu troops. Uwilingiyimana's vision of constitutional accommodation was ultimately to regain influence in Rwanda, but only after it had been bloodied by unspeakable oppression. The prime minister was cut down in the name of another vision, that of *ethnic cleansing*, also emerging in the aftermath of democratization movements.

Colonel Théoneste Bagosora contributed as much as any individual to developing the vision of *ethnic cleansing* in Africa, in linking the elements that began the massive killing of Tutsi and moderate Hutu in Rwanda in 1994. Bagosora, a high official in the army with close ties to the Interahamwe militias and the propagandistic radio of RTLF, announced, after one of the negotiating sessions in Arusha, that he was returning to Rwanda "to prepare the apocalypse." His plan for genocide, once implemented even in part, seemed to poison all around it.

The experience of Benin, that small but pivotal country in the politics of the 1990s, presented a complex mixture of continuity and change. In the presidential election of 1996, which followed on schedule the election of 1991, President Nicéphore Soglo was defeated by none other than the man removed from power by the democratization movement, Mathieu Kérékou. Soglo's administration had been successful in some ways, but relied too much on old clientelist politics and lost popular favor. Kérékou, "the chameleon," came out of the shadows, campaigned quietly, promised an alternative, and won the balloting. He presented himself as the democratic alternative, though he had support from all the dictators in the surrounding countries. Soglo, in the weeks following the election, presented the strange phenomenon of a government in power complaining that it had lost because of electoral irregularities. The whole transformation was, in a curious way, a validation of the democratization movement.

In the interconnected world of the late twentieth century, Africans had to construct their visions of the future with attention to the ideas of people from other regions. Africans had gained wide recognition of their rights to form nations. Though people from other continents were often confused by the number of African nations, they came increasingly to identify people of African birth by nation ("Senegalese" or "Chadian") rather than by race or by colonial heritage ("Negro" or "French African"). The colonial era was nearly forgotten, and African nations were known not as ex-colonies but as "poor countries." This terminology represents a change from the 1960s and 1970s, when African countries were labelled as "new nations," a term suggesting that Africans were relative youngsters, new to the world scene, who needed time and guidance to mature.

The global acknowledgment of Africans as adult members of the human family, rather than as aliens, sat in dramatic contrast to the categorization of Africans, at the turn of the twentieth century, as the lowest order of humanity. By the 1990s, an accumulation of research in archaeology, human biology, and history had confirmed Africa not only as the cradle of mankind but also as the site of many important developments in human society. Such evidence of the long-term importance of Africa in the human community, along with recurring evidence of the vitality of African cultural expression, reaffirmed the recognition of African nations.

This greater recognition of Africa in world affairs did not, however, extend to economic affairs. There, Africans in the 1990s became in some ways more marginal than previously. They were neglected in global economic statistics and economic diplomacy, and they were left dependent on the massive free-trade blocs growing up in North America and Europe.

More important than the view of Africans from the outside, however, was the question of how Africans would view themselves in the twenty-first century. By the end of the twentieth century, Africans had gained the power publicly to debate their future, though not yet really to choose that future. No African nations or groups of nations had established a common plan of action, nor even a consensus in their vision for the future, except at the most basic level. If there was any vision of African destiny shared widely across the continent, it was a vision of *dignity* for Africa and Africans. That vision summed up the achievements of Africans in the twentieth century, and many hopes for the century to come.

Africa's twentieth century was dominated by *indignity* – the indignities of conquest, continuing slavery, rampant racism, colonial rule, and the denigration of African culture by European conquerors. The achievement of independence in the years around 1960 brought a great step toward dignity. But indignity returned, marring the first generation of political independence with political autocracy and economic dependency. The memories of massacre, of civic anarchy, and of oppression within families lay all too freshly in the minds of many.

In francophone nations as elsewhere on the continent, the men, women and children of Africa did much to win back their dignity in the course of this long century. They gained, under conditions of considerable difficulty, an opportunity to add to the quality of their own lives. In politics, the experience of the democratization movements anchored a proud tradition of building national political institutions in continental and global context. The communities are not yet built, but the events of 1990–92 provided a memorable start. In nation after nation, Civil Society organized itself, recognized its diversity and its potential unity, and pressured the Power to rule not by fiat, but by consent of the governed. In economic life, ties among nations grew, especially through informal commerce, but also through officially recognized trade. The result helped to bring many economies back to growth for the first time since the 1970s.

It was in cultural affairs, more than any other area of life, that Africa had suffered the greatest stigma during the twentieth century. During the colonial era, people around the world accepted stereotypes of African society as uncivilized, backward, and unchanging. Yet it is precisely in cultural affairs that Africans have rebounded most effectively, developing vibrant combinations of new and old concepts in music, literature, philosophy, dance, religion, and dress, and winning recognition and emulation elsewhere as a result. The debates on culture in Africa, so destructive in earlier years, were eventually productive in developing a composite, cosmopolitan culture, be it national, francophone, anglophone, or pan-African.

The achievement of a position of dignity should not be confused with a dream of dominance in world affairs. It seems unlikely that Africans will dominate the world in very many fields of human endeavor – dominating even their home continent would seem to be a major task. Wealth will come slowly to all but a few Africans. Still, the richness of African cultural creations during this difficult century raises the possibility that African soil may be nursing further remarkable achievements in that and other areas. Life in the twentieth century has been a struggle, not least for the peoples of Africa. The twenty-first century holds no promise for the end of struggle, but only for transformation in the nature of the crises and in the tools with which we face them. Yet in this struggle Africans, building on their strengths at home, may reclaim a space on a crowded global stage.

Bibliographical essay

This guide to further reading is restricted almost entirely to books. In addition to these books, many excellent articles may be found in the pages of the journals listed in the second section. The books listed here give emphasis to those in English, including many which have been translated from French. The works are listed within topical sections: each work is listed only once, though some address more than one topic or time period. Within each section, the most general sources are listed first, followed by those which are more specific. In addition, each section begins with books on the nineteenth century, and works its way toward the present, listing works on the colonial era, the era of decolonization, and recent years.

GENERAL AND REFERENCE WORKS

The best one-volume histories of Africa are John Iliffe, *African History* (Cambridge, 1995); Roland Oliver and Anthony Atmore, *Africa Since 1800*, 4th edn (Cambridge, 1994); Philip Curtin, Steven Feierman, Leonard Thompson and Jan Vansina, *African History*, 2nd edn (New York and London, 1995); Bill Freund, *The Making of Contemporary Africa* (Bloomington, 1984); Catherine Coquery-Vidrovitch and Henri Moniot, *L'Afrique noire de 1800 à nos jours*, 2nd edn (Paris, 1988); and, for a focus on social and economic history, Catherine Coquery-Vidrovitch, *Afrique noire, permanences et ruptures* (Paris, 1985).

On the French territories, a broad and informative survey is Jean Suret-Canale, *Afrique noire, occidentale et centrale*, 3 vols. (Paris, 1958, 1964, 1972); volume 2 has been translated into English as *French Colonialism in Tropical Africa 1900–1945*, trans. Till Gottheimer (New York and London, 1971). For a comparison of colonial regimes in West Africa, see Michael Crowder, *West Africa under Colonial Rule* (Evanston, 1968); on Central Africa, see David Birmingham and Phyllis M. Martin, eds., *History of Central Africa*, vol. 2 (London, 1983).

The standard reference work on African history is J. D. Fage and Roland Oliver, eds., *The Cambridge History of Africa*, especially vol. 6, *From 1870 to 1905*, eds. Roland Oliver and G. N. Sanderson (Cambridge, 1985); vol 7, *From 1905 to 1940*, ed. A. D. Roberts (Cambridge, 1986); vol. 8, *From c. 1940 to c. 1975*, ed. Michael Crowder (Cambridge, 1984). The UNESCO *General History of Africa* is a second standard history. See especially vol. 7, *Africa under Colonial Domination, 1880–1935*, ed. A. Adu Boahen (London and Berkeley, 1985); and vol. 8, *Africa since 1935*, ed. Ali A. Mazrui. A third standard history is L. H. Gann and Peter Duignan, eds., *Colonialism in Africa*, 5 vols. (Cambridge, 1969–75), of which the fifth volume is a detailed bibliography.

Other important and readily available reference works are Colin Legum, ed., *Africa Contemporary Record*, an annual survey of current events in each African country up to 1990, and the *Historical Dictionary* series (Scarecrow Press, Metuchen, NJ), which include capsules of events and good bibliographies for most francophone African countries.

JOURNALS

The main English-language journals carrying articles on francophone Africa (some of which appear in French) are: *The Journal of African History, International Journal of African Historical Studies, Canadian Journal of African Studies* (a bilingual journal), *Journal of Modern African Studies, African Affairs, History in Africa*, and *African Economic History*. The main French language journals (some of whose articles appear in English) are *Cahiers d'études africaines, Journal de la Société des Africanistes, Revue française d'histoire d'Outre-Mer, Revue française d'études politiques africaines, Présence africaine*, and *Cahiers du CEDAF*.

AFRICA BEFORE 1880

Good general texts covering precolonial Africa include Roland Oliver and Anthony Atmore, *The African Middle Ages, 1400-1800* (Cambridge, 1981); and Basil Davidson, *Africa in History* (New York, 1968). On Central Africa, see David Birmingham and Phyllis M. Martin, eds., *History of Central Africa*, vol. 1 (London, 1983). On slavery, slave trade and their impact, see Patrick Manning, *Slavery and African Life* (Cambridge, 1990).

On West Africa, the epic of ancient Mali is brilliantly retold in D. T. Niane, *Sundiata, an Epic of Old Mali*, trans. G. D. Pickett (London, 1965); the historical background is summarized in Nehemiah Levtzion, *Ancient Ghana and Mali* (London, 1973). For later years, see Philip D. Curtin, *Economic Change in Pre-Colonial Africa: Senegambia in the Era of the Slave Trade*, 2 vols. (Madison, 1975); I. A. Akinjogbin, *Dahomey and its Neighbors, 1708-1818* (Cambridge, 1967); and David Robinson, *The Holy War of Umar Tal* (Oxford, 1985).

A Central African epic is expertly presented in Daniel Biebuyck and Kahombo C. Mateene, eds. and trans., *The Mwindo Epic* (Berkeley, 1971). For details on the politics of the southern savanna, see Jan Vansina, *Kingdoms of the Savanna* (Madison, 1966); for precolonial history of the Zaire River, see Robert Harms, *River of Wealth, River of Sorrow* (New Haven, 1981).

HISTORIES OF FRANCE AND BELGIUM

Three of the many good general histories of France are Roger Price, *A Concise History of France* (Cambridge, 1993); Gordon Wright, *France in Modern Times*, 2nd edn (Chicago, 1974); and Ernest John Knapton, *France, an Interpretive History* (New York, 1971). Histories of Belgium in English are neither as numerous nor as strong, but see Margot Lyon, *Belgium* (New York, 1971); John Fitzmaurice, *The Politics of Belgium* (New York, 1983); and Stephen B. Wickman, ed., *Belgium: A Country Study* (Washington, D.C. 1984). A fine study of the early relations between French and Africans is William B. Cohen, *The French Encounter with Africans* (Bloomington, Ind., 1980). For surveys of the francophone community, see Auguste Viatte, *La Francophonie* (Paris, 1969); Xavier Deniau, *La Francophonie* (Paris, 1983), in the "Que sais-je?" series; and Jean-Jacques Luthi, Auguste Viatte, and Gaston Zananiri, eds., *Dictionnaire général de la francophonie* (Paris, 1986).

ECONOMIC AND SOCIAL HISTORY

The economic history of francophone sub-Saharan Africa has been studied more thoroughly than social history. Major studies of economic history in West Africa include A G. Hopkins, *An Economic History of West Africa* (London, 1973); Patrick Manning, *Slavery, Colonialism and Economic Growth in Dahomey, 1640–1960* (Cambridge, 1982); Stephen Baier, An Economic History of Central Niger (Oxford,1980); Monique Lakroum, *Le Travail inégal* (Paris, 1982); Odile Goerg, *Commerce et colonisation en Guinée (1850–1913)* (Paris, 1986); and Emil

Schreyer, *L'Office du Niger au Mali 1932 à 1982* (Wiesbaden, 1984). For an important collective work with many contributions on West Africa, see Catherine Coquery-Vidrovitch, ed., *Entreprises et entrepreneurs en Afrique, XIXe et XXe siècles*, 2 vols. (Paris, 1983). For social history in West Africa, see Denise Bouche, *Les Villages de liberté en Afrique Occidentale Française, 1887-1910* (Paris, 1968); Myron Echenberg, *Colonial Conscripts: The Tirailleurs Sénégalais in French West Africa, 1857-1960* (Portsmouth, NH, 1991); and Majhemout Diop, *Histoire des classes sociales dans l'Afrique de l'Ouest* (Paris, 1985).

On Central Africa, Michel Merlier, *Le Congo de la colonisation belge à l'independance* (Paris, 1962) is a good general history with special emphasis on economic affairs. The definitive study on the economy of French Equatorial Africa is Catherine Coquery-Vidrovitch, *Le Congo au temps des grandes compagnies concessionnaires 1898-1930* (Paris, 1972). For further information on the economy of colonial Zaire, Marvin P. Miracle, *Agriculture in the Congo Basin* (Madison, 1967); J P. Peemans, *Diffusion du progrès et convergence des prix. Congo-Belgique, 1900-1960* (Louvain and Paris, 1970); and P. Joye and R. Lewin, *Les Trusts au Congo* (Brussels, 1961). See also the many important articles of Bogumil Jewsiewicki, including "Zaire enters the world system: its colonial incorporation in the Belgian Congo, 1885-1960," in G. Gran, ed., *Zaire: The Political Economy of Underdevelopment* (New York, 1979). On social history in Central Africa, see Bruce Fetter, *The Creation of Elisabethville, 1919-40* (Stanford, 1976).

For the era of decolonization, studies of social history are more numerous. Two excellent studies on the Mourides of Senegal are Jean Copans, *Les Marabouts de l'arachide. La confrérie mouride et les paysans du Sénégal* (Paris, 1980); and D. B. Cruise O'Brien, *The Mourides of Senegal* (Oxford, 1971). For a study of social change in decolonizing Guinea, see William Derman, *Serfs, Peasants and Socialists* (Berkeley, 1973). Other useful studies of social conditions include Elliott P. Skinner, *The Mossi of Upper Volta* (Stanford, 1964); H. Derrienic, *Famines et dominations en Afrique noire* (Paris, 1977); and I. Deblé and Ph. Hugon, *Vivre et survivre dans les villes africaines* (Paris, 1982). On recent economic conditions in West Africa, see Samir Amin, *Neocolonialism in West Africa* (New York, 1974); Samir Amin, *Modern Migrations in West Africa* (London, 1974); Rita Cruise O'Brien, ed., *The Political Economy of Development: Dependence in Senegal* (Beverly Hills, 1979); I. William Zartman and Christopher Delgado, eds., *The Political Economy of Ivory Coast* (New York, 1984); and, for an insightful micro-study, Abdou Touré, *Les Petits Metiers à Abidjan* (Paris, 1985). An important econometric analysis of the former French territories of West and Central Africa is Boris Maldant and Maxime Haubert, *Croissance et conjoncture dans l'Ouest africain* (Paris, 1973). On environmental problems, see Lloyd Timberlake, *Africa in Crisis: The Causes, the Cures of Environmental Bankruptcy* (London, 1985).

For social conditions in Central Africa after 1940, two major works are by the sociologist Georges Balandier, *The Sociology of Black Africa* (New York, 1970); and by the geographer Giles Sautter, *De l'Atlantique au fleuve Congo. Une géographie du souspeuplement* (Paris, 1966). Other significant studies of social conditions include Wyatt MacGaffey, *Custom and Government in the Lower Congo* (Berkeley, 1970); Suzanne Comhaire-Sylvain, *Femmes de Kinshasa* (Paris, 1968); Jeanne-Françoise Vincent, *Femmes africaines en milieu urbain* (Paris, 1966); and J. P. Chretien, ed., *Histoire rurale de l'Afrique des Grands Lacs* (Paris, 1983). A number of authors have successfully combined social and economic analysis. These include Jane I. Guyer, *Family and Farm in Southern Cameroon* (Boston, 1984); Pierre-Philippe Rey, *Colonialisme, néo-colonialisme er la transition au capitalisme : exemple de la 'Comilog' au Congo-Brazzaville* (Paris, 1971); Michael Schatzberg, *Politics and Class in Zaire* (New York, 1980); Nzongola-Ntalaja, ed., *The Crisis in Zaire: Myths and Realities* (Trenton, N.J., 1986). On the misadventures of the great Inga dam project, see Jean-Claude Willame, *Zaire: l'épopée d'Inga* (Paris, 1986).

On economic affairs in recent years, two excellent local studies are John Igué and Bio G. Soulé, *L'Etat-entrepôt au Bénin: commerce informel ou solution à la crise?* (Paris, 1992), and P.

Canel, Ph. Delis and Ch. Girard, *Construire la ville africaine: chroniques du citadin promoteur* (Paris, 1990), which centers on Douala. Useful national studies include Gilles Duruflé, *Le Sénégal peut-il sortir de la crise? Douze ans d'ajustement structurel au Sénégal* (Paris, 1994); and Peter Geschiere and Piet Konings, *Itinéraires d'accumulation au Cameroun* (Paris, 1993). For economic affairs in francophone Africa generally, see Alain Delage and Alain Massiera, *Le Franc CFA: bilan et perspectives* (Paris, 1994); Axelle Kabou, *Et si l'Afrique refusait le développement?* (Paris, 1994); and Eugène Nyambal, *Afrique: quels changements après la faillite* (Ivry-sur-Seine, 1994).

For social conditions in recent years, Anne-Sidonie Zoà has written a brilliantly incisive study of urban refuse in *Les Ordures à Yaoundé: Urbanisation, environnement et politique au Cameroun* (Paris, 1995). For other studies of urban life, see Yves Boulvert, *Bangui 1889–1989* (Paris, 1989); Annick Combier, *Les Enfants de la rue en Mauritanie* (Paris,1994); Pierre-André Krol, *Avoir 20 ans en Afrique* (Paris, 1994); Yves Marguerat and Tchitchékou Pelei, *"Si Lomé m'était contée ...": dialogues avec les vieux Loméens* (Lomé, 1992); and Jean-François Werner, *Marges, sexe et drogues à Dakar: enquête ethnographique* (Paris, 1993).

POLITICS AND GOVERNMENT

A good introduction to the politics of francophone West Africa is John D. Hargreaves, *West Africa: The Former French States* (Englewood Cliffs, NJ, 1967). For an authoritative overview of French colonialism, see Henri Brunschwig, *French Colonialism 1871–1914: Myths and Realities* (1961). On the French wars of conquest and the African responses, see Martin Klein, *Islam and Imperialism in Senegal* (Stanford, 1968); A. S. Kanya-Forstner, *The Conquest of the Western Sudan* (Cambridge, 1969); and the massive study of Yves Person, *Samori: une révolution dyula*, 3 vols. (Dakar, 1968–75). For a narrative of French conquests and wars, see Marcel Chailley, *Histoire de l'Afrique Occidentale Française 1638-1959* (Paris, 1968). On the French and African administrators, see William B. Cohen, *Rulers of Empire* (Stanford, 1971); and Henri Brunschwig, *Noirs et blancs dans l'Afrique noire française, ou comment le colonisé devient colonisateur (1870–1914)* (Paris, 1983). On French administrative policy and the political relations between French and Africans, see Michael Crowder, *Senegal, A Study in French Assimilation Policy* (London, 1962); and Robert Delavignette, *Freedom and Authority in French West Africa* (London, 1950). For an excellent study of World War I and its impact, see Marc Michel, *Appel à l'Afrique, Contributions et réactions à l 'effort de guerre en AOF, 1914–19* (Paris, 1982); on the same era, see G. Wesley Johnson, *The Emergence of Black Politics in Senegal* (Stanford, 1971). For two useful studies outside of Senegal, see Finn Fuglestad, *A History of Niger 1850–1960* (Cambridge, 1983); and Timothy Weiskel, *French Colonial Rule and the Baulé Peoples* (Oxford, 1980). For African critiques of colonialism, see Philippe Dewitte, *Les Mouvements nègres en France* (Paris, 1985).

Aspects of the political history of early colonial Central Africa have been analyzed in great detail. On the European exploration and conquest, see Henri Brunschwig, *Brazza Explorateur. L'Ogooué 1875-1879* (Pans, 1966); Brunschwig, *Brazza explorateur: les traités Makoko, 1880–1882* (Paris, 1972); Catherine Coquery-Vidrovitch, *Brazza et la prise de possession du Congo* (Paris, 1969); Ruth Slade, *King Leopold's Congo* (London, 1962); and, for a biography of Leopold II, Neal Ascherson, *The King Incorporated* (London, 1963). Henry Morton Stanley chronicled his own activities in great detail: see, for example, *In Darkest Africa*, 2 vols. (New York, 1890). On the African participants in these events, see Leda Farrant, *Tippu Tip and the East African Slave Trade* (New York, 1975); Jan Vansina, *The Tio Kingdom of the Middle Congo 1880–1892* (London, 1973); and Dennis D. Cordell, *Dar al-Kuti and the Last Years of the Trans-Saharan Slave Trade* (Madison, Wis., 1985). On early administration in Central Africa, see William Roger Louis, *Ruanda-Urundi 1884–1919* (Oxford, 1963); L. H. Gann and Peter Duignan, *The Rulers of Belgian Africa 1884–1914* (Princeton, 1979). On the later colonial era, see Roger Anstey, *King Leopold's Legacy*; and

Pierre Kalck, *Histoire de la République centrafricaine* (Paris, 1974). Pierre Ryckmans, *Dominer pour servir* (Brussels, 1931), presents the rationale of paternalism as well as useful detail on the administrative problems of Ruanda-Urundi.

For West Africa after 1940, a sound and detailed study of administration is Virginia Thompson and Richard Adloff, *French West Africa* (Stanford, 1958). The essential study of post-war politics is Ruth Schachter Morgenthau, *Political Parties in French-Speaking West Africa* (Oxford, 1964); also useful is William J. Foltz, *From French West Africa to the Mali Federation* (New Haven, 1965); and, for a more personal account, see Gabriel Lisette, *Le Combat du rassemblement démocratique africain* (Paris, 1983). For two hagiographic but informative biographies, see Paul Henri Siriex, *Félix Houphouët-Boigny, l'homme de la paix* (Paris, 1957); and Siriex, *Houphouët-Boigny, ou la sagesse africaine* (Paris, 1986). For journalistic biographies, see Ibrahima Baba Kaké, *Sékou Touré* (Paris, 1987); and Sennen Andriamirado, *Sankara le rebelle* (Paris, 1987). Leopold Senghor's political philosophy is set forth in Senghor, *On African Socialism*. John D. Hargreaves, *The End of Colonial Rule in West Africa* (London, 1979), provides a thought-provoking survey of decolonization, while a good country study may be found in Sheldon Gellar, *Senegal, an African Nation between Islam and the West* (Boulder, 1982). On military coups in francophone and other nations, see Jean-Pierre Pabanel, *Les Coups d'état militaires en Afrique noire* (Paris, 1984).

On Central African politics after 1940, Virginia Thompson and Richard Adloff, *The Emerging States of French Equatorial Africa* (Stanford, 1960) is even more useful than their survey of French West Africa. Brian Weinstein's biography, *Eboué* (New York, 1972), portrays this key figure in readable prose; a more thorough biography is Elie W. Castor and Raymond Tarcy, *Félix Eboué* (Paris, 1984). René Lemarchand, *Rwanda and Burundi* (New York, 1970), provides a detailed analysis of politics and society in the era of decolonization. Three strong studies on politics in Cameroon are Victor T. Le Vine, *The Cameroons from Mandate to Independence* (Berkeley, 1964); Le Vine, *The Cameroon Federal Republic* (Ithaca, 1971); and Richard Joseph, *Radical Nationalism in Cameroun* (London, 1977). Other useful country studies are Brian Weinstein, *Nation-Building on the Ogooué* (Boston, 1966); Hughes Bertrand, *Le Congo* (Paris, 1975); and Virginia Thompson and Richard Adloff, *Conflict in Chad* (Berkeley, 1981). On the decolonization of Zaire, see Crawford Young, *Politics in the Congo* (Princeton, 1965); René Lemarchand, *Political Awakening in the Congo* (Berkeley, 1964); Herbert Weiss, *Political Protest in the Congo* (Princeton, 1967); Robin McKown, *Lumumba* (New York, 1969); Crawford Young and Benoit Verhaegen, *Rebellions au Congo*, 2 vols. (Brussels, 1966–69). On later politics in Zaire, see Crawford Young and Thomas Turner, *The Rise and Decline of the Zairian State* (Madison, 1985); and Thomas Callaghy, *The State–Society Struggle: Zaire in Comparative Perspective* (New York, 1984)

For more recent years, it is unfortunate that no major study has yet appeared on the first national conference, that of Benin. René Dumont's *Démocratie pour l'Afrique* (Paris, 1991) sounded the call for social change; some general studies of democratization movements and national conferences include F. Eboussi Boulaga, *Les Conférences nationales en Afrique noire: une affaire à suivre* (Paris, 1993); Gérard Conac, ed., *L'Afrique en transition vers le pluralisme politique* (Paris, 1993); Thierry Perret, *Afrique: voyage en démocratie, les années chacha* (Paris, 1994); P. J. M. Tedga, *Ouverture démocratique en Afrique noire?* (Paris, 1991); and Philippe Decraene, *L'Afrique centrale*, 2nd edn (Paris, 1993). For useful country studies on the era of democraization movements, see Nadine Bari, *Chroniques de Guinée* (Paris, 1994); Calixte Baniafouna, *Congo démocratie*, 2 vols. (Paris, 1994); Cheikh Oumar Diarrah, *Vers la IIIe république de Mali* (Paris, 1991); Jean-Noel Loucou, *Le Multipartisme en Côte d'Ivoire* (Abidjan 1992); and Valentin Ndi Mbarga, *Ruptures et continuités au Cameroun* (Paris, 1993). For two important national studies centering on the 1980s, see Ludo Martens, *Sankara, Compaoré et la révolution Burkinabè* (Antwerp, 1989); and Gauthier de Villiers, *De Mobutu à Mobutu, trente ans de relations Belgique-Zaire* (Brussels, 1995). The disastrous politics of Chad, Rwanda, and Burundi are chronicled in Varsia Kovana, *Précis des guerres et conflits au*

Tchad (Paris, 1994); Filip Reyntjens, *Rwanda, trois jours qui ont fait basculer l'histoire* (Brussels, 1995); René Lemarchand, *Burundi: Ethnocide as discourse and practice* (Cambridge, 1994); and Gérard Prunier, *The Rwanda crisis: history of a genocide* (New York, 1995).

CULTURE AND RELIGION

Studies of religion dominate the studies of culture for the early colonial years. For West Africa these include the numerous studies of Islam by Paul Marty, including *Etudes sur l'Islam au Dahomey* (Paris, 1926). A general study written in later colonial years is Alphonse Gouilly, *L'Islam dans l'Afrique occidentale française* (Paris, 1952). Vincent Monteil, *L'Islam noir*, 4th edn (Paris, 1980), is an authoritative overview. On Christian missionaries, see Andre Picciola, *Missionaires en Afrique, 1840–1940* (Paris, 1987). Other studies of religion include D. B. Cruise O'Brien, *The Mourides of Senegal* (Oxford, 1971); and Gordon Halliburton, *The Prophet Harris* (London, 1971). For a study of rural culture which yields surprising conclusions on the impact of Islam, see René Bravmann, *Islam and Tribal Art in Africa* (Cambridge, 1974). Marcel Griaule, *Conversations with Ogotemmeli* (London, 1965), has become an important text in the discussion of African philosophy. Jahnheinz Jahn, *Muntu: The New African Culture*, uses materials from West and Central Africa as well as the New World to propound a theory of African cultural change. Early writings by West Africans included Paul Hazoumé, *Le Pacte de sang au Dahomey* (Paris, 1937); Hazoumé, *Doguicimi* (Paris, 1938); and Kojo Tovalou-Houénou, *L'Involution des métamorphoses et le metempsychose de l'univers* (Paris, 1922).

On missionary work in Central Africa, see Marvin Markowitz, *The Cross and the Sword: The Political Role of the Missions in the Congo, 1908–60* (Stanford, 1973). Major literary works on Central Africa include Joseph Conrad, *Heart of Darkness* (New York, 1910); René Maran, *Batouala* (Paris, 1921); and André Gide, *Travels in the Congo* (New York, 1937). Two major philosophical texts are Alexis Kagamé, *La Philosophie bantu-rwandaise de l'être* (Brussels, 1956); and Placied Tempels, *Bantu Philosophy* (Paris, 1959). For an excellent introduction to art history focusing on Central Africa, see Jan Vansina, *Art History in Africa* (London, 1984). See also the beautifully produced first part of a comprehensive series by Daniel Biebuyck, *The Arts of Zaire. Volume 1: Southwestern Zaire* (Berkeley, 1985).

For recent years, studies of religion have given way to studies of literature and philosophy, though René Bravmann, in *African Islam* (Washington, DC, 1983) continues his earlier analysis of Islam and art. Other studies on religion include C. Coulon, *Les Musulmans et le pouvoir en Afrique noire* (Paris, 1983); and A. Traoré, *lslam et colonisation en Afrique: Cheikh Hamahoullah, homme de foi et résistant* (Paris, 1983). For a critique of African literature, see Locha Matess, *La Littérature africaine et sa critique* (Paris, 1986). On cultural change more generally, see Jean-Pierre Dozon, *La Société bété: Cote d'Ivoire* (Paris, 1985); Abdou Touré, *La Civilisation quotidienne en Côte d'Ivoire (procès d'occidentalisation)* (Paris, 1981); and G. Blanchet, *Elites et changements en Afrique et au Sénégal* (Paris, 1983). A widely available study of Senghor is Jacques Hymans, *Leopold Sedar Senghor, an Intellectual Biography* (Edinburgh, 1971). For major political and philosophical tracts, see Frantz Fanon, *Wretched of the Earth* (New York, 1966); Paulin Hountoundji, *African Philosophy* (Bloomington, Ind., 1983); and Pathé F. Diagne, *L'Europhilosophie face à la pensée du Négro-africain* (Dakar, 1981). On film, see Françoise Pfaff, *The Cinema of Ousmane Sembène* (Westport, Conn., 1984); Victor Bachy, *La Haute Volta et le Cinéma* (Paris, 1983); and Victor Bachy, ed., *Camera Nigra: le discours du film africain* (Paris, 1985). For a study of language instruction in Senegal, see Pierre Dumont, *L 'Afrique noire peut-elle encore parler français?* (Paris, 1986).

Three important studies of religion in Central Africa are Wyatt MacGaffey, *Modern Kongo Prophets: Religion in a Plural Society* (Bloomington, Ind., 1983); James Fernandes, *Bwiti: An Ethnography of Religious Imagination* (Princeton, 1982); and Ian Linden, *Church and Revol-*

ution in Rwanda (Manchester, 1977). Zairian philosopher Valentin Mudimbe has also written several novels, including *Entre les eaux* (Paris, 1973) and *Le bel immonde* (Paris, 1976). Novelist Makombo Bamboté, from Central African Republic, is noted for his *Princesse Mandapu* (Paris, 1972).

In recent years, the most forceful critic of "francophonie" has been Guy Ossito Midiohouan of Benin, in *Du bon usage de la francophonie* (Cotonou, 1994). For a collection of empirical studies on Zaire, see Sully Faik et al., *La Francophonie au Zaire* (Lubumbashi, 1988). Solid studies have now appeared on many aspects of education and popular culture: Adoum Mbaiosso, *L'Education au Tchad: bilan, problèmes et perspectives* (Paris, 1990); Bogumil Jewsiewicki, ed., *Art pictural zairois* (Quebec, 1992); Pierre Saulnier, *Bangui chante: anthologie du chant moderne en Afrique centrale* (Paris, 1993); and Andre-Jean Tudesq, *L'Afrique noire et ses télévisions* (Paris, 1992).

For an excellent anthology of francophone African writings, see Lilyan Kesteloot, ed., *Anthologie négro-africaine: histoire et textes de 1918 à nos jours* (Vanves, 1992). The creativity of francophone African novelists in the post-independence years is reviewed in Sewanou Dabla, *Nouvelles écritures africaines: Romanciers de la seconde génération* (Paris, 1986). Of the accelerating literary output of francophone African authors in years thereafter, some notable volumes are Achille Ngoye, *Kin-la joie, Kin-la folie* (Paris, 1993); Véronique Tadjo, *A Vol d'Oiseau* (Paris, 1992); Cheick Oumar Kanté, *Fatoba, l'archipel mutant* (Paris, 1992); and Nouréini Tidjani-Serpos, *Bamikilé* (Paris, 1996). For a recent study of films, see Imruh Bakari and Mbye B. Cham, eds., *African Experiences of Cinema* (Bloomington, 1996).

Index

Please remember that this is a library book,
and that it belongs only temporarily to each
person who uses it. Be considerate. Do
not write in this, or any, library book.